IS IT TOO LATE TO RUN AWAY AND JOIN THE CIRCUS?

IS IT TOO LATE TO RUN AWAY AND JOIN THE CIRCUS?

finding the life you really want

MARTI D. SMYE, PH.D.

KEY PORTER BOOKS

Canadian Cataloguing-in-Publication Data

Smye, Marti D., 1950 –
    Is it too late to run away and join the circus?

    Canadian ed.
    Includes index.
    ISBN 1-55013-977-0

    1. Career changes.   2. Success in business.   I. Title.

HF5384.S68   1998   650.14   C 98-931396-4

Key Porter Books Limited
70 The Esplanade
Toronto, Ontario
Canada M5E 1R2
www.keyporter.com

Printed and bound in Canada

 99 00 01 4 3 2

Originally published in the United States by Macmillan USA

dedication

I want to dedicate this book to Bill Weafer, a former executive with The Cooperators. Bill died the year in which I was working on this book. It was Bill who first gave me the opportunity to work in this area twenty years ago. He asked me to develop a program to help managers make more lateral moves because the company was delayering. The program helped retention and improved people's job and personal satisfaction. Bill was one of the best supporters, mentors, and friends I have ever had. His death is a loss for all of us who knew him.

acknowledgments

This book contains the collected wisdom of dedicated and gifted career counselors and my support team.

Bill Ames helped me understand something about confidence and the cyclical nature of our lives.

Joel Aron made me think about what work and success mean.

Judy Barton reminded me that even involuntary career change can be good news.

Dr. David Blank made me reconsider what I thought I knew about networking and working from home.

Joe Bowden advised me about not jumping too quickly and leaving options open.

Bud Bray reminded me that mountains seldom come to Mohammed and thereby changed the whole shape of this book.

Richard Chagnon spent a whole day talking about the ideas in this book and giving me the benefit of his wit and wisdom.

Brenda Eddy explained the difference between aptitudes and skills and suggested how to identify aptitudes.

Rob Fish challenged me to re-examine some of the myths that surround jobs and the future of work.

Joan Hanpeter emphasized the importance of thinking about the dreams we used to have.

Kenneth "Pete" Henderson helped me think about work settings and preparing for retirement.

Joe Jannotta told me about 360-degree feedback and the essential importance of the work environment in job satisfaction.

Lee Lindeman suggested many useful sources and books and helped me to understand some of the processes of career management.

Rebecca Maddox debunked some of the myths of change and gave my ideas some needed reality therapy.

Dave Maguire told me how not to be a pinball in a machine but to take charge of my career.

Doug Matthews reminded me that we all need to prove ourselves again and again.

Dr. Leslie Mayer explained some of the personal and emotional aspects of change and reminded me that change means leaving some things behind.

Tom Mullaney made me realize that retirement isn't what it used to be.

Carol Pomerantz made some important links between work life and family life.

Warren Radtke got me thinking in terms of verbs rather than nouns.

Carl Samuels reminded me about mentoring and the need to leave a legacy in the work world.

Boardy Thompson talked good sense about what drives people in their careers.

Gil Wetzel suggested ways in which career change is affecting corporations and how employers need to respond to the new career paths.

Lis Hugh took time to read this book before it was readable.

Philippa Campsie provided ideas, research, writing skills, and editorial advice.

Patrick Withrow gave the book his own unique style.

Sarah Withrow interviewed many of the people whose stories appear in the book.

Lee Downs stepped in when I needed her.

Nelrene Dunleavy and Howard Shulman helped pull together all the pieces.

Zella Hayman reminded me of who I am and kept me grounded.

Marian Marshall as always provided advice and support throughout the book.

Manville Smith not only shared his own wisdom with me, but also provided me with access to many of the wonderful people mentioned above.

contents

part three: at the circus, there be tigers

foreword

When I was a young professional in the late 1960s, I had the good fortune to learn a fundamental truth from the educator Malcolm Knowles. I vividly remember his telling us that the people who were children at the time were destined to live through seven complete cultural changes as they grew up. Not just career changes or organizational changes, but cultural changes, the kind of changes that fundamentally alter one's frame of reference.

The children of the 1960s are now in their thirties and are probably somewhere in the middle of their second or third cultural change by now. In addition, what they experience now will undoubtedly shape and position their next changes as well.

Those of us who were born before the 1960s might find the adjustment a little harder to make, but we have to do it anyway. Whoever we are, whatever we do now, there's a cultural change in our future that is going to make our original plans obsolete. Even if we are facing retirement, the question is pressing because studies show that those who choose non-activity in retirement have a shorter life expectancy than those who choose to keep learning and reinventing themselves.

The book you are holding contains wonderful stories of people who have reinvented their work lives. Some of them chose to change and some had change thrust upon them, but all of them have found new levels of satisfaction in work that wasn't part of their original career planning when they left school.

In doing so, many of them have helped to reinvent the organizations they work for. This is as it should be. For years we've been hearing talk about organizational reengineering and restructuring. Now it suddenly seems that the gurus have discovered that there are people involved. Some of us, Marti Smye included, have known this all along. That is why, after writing two books on organizational change, she has written this book. And also why, after about 30 years of counseling people in various ways, I want to recommend it to those who are trying to bring about change in their own lives and to those who recognize the profound implications of new career paths on organizations and of renewed organizations on career direction.

But there is more than organizational change involved here. In reinventing our relationship to work, we reinvent our relationships to our families, our communities, ourselves. We cannot separate work from the rest of our lives. In fact, of the two phrases that people most long to hear, "Good job!" is right up there as a powerful confidence-builder as "I love you."

Reinventing yourself is a fundamental act of creativity. It represents forward movement in a world that never stands still. I hope that this book will help you take the next step in choosing who you are and what you are going to do with the next cultural change that is coming your way.

RICHARD CHAGNON

Group managing vice-president
Right Management Consultants, Philadelphia
and author of *Essential Facts: Termination of Employment*
(Warren Gorham & Lamont, New York, 1995)

introduction

The Trouble with Even Good Scotch in a City Where You Don't Live

---

In which you will find out that:

1. If your life feels like a shoe that's too tight, you are certainly not alone.

2. You're probably going to have to change your life whether you plan it or not.

"Well, here we are, another day closer to the grave," the tall guy said. I was at an executive 10K run for charity. Executives like these things because it's another outlet for the eternal competitor. I'm a bit diffident about these events: I'm 5'2", so the average six-foot executive's 10K means 12K for me. I've tried to have the length of the runs adjusted downwards so they take my size into account. "Affirmative action for the short," I say. But nobody listens. Size-ist creeps.

One man had "Born to Downsize" silk-screened on his singlet. He meant it, too. The last time I looked in the *Wall Street Journal*, he'd just disappeared another 1,700 of his employees, apparently with gusto. Another had a cell phone with him, although how he planned to use it was beyond me. Carrying on a conversation with the man who'd first spoken to me was impossible over the pattering of about 500 executive Nikes and the straining of 250 executive-sized lungs.

I met the tall guy again three months later at an industry conference. I gave a speech on successful and unsuccessful management of corporate change. He gave one of the keynote speeches—unusual for somebody who was younger than most of the people in the room—and he put a lot of zest into the presentation.

At the cocktail party afterwards (if they make you listen to some of the speeches at these things, they figure they owe you a drink), I had a chance to talk with him again. He repeated what he'd said the first time: "Another day closer to the grave." The comment was so much at odds with the man I'd seen on the podium that I wanted to find out more about him.

We started a long conversation. This was one of those industry events where the participants are all from out of town and are trying to avoid going back to their rooms and watching what passes for late-night television these days.

Take some Scotch, mix with an out-of-town industry conference, and you get somebody's life story.

He'd wanted to be a historian. He loved digging through archival documents looking for the truth of who did what to whom at Yalta and the effect of the Rothschilds on the Franco-Prussian war. The past was present to him, and more interesting than the Super Bowl.

He was in college when he bought a pipe to let everybody know he was serious about history. Unfortunately, he'd also fallen in love with an anthropology major who kept bumping into walls because she was too vain to wear her glasses—these were the days before contact lenses. They were also the days before college students had acquired a thorough and accurate knowledge of contraception. One thing led to another thing and that led to a June marriage. After the confetti, came the job offer from the father-in-law, whose occupation I'll give as "developer." It was a generous offer: work through the summer and then part-time and we'll get you through college, "Although I don't see much profit from the history thing."

September came, and he went back to school. Then December came with the baby girl and the medical problems. Things were tight with the developer: He'd gotten in a little over his head and couldn't come up with the money for the doctors. He could give a little help, but our man was going to have to work, too. There was a job open with another developer. He took the job. No choice.

Somehow the following year there was another baby girl: The inventors of the diaphragm have a lot to answer for. There were no medical problems, but obviously, there was no going back to college. But they had a plan. They drew it up one night. If they cut down here and there, then five years from that date, if the stars were in the right position, interest rates went down, taxes didn't go up . . .

What actually happened is that he went back to his father-in-law's business five years later. This time he went in with a more senior position because he went in with money he inherited. The idea was that with partial ownership, pretty soon he could go to college on the dividends.

Twenty-odd years later he still hadn't made it back to the classroom. Sure, he had an Audi, three kids, a 26-foot boat, and the occasional four-day weekend in Lake Tahoe. He got to make keynote speeches. He was respected by his employees, and the company was now his. His banker thought he was solid. And, occasionally, he'd get his hands on some documents that put a new light on some part of history that interested him and, with luck, he'd get time to read them.

There was talk of running him for city council, but he thought there were probably too many developers around that table already. And, you know, housing development was getting a little more interesting these days. There was some innovation happening. The New Urbanism was making small towns look like small towns again instead of anonymous subdivisions—or at least it was trying to. There were interesting new building techniques that meant you could put a house together in three weeks if you really knew your stuff. That would cut down the length of time you'd have to finance unsold inventory, which meant you could actually make a decent profit. They were wiring smart homes for computers and modems and the rest of the convergent technology: you could phone your house and have your computer turn your air conditioning on.

"You know," he said, "Some interesting things." Then he finished his drink and repeated what he'd said before: "'Nother day closer . . ."

Now, the first obvious lesson here is probably beware of after-seminar Scotch in cities where you don't live. I ought to know. I travel more than a hundred days a year talking about corporate change techniques and I spend a lot of evenings at cocktail parties at which I've learned to drink Perrier out of a Martini glass so I don't start into my own autobiography.

But the phrase stuck with me. I was planning a new book to follow up on my first book on organizational change and my second book on corporate abuse. I wanted to talk about market value replacing market share and value migration and value management and related topics. I'd started scribbling notes to myself and talking into a tape recorder. But I kept tripping over people's stories, a lot of them very much like this.

I have written about the problems of people in abusive cultures, but what I was hearing wasn't about abusive cultures or bullying bosses.

"Another week on the gerbil wheel," said one CEO. He worked for a U.K.-based packaged goods company. Gerbil wheel? The guy has a company-provided Turbo Bentley. He also has the respect of his colleagues, a charming wife, generous use of a company-owned jet, and a yearly performance bonus equal to the lifetime salaries of many of his countrymen. "Gerbil wheel," he said, and that's the way he really felt.

I kept waking up in the middle of the night and remembering phrases like that. Somehow corporate market value seemed less and less important. People always come first (in my work, in the name of the company I started), and what the people were saying belied all the rosy predictions about twenty-first century business.

I started asking people, quite seriously, "How are you feeling today?" "First of all I want to scream. Then I want to kick someone. Then I'd like a bottle of bourbon and a quiet dark room." This answer is from someone who over the last ten years has built up a chain of eleven paint stores. He owns them all—no franchisees. Again, he has the respect of his colleagues. He certainly has the respect of his competitors. Good family life. Fishing trophies. But "That's the way I feel most days. And what's frightening is that someday I suspect I'm going to do it: the scream and the bourbon and the small dark room."

"How's it going with you?" "They're scaring me. I've been eighteen years with this company and I know someday soon somebody from some consultancy is going to draw an orange circle around my part of the organizational chart and say something like 'downsize' or 'outsource' and they'll make me vanish." Solid, intelligent, church-going, a relative of mine.

"I have a feeling they promised me something better than this for a life, but I can't find the original contract." I didn't know whether she was talking about her family or her university job or both.

"I'm tired, and I've been tired forever and I'm tired of it. This is some kind of sleep-deprivation experiment. I'm four hours short, permanently." The people who work with him at the hardware company buying team think of him as energetic.

"I get myself up in the morning. I shave my face. I dress in my clothes. I go to my office. I do my work. I come back to my house. But I feel like I'm only doing an imitation of myself, and it's not a terrific impersonation." His picture's been on a couple of business magazines.

"Been there, done that. Have to go there again and do it again. Same stuff tomorrow." Like me, she travels a lot, and I'd always thought of her as having a remarkably varied job.

"They asked me to get more productive. I showed them productivity. They asked me to be a team player. I gave them team. They asked tech, I gave them tech. They asked global, I gave good global. I gave them all this and in return they give me twenty-five minutes a day to spend with my wife and family." A neighbor.

"You know, I spent a few years as a hippie before all this. I'm thinking of taking it up again. Better gig." I was at grad school with her.

"The prime leisure activity of America according to research reports is lawn care: mowing, fertilizing, and weeding. I'm with them. The best part of my week is spent on a John Deere. Nobody talks to you when you're on a riding mower, and you don't have to talk to anyone else. You know what to do and it gets done." Jeepers, I could have sworn that he loved his day job.

"What do you have to do to be allowed to be in a rage? My kids are allowed to be in a rage sometimes. My wife is allowed to be in a rage sometimes. Why can't I? When do I get my mid-life crisis?" He's still in the Young Presidents' Organization. I think he's forty-two.

I've always asked people how they were. It used to be a simple matter of civility. But lately it seems people have been giving me much more than the usual "Fine, thanks." Maybe I'm asking with a little more interest these days. Or maybe it's that they really don't actually feel just fine, okay, or real good any more and they want to talk about it with someone from outside the company and outside their office and family.

Once in a while you do get different answers. "Dynamite. We're opening up a new plant in New Zealand. I'm learning the culture, I'm learning new ways to do things, different ways to look at stuff. I may even be able to learn to speak New Zealand."

"Feeling good ever since I learned not to keep score when I played golf."

"Great. I just got fired. Somebody said it would be the best thing that ever happened. It is. Really, I'm not kidding. It's like a weight has been taken off my chest."

However, there is a lot of gloom out there, even with the economy on the way up. There always has been. Translations of the hieroglyphics on Egyptian tomb walls reveal some similar sentiments.

The people who are having a rough time are not wallowing in self-pity. They're tough. They're simply looking at their situation in wonder. Some of them even laughed when they said what they said. But how do you get the sad people as happy as the happy people? Has anybody ever pulled off that trick? Is it possible? Should it be possible, or does the world need a steady supply of angst to make it run? Did the inventor of insulin or the measles vaccine require dismay to get the project going? Was the man who invented champagne depressed? Did the person who came up with the first fishing lure feel under relentless pressure?

And I kept waking up in the middle of the night, hearing their voices and remembering how they looked when they said that things hadn't quite turned out as they'd planned. I stopped making notes about value migration and started putting down some of the stories on my tape recorder. Here are three of them. No names, please.

One. The guy at the next desk in business school. Back then, business was a science for him and a lot of others. Do "A" and you'll get "B," the case studies said. Failure meant that somebody was messing up along the way. Because all you had to do was determine the needs hierarchy, order the priorities in terms of profitability and underutilized present capacity, produce, and sell. It was as simple as astronomy: the planets would move in their orbits.

He did very well, moving steadily from salesman to assistant product manager to product manager to group product manager until the recession hit, when everything, including the economy and his wife, dropped out of bed.

He adjusted quickly. After he'd been downsized from his family, he was frightened of being downsized from his company. Because he was making a lot of money, he saw himself as a big target for the bean counters. So he took the initiative: He rationalized his corporate operation, cutting budgets by over a third. He did this so effectively, in fact, that his cascading process was adopted as a model by the management of his corporation which, in the end, used it to outplace him.

"I was the boy they called in for the magic answers. Then they changed their ideas about magic. Later I realized that where I'd been working was a tribal situation and that tribes can and do change their ideas about God and magic."

Between 1980 and 1995, 4.6 million Americans were downsized, smart-sized, right-sized, merged, purged, dehired, or rationalized out of their jobs—what we used to call fired in the old days. Never mind that most of us found jobs again: we were spurned, dislocated, unloved, and wondering when it would happen again.

And nothing I've read says it won't happen again. What's happened in the financial world—the oil crisis, the recession, the shifts in trade patterns, the savings and loan blowups, the massive adjustments in employment patterns—has affected our plans. What the sheik decides in the Emirates and the broker decides in Malaysia and the car maker decides in Korea gets in the way of our deciding to buy three tick hounds and start a chicken farm in Mississippi—or even moving over to the new plastics division of your own company.

The flux has become normal. The question at this point is not what the flux has done to your first life, it's how will it affect plans for your second life (or your third or fifth life)?

Two. "My family didn't have enough money for me to be a doctor, but they thought that there'd be enough so I could be a dentist. That was sort of a breakthrough thing for a girl to get to be at that time. A lot of the other students thought I was just husband-hunting. But I graduated and I took out a huge loan to get an office equipped. Things went just terrifically for a long time.

"I don't know if you know about Deaf Smith county in Texas. Years and years ago they began noticing that very few people in Deaf Smith county got cavities. So they did a lot of research and it turned out that there was natural fluoride in the water. And that's when we started putting fluoride in our water supplies and into toothpaste. And kids started drinking the water and using their toothpaste. And now all those kids have grown up. And they just don't have cavities the way people used to have cavities.

"What that means is that, as a dentist, I now have to have two to three thousand steady customers to make a living, whereas a dentist in my father's day would need only a half to a third of that. So what they found in Deaf Smith County snuck up and changed my whole life."

Technology isn't just something that changes the lives of bookkeepers or people on assembly lines. It's happened to all of us: dentists, shinglers, mechanics, economists, and mushroom farmers. And new technology is going to continue to happen to us. What are your plans to deal with that?

Three. "I had four years of sociology, two children, and a divorce. I planned the sociology, I planned the children, but I didn't plan the divorce. I should have.

"I mean, a sociologist should know from reading the stats that the chances are fifty-fifty that you're going to end up arguing about who pays for what and whether to sell the house and who gets custody of the damn cat. And what's happening to me now means I don't get to plan anything. I don't have the time. I don't have the money. I don't have the energy. I'm rushing, day after day after day. Life is what's inflicted on me."

The unpredictability of our personal lives has become, well, predictable. It's as predictable as technology changes, culture shifts, the fluxes in world finances, the mobility of acceptable morality, and the changes in the ways our corporations behave.

This means that the real problem is that you are very likely to have a second (third, fifth) life thrust upon you whether you want it or not. Somebody's going to invent a new way to do your job, some manager is going to decide that your career needs a new direction, some banker is going to adopt a new strategy, or some family member is going to decide to start paying attention to a previously silent bit of karmic whispering. Or—and you can probably think of some personal examples—all of these things will happen to you, probably all in the same week.

I had spent the best part of my adult life helping companies in transition: organizations going through corporate versions of the problems individuals were telling me about. Companies go through divorces. Organizations find themselves out of a job. Multinationals find themselves losing control of their own agendas. Boards of directors find themselves bored and stale and on what seems to be a treadmill. And in working with organizations, my colleagues and I had found sound and useful techniques for dealing with corporate problems successfully.

I began to wonder if those techniques for organizational change could be applied personally. Would what worked for General Foods work for Joe/Joan Average? Did the lessons learned by a major insurance company carry any messages for people who wanted change or were having change inflicted on them? Did what my organization had learned in thousands of person-years of helping organizations adapt have something of value for someone like you?

Being at a transitional stage of my life myself, I decided to find out.

- I talked to career transition counselors and outplacement consultants at our sister division, Right Associates. I asked about what they were seeing, whom they were seeing, and what happened to people after they left the counselor's or consultant's office. What they had to say was always intriguing and sometimes downright amazing.

- I asked my friends and colleagues to introduce me to people who had found a second life and who, when asked how they were that day, usually said, "Just great" and meant it. Then I asked when they started to feel that way and how.

- I paid attention to a 1995 Gallup poll in which one-third of employed, college-educated adults said they would, if given the chance to start over again, opt for a different line of work. And a 1996 poll carried out for the National Career Development Association in which barely half of those who responded said that they liked their jobs enough that they didn't want to leave.

- I clipped an article from *Fortune* magazine that contained a survey of 300 career women between 35 and 49: 87 percent had made or were planning a major change in their lives, such as taking a sabbatical, starting a business, returning to school, or changing to a new career; 40 percent said they felt trapped.

- I read psychology and self-help books and biographies of people who'd changed their lives. I waded through some fairly dense academic papers, only to find that they said much the same thing as the polls and the articles in *Business Week* and *Psychology Today*, but using a more esoteric vocabulary.

As I got deeper into the idea of applying corporate change management techniques to individual lives, I noticed something interesting: I was not moving away from my abiding interest in organizational change, I was getting closer to it.

We've always accepted that what happens to organizations affects what happens to people. From my conversations and my rereading of what had been written, however, I was also struck by the fact that what happens to people is eventually going to change how companies function. As people plan second, third, and fourth lives, their individual decisions, taken all together, add up to a new force for organizational change. If enough people run away and join the circus, the circus, in all its various manifestations, is going to become an economic force to be reckoned with.

Futurist Watts Wacker has suggested that what comes after the Information Age is the Dream Society, in which status is based, not on consumption, but on contentment, and the great motivator is self-esteem. If he's right, we're in for a highly interesting twenty-first century.

Get a jump on the trend and start now to organize your work around satisfaction, serenity, and self-esteem. You don't have to be at the mercy of technology, economic decisions made five time zones away, or some-one else's manifest destiny. Whatever happened in your first life, you can plan a successful and satisfying second life: you still can run away to the circus. And you'd better do your planning now because the future is going to happen to you whether you're ready or not.

part one

---

watching
the circus
pass by

1

is it too late to run away and join the circus?

In which you will find out that:

1. There's a good chance your boss, your next-door neighbor, and your car mechanic want to change their lives as much as you do.

2. When you feel like a square peg in a round hole, don't try to round off your corners, go find a square hole instead.

Before I sat down to write about people's second lives, I wanted to find out if it would be a book that people actually wanted to read. First, I compiled a list of business leaders I knew well enough to have cognac or coffee with and asked them which book from a list of titles they would pick up first in the privacy of their own bedroom, not at work. The titles were:

> How difficult it is to accept that behind the facade of our tidy narratives rages the aimless human circus.
>
> —JACK HITT

The Joy of Self-Renewal

Re-engineering Yourself

Your Second Life

Empowering Yourself

Is It Too Late to Run Away and Join the Circus?

This Time I Get It Right

Up the Mountain: Achieving the Best

Change Management in Personal Life

Lessons from the Corporations: How to Take Charge of Your Own Life

The business leaders were serious people, any one of whom you would be glad to have to dinner in your own home. They had serious career strategies, good tailors, sound work ethics, major incomes, and impressive intelligence. You would not only have them to dinner, you would hire them. You would even let them drive your car.

The result? Sixty percent of them chose the title, *Is It Too Late to Run Away and Join the Circus?* These people were captains of globally integrated companies, commanders of Fortune 500 companies. People you would golf with, voluntarily.

I'd simply sent out a couple of hundred faxes, but about 120 people replied, showing a rather astonishing level of interest. That sample admittedly is not large, and as a matter of fact the whole survey was a tad unscientific: I designed it myself. And what research people call the universe was skewed because the respondents were not typical. I just went through my Rolodex.

So I thought I'd test the idea again, with a different group. I looked up the numbers for all the people with whom I deal on a day-to-day basis: dry cleaners, fridge repair guys, the man who poisons my dandelions, and the woman who painted my living room. I asked the same question.

I got the same answer: about 60 percent of these people apparently want to run away and join the circus too. Lesson one: the phenomenon crosses class lines. The Colonel's lady and Sadie O'Grady are sisters under the skin, and they both want to run away to the circus.

This thought kept me up nights. Imagine: you could be cutting a merger deal, putting together two mega-corps, and as you look across the desk at the other CEO, you know that there's a 60 percent chance this person has secret fantasies about running away and shoveling up after the elephants have finished their parade.

You're in the middle of your kitchen renovation. The renovator is talking about running 220 for the oven and installing halogen lights and a granite countertop, but there's a 60 percent chance he'd rather be on the midway yelling "Hey, Rube! Five for a dollar. Show the little lady a treat."

She's wearing a navy power suit and talking optimization of market share in a declining market. But there's a 60 percent chance she's imagining herself in shocking pink spangles, putting rosin on her hands, getting ready for the trapeze act.

There's evolving technology on his lips, but there's, "Yo, I'm Bozo" in his heart. It makes you stop and think. Is the whole future of ethical capitalism in the hands of people who, by and large, are unfulfilled roustabouts?

And is the President himself secretly a repressed lion tamer? "It happened on my watch. During a National Security meeting about the future of Bosnia, I decided that my future was really in selling corn dogs in some carnie in Mississippi."

Think about this. Then take a look at your boss, your doctor, your bank teller, your spouse, your neighbor. Check the mirror. Is it too late to run away and join the circus?

What Do They Mean by That?

I'm personally and professionally analytical, which often annoys other people. But I began wondering what all those people meant when they said they wanted to run away to the circus. After all, polls can be misleading. The classic example is the one that Ford took of potential buyers about whether they'd buy a car like an Edsel. People answered yes in sufficient quantities that Ford bet the farm and produced a car that failed. The people who were polled didn't lie. It's simply that the researchers didn't find the truth in the survey. People wanted a car like an Edsel. But the car that was most like the Edsel turned out to be a Pontiac that year.

So what did my poll mean? Did it mean that the population of my Rolodex honestly wanted to wake up smelling the popcorn? I had a longish debate with myself about this and decided the answer was no. If I'd substituted something like "Is it Too Late to Run Away and Become a Working Cow Poke?" or "Is It Too Late to Run Away and Have a Second Career as a Caribbean Charter Captain?" I think I would have gotten a similar 60 percent result.

Those two words, *run away*, were probably as far as most people got. Maybe a few of them really would prefer to ride bareback on a galloping pony in a sparkly costume, but I think most of them just found the idea of the circus appealing compared with what they do every day. They don't really know what they should run to, but they are often surprisingly specific about what they want to run from. At parties and in casual conversations, I often hear people say things like:

"I don't want be employed by an organization that can't state its objectives clearly."

"I can't take the two-and-a-half-hour commute much longer."

"I've had it up to here with automated voice mail systems."

"I never want to work with politicians again."

"Get me off this nine-to-five treadmill. If there's something to be done, I'll work longer. If there's nothing to be done, I'll do that."

"I won't lie to customers and I don't want to be in a position where I have to."

"If I don't understand why it's being done, I don't want to do it."

"I never want to have to fire anyone ever again."

"Please don't give me a dirty slate and expect me to clean it."

"I never again want to work with someone else's policies and procedures manual, especially if it's more than ten years old."

"Just once I'd like to start the day without 37 e-mails waiting for me."

"I'd be happy if I never had to do another dog-and-pony show again."

"Get me out of this cubicle. I haven't seen sunlight in eight days."

"If I'm not in charge, don't pretend I'm in charge."

"If people can't tell me why they want a report, I'm not going to do a report."

"If I never had to wear another suit, it wouldn't be soon enough for me."

"I don't know if I can take another freezing cold winter here."

So when the President of MegaCorp says softly that running away to the circus is a splendid idea, he means he feels trapped by what he's doing now—trapped by the schedules, the expectations, and the job.

When the assistant manager of the local electronics store confesses that she would rather be running a bed and breakfast on an island off Nova Scotia, she'll break down after questioning and tell you that she isn't precisely sure about the bed and breakfast bit, but that she sure as hell wants to be doing something else, in another way, in a different atmosphere, and with different people.

When the top local sales guy at HugeCo says he'd rather be working an organic farm, that's not really what he means either. If you talk to him for two hours, you'll find he means he wants a looser world, looser clothes, looser relationships.

According to a recent survey, even 50 percent of the Japanese—the workcentric, loyal-to-the-company-no-matter-what Japanese—would grab the chance to walk out of the door of their large company, shuck the uniform, forget the company song, and find something better.

People crave change. But they are afraid of leaving the familiar behind. They want to do something different, but they don't know how different they want it to be. So they stay where they are. And day after day, they feel more and more boxed in by life.

WHAT IF IT'S ALL IN YOUR HEAD?

When we find ourselves sensing something wrong with our lives, many of us head toward the self-help section of the bookstore. There are shelves of books, tapes, and CD-ROMs aimed at you; the carpet on the pathway to that part of the store is worn to a nubbin. There is even a self-help cable channel.

As I trudged through what was available, the books and the tapes began to annoy me. They were all about altering the inner me and contained very little about the outer reality in which I live. They wanted me to change my attitudes, goals, and percentage of body fat. They wanted me to slow down, smell the roses, and rearrange my character. They assumed that there was something wrong with my genes, my personality, and my upbringing—everything my life so far had imprinted on me.

Forget it. I am extroverted, talkative, demanding, and energetic. If I'm going to smell the roses, I'm going to do it on the run. But there's a place for me in the world just as there's a place for consensus-seeking, introverted people with superior listening skills, a tendency to underweight, and an ability to contemplate roses in the lotus position.

The people I'd been talking to weren't short on self-knowledge. What they couldn't understand is that, with all that self-knowledge and talent as well as jobs they figured they should have enjoyed, they still wanted to run away to the circus.

The problem, I began to see, was that the environment they were in was wrong. They were working with the wrong people, working in the wrong place, working for the wrong incentives, or involved with the wrong work processes.

So the books that give career advice weren't helping much because they all seemed to focus on using your skills and talents, not on finding the right environment. A friend of mine recently told me, "I bought one of those test-yourself books. It went into considerable detail. When I did the test the first time, on a long weekend at the cottage, I found out that I should probably be opening a school for creative ceramic art or something like that. I tried it again when I was stuck in bed recovering from appendicitis and found that this time I should be working overseas in international development. I'm afraid to try it a third time in case I find out I should have been an astronaut. I never seem to find my place in the world."

I remembered a report from the 1997 World Economic Forum stating that CEOs about five years ago spent 70 percent of their time focusing on internal problems, such as leading change. Now CEOs spend 70 percent of their time on external matters: customers, niches, and markets. Perhaps, I thought, the same thing applies to people. Instead of gazing at our navels and wondering what we're good at, we should be looking at where we fit, where our niche in the world is. Instead of wondering about who we are, we should spend more time wondering about where we are, why we are there, and what we should do about it.

It makes sense. If you have a large English sheepdog in a 450-square-foot apartment, you either give the sheepdog to someone who lives on a farm and get yourself a Chihuahua or you buy the farm yourself and move together. If you're a clown in a room full of bankers, navel gazing won't make much difference. Finding a good circus will.

Changing yourself is not the answer all the books and tapes have made it out to be. Changing where you are, who you're with, and how you do what you do might be a happier, more effective solution. After all, it's important to understand who we are and what we want to do. However, it's at least equally important to think about who we want our customers, partners, and colleagues to be as well as how, when, and where we want to interact with them. The problem might not be you.

It might just be that you're in the wrong place at the wrong time with the wrong folks. That's a problem most of those self-help books don't address.

RIGHT PERSON, WRONG CIRCUS

It makes sense. After all, most of those find-out-what-you're-good-at books are obsolete as soon as they are printed because so much is changing so fast. How you get to use your talents depends on the world around you, not just on what's inside your own sweet self. You might have the skills to be just a whiz-bang linotype operator, but demand for that kind of work is pretty thin nowadays.

The men and women I'd talked to were, in most cases, energetic, intelligent, directed, and ethical. And they knew it. They also were frustrated and restive, not because they didn't know themselves, but because they didn't like the situations in which they found themselves. To think that they'd change their life by becoming more self-aware would be like thinking you could repave a highway by tinkering with your carburetor.

When I talked to career counselors and outplacement counselors, I heard the same thing. These people work with a lot of clients who have to change. Whether or not the clients knew who they were or enjoyed what they did, one day they woke up and the world around them was no longer the same. They had skills, but those skills were no longer in demand. They had positions in companies, but suddenly those positions had disappeared. Finding a second life wasn't simply a matter of discovering who they were—although that was certainly a part of it. It meant taking a long, hard look at where they were, how they got there, where the rest of the world had gotten to in the meantime, and coming up with a new way to fit into a changing world.

Think back in your career and ask yourself of all the people you know who failed in a job and were terminated, how many of them failed because they lacked the right educational degree, the right job experience, or the right industry background. In all likelihood, most of them failed because of inadequate interpersonal skills, an inability to communicate, or because they just didn't fit in with the culture; in other words—bad chemistry!

—CLIFFORD E. MONTGOMERY, ADJUNCT PROFESSOR
AT ROSEMONT COLLEGE AND VICE PRESIDENT,
HUMAN RESOURCES, QUAKER CHEMICAL CORP.

Bad chemistry?

If the reason people don't do well at their job is bad chemistry, maybe the same batch of chemicals is responsible for people who are unhappy, unfulfilled, dissatisfied—you pick the word—with their current environment. Think of a person who's not thrilled with where he or she is. Is it because of education or experience or industrial background? Or is it because of chemistry?

What you want is important. Not getting it is called *organizational incompatibility* by the experts. I call it feeling like a square peg in a round hole.

I believe that the 60 percent of the people I'd polled who wanted to run away to the circus—or at least the 60 percent who admitted the craving—also felt like square pegs in round holes. And that the answer was not to try to round off their corners, but to show them where the square holes were. Or, as the case may be, square circuses.

Coming to that conclusion wasn't easy. After all, we're supposed to be able to adapt and change. We're supposed to be tough and resilient. We're professionals and we're supposed to be able to tackle any new challenge, even if it's a challenge we didn't particularly want to tackle. If we are unhappy, too bad. If we are itchy to discover something new, it is because we're inconsistent or even disloyal. If we find ourselves disappointed with the way things are, we mustn't whine, we must just pull up our socks, roll up our sleeves, wake up and smell the coffee, and put our shoulder to the wheel. Everything will be fine if we just work harder, change, and adjust. So they say, usually in the same tone of voice my second-grade teacher used to use.

> *Studies are starting to show that a poor fit between what you have and what you want is more detrimental than a poor fit between the demands of the job and your abilities.*
>
> —JEFFREY EDWARDS, ASSOCIATE PROFESSOR, MICHIGAN SCHOOL OF BUSINESS ADMINISTRATION

But . . . I don't think that working harder would have been enough to keep me in the jobs I've left behind. I don't think a lack of hard work is what is the matter with you and I don't think it's the problem with the population of my Rolodex.

Let's take it for granted that hard work is not the issue and get on with it. The fact that you're a pretty useful, serviceable kind of person still leaves us with this persistent hankering you have to join the circus or whatever. I believe that means you have to define what kind of circus you want to run away to and decide how you're going to do it.

This is how organizational change

I've always thought it absurd that people seem to be expected to make a decision early in life about a career and then stick with it for the rest of their lives. It doesn't work that way for most people. True, some people have clear goals and pursue them throughout their lives. Whatever they do—choosing a college, moving to a different city, finding a job—it is part of their pursuit of that goal. But others go from experience to experience, not always sure where it is leading them, but trusting that there is a next step. They are open to their experiences and to learning from them. For these people, there is no one goal in life.

—CAROL POMERANTZ,
CAREER COUNSELOR, SAN FRANCISCO

works. People in organizations don't wake up one morning and start doing their jobs differently. Instead, the world around them starts to buckle and heave, and they find that what used to work no longer gets the same results. Trying harder at the same things won't make the slightest difference. At the same time as they crave change, they don't want to lose what they've got: their core business strengths and capabilities. So they have to reposition themselves to keep the best of the old and keep up with the new.

It isn't a simple, straightforward process. People in organizations resist change, they learn, they fall flat on their faces, they crash into each other, they get it right, almost right, or upside down. They experiment, they go on wild goose chases and down blind alleys, and they stumble over something they weren't looking for. And at the end of all this confusion, they find that the organization is a very different place. It's got some new faces, some old faces, and some old faces with a new expression on them.

We shape our organizations, and our organizations shape us. The process never stops. We don't change ourselves in a vacuum. It seemed to me that a lot of self-help books ignore the environment in which we find ourselves. Even the articles in the psychological journals that talk about person-organization fit seem to overlook the fact that both halves of the equation are variable. Organizations aren't static; they're moving targets.

If you feel like a square peg in a round hole, it may well be that you started off round and have squared over the years or that the hole started square and has been gradually squeezing in the corners. Quite a few of the people I talked to feel that they've done everything right—the right career moves, the right spouse, and the right investments—and yet somehow wound up in the wrong place. They don't know why. I think it's because what seemed like the right place when they were 25 is not the right place for them at 40 or 50. What you used to want you don't want any more. Hence divorce. What fit you once may not fit now. Hence that Donna Karan in my third-floor closet.

> *Eleven thousand days of our lives: roughly speaking, that's the amount of time we spend at work between the ages of 21 and 65. It's a staggering amount of time to commit to any one activity.*
>
> —RICHARD KOONCE

Some day someone will come up with a mathematical equation describing the tendency of square holes to become round over time or, conversely, the tendency of round pegs to develop corners. For now, let's just take it as a working hypothesis that the fit between you and your situation is a constantly changing relationship. You grow into and out of jobs, marriages, houses, interests, and lives.

All this complicates the process of finding a second life, it's true. But it's also liberating to start down the road with the idea that, after all, it's not entirely or mostly your fault. And it's liberating, too, to realize that you don't have to live just one life or join one circus. After all, your second life might just be the route to a third and fourth. Nobody's going to make you sign in blood that what you do next you're going to have to do forever. All you have to do at this point is take the next step. The step after that may not exist yet, but later on we'll teach you how to build as many steps as you want or need.

Let's start by looking at what the world's been doing while you were on your last coffee break.

2

the future isn't what it used to be

In which you will learn that:

1. Whatever you predicted for your life 10 or 20 years ago is 10 or 20 years out of date.

2. Your personal predictions were probably as accurate as the forecasts produced by the Department of Labor, the Club of Rome, and most of the Fortune 500 companies.

3. Planning is not the same thing as prediction. You can still plan.

4. If you don't plan your career, someone else will plan it for you.

Maybe you even took out a piece of paper when you designed your life: I know I did. I used very formal graph paper and a bold black pen. No pencils: we were sure of what was going to be happening. By such-and-such a year, we'd be in such-and-such a position, with such-and-such a

13

> *What we anticipate seldom occurs; what we least expected generally happens.*
>
> —BENJAMIN DISRAELI

salary, which would allow us to live in such-and-such a neighborhood and send our children to such-and-such schools. We'd vacation in this spot and buy a country property in that spot. Some of us even had ideas about what we'd be doing in our retirement—at 55, of course. Either we'd be sitting on a porch in the Berkshires watching our organic French market lettuce growing or we'd find ourselves a bijou duplex in Manhattan and keep up with the latest shows and exhibitions. These dreams rocked us to sleep every night. They had a reassuring predictability and were about as durable as the Berlin Wall, the fact that the Japanese would never build a real American-sized pickup, and the heart-healthy properties of margarine. Things were all set.

FROM INDUSTRIAL REVOLUTION TO INFORMATION REVOLUTION TO . . . ?

There are eras when you can choose what you do and eras when your life—slam, bam, thanks—is apparently chosen for you. For most people in most periods of history, the luxury of choosing has not been available. In most periods, your future was assigned to you by your class, your sex, and your country, and you accepted it. Doing anything else was madness.

About 150 years ago, the North American population was 90 percent rural. If you were born on a farm, your future was to walk behind a horse or stand by a stove: you would always work within sight of where you lived. Your tomorrows were formed the day the woman from the neighboring farm slapped the phlegm out of your throat and told your mother whether she had given birth to a future field hand or the future wife of a field hand. The only possible change in that future would have been caused by a war. Your primary expectation in life was survival and the occasional good cash crop that the weevils didn't get.

With mechanization, the economy shifted rapidly from rural to urban production. Tractors and threshers enabled one person to produce 20 times the agricultural output of before. But somebody had to build the tractors and threshers, and that brought field hands into factories. This was the Industrial Revolution—a revolution which, it should be noted, has not yet happened uniformly all over the world.

Like all revolutions, it was dislocating and bitter. It piled workers up in tenements, strained the family unit ("Mom'll be working at the Triangle Garment Factory today. You kids'll have to look after yourselves"), and rearranged the class structure. It took a long time to sort itself out. But by the end of the Second World War, it looked as if the benefits were starting to trickle down to the working classes. You could hope for an automobile and a house. You could even hope for a retirement some day.

For the middle classes, the house, the car, and the retirement were not dreams anymore, they were expectations—and expectations for middle class children were even more extravagant. America would be populated almost entirely by managers, doctors, and lawyers with the occasional movie star. To paraphrase Garrison Keillor, we'd all be above average.

Just as we were getting comfortable, the Information Revolution whacked us. Although we're still going through it, it's obvious that the effects will be as profound as what happened a century ago when the Industrial Revolution picked the country up by the scruff of its neck and began shaking it.

You know what happened during the Industrial Revolution: you studied it in school. But it was sanitized, safe, preserved within the covers of textbooks. It wasn't real. You can't really imagine a world before industrialization, before widespread home ownership, before children had their own TVs.

It's just as hard to understand what's happening to you during the Information Revolution, during globalization. Few of the participants in a revolution get a clear view of what's happening. It's particularly hard for you because your mindset is likely still industrial, mechanical, and rooted in a real place, not in cyberspace. Your kids are another matter. Kids accept whatever reality they find, and what they find is information-based, electronic, and placeless. That's why your child takes to a computer with an alarming alacrity while you're still trying to get the VCR to stop flashing *12:00*.

The transistor is now half a century old. I remember my first six-transistor radio, something that would have cost a cook at a diner half a week's wages at the time. It weighed the same as a can of beans and fit in my purse only if I took out all of my makeup. The transistors, I read, cost the equivalent of seven dollars each to make in those days. These days my dog Bailey has a computer chip embedded under her skin in case she goes astray. There are more transistors in it than I could count in an hour. I can't remember the cost because it wasn't much. Bailey doesn't notice it.

How You Ended Up in the Wrong Circus and Why You Might Be Given the Boot

You thought your reality was set, say, twenty years ago, when you took out the graph paper and began designing your future in bold, black pen. The new reality has not yet sunk in. You're still in a denial phase, hoping that what we're going through right now is some kind of anomalous economic blip and that everything is going to be all sorted out and life will return to the way it should be. Secure and stable jobs will return. You can get control over your life.

As my grandfather used to say, "Ain't gonna happen." Knowing that it won't happen helps you plan what's going to happen to you and yours. Look at the chart below and see what has happened to jobs:

FASTEST GROWING OCCUPATIONS

PREDICTED FROM 1972 TO 1980	PREDICTED IN 1984 TO 2000	PREDICTED IN 1995 TO 2005
Secretaries	Paralegal personnel care	Personal and home aides
Cashiers	Medical assistants	Home health aides
Registered nurses	Physical therapists	Systems analysts
Cooks	Data processing equipment repairers	Computer engineers
Truck drivers	Home health aides	Physical and corrective therapy assistants
Accountants	Podiatrists	Electronic pagination systems workers
Engineers	Computer systems analysts	Occupational therapy assistants

PREDICTED FROM 1972 TO 1980	PREDICTED IN 1984 TO 2000	PREDICTED IN 1995 TO 2005
Computer operators	Medical records technicians	Physical therapists
Bookkeepers	Employment interviewers	Residential counselors
Computer specialists	Computer programmers	Human service workers

SOURCE: MONTHLY LABOR REVIEW, 1982, 1985, 1995.

Hey! What happened to engineers? Unfortunately the Cold War ended, and money for defense-related projects is drying up. How do you feel about being a home health aide? Universal product codes happened to cashiers. A universal ability to keyboard and use spell-check software happened to secretaries. The fact that computers started to become outdated before they broke down happened to data processing equipment repairers. Each job has had its own particular disaster along with the changes we all encountered.

America's employment figures are better than they have been in some years. In fact, some economists are asking if the country has a big enough labor force to continue the current growth. The problem is that the growing number of jobs may not be in areas that match your skill set or in the industry you're now in. Your industry and your current job may be teetering, even as recruiters are having difficulty hiring and retaining people in other sectors. After all, more than 40 percent of the 1980 Fortune 500 no longer exist.

What's the biggest threat to your own industry and your own current job?

- **Technology.** Have they invented a box or a disk to replace you, what you do, or what you make? Is that five years away? Or two?

- **Global competition.** Where are they going to start doing what you do for half of what you do it for? Japan was one thing. What's going to be the impact of China?

- **Government downsizing.** Bureaucracies are slimming down. Programs are being cut back. Grants are evaporating. If you depend on the government as a client, funding source, or employer, think again.

- **Fashion.** Felt hats—the kind Bogie wore—were fashion. So were macramé, opera windows in cars, turntables, that orange stuff the astronauts drank, digital watches, deep fryers, fondue pots, girdles . . . . Look around your kitchen, office, and car. What's missing that was there ten years ago?

- **Environmental protection.** Is what you produce recyclable? If not, will it be required to be recyclable by the year 2005? Are your waste products biodegradable? Are any of your raw materials likely to become unobtainable in the next ten to twenty years? Is some consumer group likely to boycott your products because they fail to meet environmental audit standards?

- **Demographics.** The baby boomers still dominate the market. They're all buying minivans, aren't they? Well, actually, now they're nudging fifty, they're starting to buy sporty cars because their kids have moved out. Minivan sales are down. What will they want next and what will it do to you? And after that, what will the baby bust generation do?

The Department of Labor does its best to predict trends, but never gets it quite right. Futurists, economic forecasters, demographers, and trend spotters write books and articles about what's coming next and they have their hits and misses, just like the psychics quoted in the tabloids who predict that the Loch Ness monster will be abducted by aliens.

Look around you. People are doing things we didn't have names for twenty years ago: Web masters, genetic counselors, industrial anthropologists, diversity consultants, virtual reality designers, cognitive ergonomists, messaging engineers, and on-line sales logisticians, to name a few. I have at least half a

> *What the future predictors, the change-analysts, and trend-tenders say in effect is that with the aid of institute resources, computers, linear programming, etc., they will deal with the kinds of change that are not the consequence of the Random Event, the Genius, the Maniac, and the Prophet. To which I can only say: there really aren't any; not any worth looking at anyhow.*
>
> —ROBERT NISBET

dozen business cards people have given me that bear titles like director of workplace evolution and vice-president, organizational paradoxes. There are courses listed in every college calendar on subjects that don't fit into the disciplines I remember when I went through college. Feminist Issues in Artificial Intelligence. The Cultural Archaeology of Tomorrow's Global City States. The seven-year-old daughter of a friend of mine told me solemnly the other day that she wants to be a cyber-architect when she grows up. I didn't tell her that the job will be passé when she's through grad school and we'll all probably be exchanging ideas telepathically with implanted microchips. She'll find out soon enough.

As for the rest of us, whoops, we got it wrong all those years ago. Things happened. All we can safely predict for tomorrow is that there will be more changes and that we can't predict what changes they are going to be. Or, to put it another way, we know something's going to happen, we just don't know what.

WHAT DID YOU PREDICT FOR YOURSELF?

Looking at the trends tells us only what's happening to the population in general instead of what's happening to us in particular. It's tempting to think that trends don't really have anything to do with us, just like accidents always happen to someone else. After all, we aren't average North Americans. Our mothers told us that, and Mom was always more credible than, for example, the U.S. Bureau of Statistics, the Gallup organization, or any Silicon Valley think tank. Mom raised us to be Masters of Our Fate and not the helpless playthings of statisticians.

It's useful to do a couple of exercises that show just how quantum our leap has been in the past while. That's important because the next leaps are apt to be just as quantum.

The first table compares where you thought you'd be by now with the situation in which you actually ended up. To create this type of table, all you have to do is cast your mind back ten or twenty years. A couple of glasses of wine might help. What kind of company did you think you'd be working with? What kind of position did you think you'd have? What kind of income (adjusted for the deadly realities of inflation) did you think you'd have? And, because we're not merely careerists, I've included personal questions.

This makes an excellent, if sometimes too-revealing and too-frustrating, party game. In fact, the exercise gets more honest and more complete if you're prompted by others' revelations. Their memories will improve yours. Try it, although you should be ready to step in to put a stop to the process if somebody begins weeping inconsolably or if couples begin a meltdown over mismatched memories.

	10 OR 20 YEARS AGO I THOUGHT . . .	TODAY I GOT . . .
Position	_____	_____
Company type	_____	_____
Prime mission	_____	_____
Location	_____	_____
Number of staff	_____	_____
Salary (adjusted)	_____	_____
Status	_____	_____
House	_____	_____
Car	_____	_____
Marriage	_____	_____
Children	_____	_____
Vacations	_____	_____
Happiness quotient	_____	_____
Retirement plan	_____	_____
Hobbies	_____	_____
Spiritual life	_____	_____
Community life	_____	_____
Health, fitness	_____	_____

Measuring the difference between what we thought would happen to us personally and what actually did happen reinforces the central message of this chapter: Change is going to happen and it's not necessarily predictable. Specific changes are not predictable because the real world does a kind of joyful random violence to predictions. Consider the august Club of Rome's earnest and well-researched projection that, by the year you're reading this, the world would be, for practical purposes, out of oil and that we'd all be scrambling to get our solar-powered cars into a sunny spot in the company lot.

There have been a thousand similar predictions by a thousand similarly expert bodies with a thousand similarly contradictory implications. Henry Ford thought that the future of his business would be in tractors. Alexander Graham Bell saw limited usefulness for the telephone. Sony thought buying MGM was a good idea. Professional economists have learned to live with the absolute certainty of getting it wrong at least half the time.

Global predictions are tough. That makes predicting what happens to you even tougher. You don't live in a vacuum: you're increasingly at the mercy of what happens globally. Things such as recessions, technology, inadequate superiors halfway around the world, computer failures, new laws, software platforms, foreign competition, downsizing, LBOs, and earthquakes happen. You can stand at the shore singing "I've Got to be Me" as loudly as you can, but you're still going to end up pretty soggy when the tide changes. And it will.

Personal changes also affect the accuracy of your predictions. If you suddenly decide to be Mick Jagger instead of remaining Ward Cleaver, that's going to have an impact one way or another on your finances. If your doctor detects an ulcer, that's going to dictate a course change. If your spouse decides to run off with a performance artist leaving you with the kids, the dog, and the mortgage, life is going to be different. Then there are inconvenient progeny, bad hair days, the danger of being run over by a Subaru, faltering sight, shin splints, hormone surges, and the other vast impedimenta involved with being human.

How to Plan for the Unforeseeable Future

Abandoning hope isn't a particularly useful option. Neither is passive acceptance of what the world is doing to you: you can't merely shrug your shoulders and mutter, "It is God's will." What you have to do is to learn to plan a place for yourself—a place where you fit—within a world you know is going to change.

But didn't I just finish saying—at length—that we don't know what changes are being aimed at us? Yes, that was me. And I meant it: you can't predict the particular changes that will affect you. But you do know that change is coming. My company, People Tech, has observed some basic general changes in companies that are adjusting to the information age. So have magazines like *Business Week*, which in 1992 published the table below noting the trends affecting the working and personal lives of people in organizations.

	FROM . . .	TO . . .
Organization	Hierarchy	Network
Structure	Self-sufficiency	Interdependencies
Worker expectations	Security	Personal growth
Leadership	Autocratic	Inspirational
Quality	What's affordable	No compromises
Workforce	Homogenous	Culturally diverse
Work	By individuals	By teams
Focus	Profits	Customers
Markets	Domestic	Global
Advantage	Cost	Time
Resources	Capital	Information
Knowledge base	What worked in the past	Continuous learning

The organization you're working with may not have made, or even started, all these changes. Some companies will never make them. Some organizations will stay in the industrial age, just as some people stayed on the farm. However, most successful organizations will have these transformations in place or in progress. These ongoing global organizational shifts mean you have to make some changes yourself to keep up with the information age. Here are some of the changes you should be prepared for:

- Being more information-oriented. If it's information that's propelling companies, it'll be information and knowing how to access it that'll grant you your independence.

- Being more self-responsible. If companies aren't offering security any more, your personal mandate has to include being continuously re-educated to prepare for your next position.

- Having more real people skills. If your success is going to involve your achievements being measured on a team basis, you'd better learn what it takes to work well on a team. Those skills will also help your leadership potential, your ability to work in a culturally diverse environment, and your success with customers.

This is not just me talking. There are others in the chorus, like Charles Winslow and William Bramer or Sally Lerner, who have tracked shifts in the way our economy is organized:

- The new economy will return to a hunter-gatherer society. The hunt will be for knowledge; the fields and the forests where we hunt and gather will be the global telecommunications network.

- Smaller organizations, as small as one person, will find new ways to work through innovation, creativity, and efficiency.

- People are beginning to ask whether secure, full-time, adequately waged employment will be available to much of the North American workforce, at least over the next thirty to sixty years.

Joseph Coates has mapped emerging trends on the job in his book *Future Work*. Here are some of the changes he has noted:

- Work is moving to unconventional sites and arrangements. You're going to have to be ready to move out of the factory or the office tower and find a work arrangement that's vastly different from the show-up-Monday-to-Friday model. You may no longer be hired, you may be leased or rented as an employer's circumstances change.

- The people driving change aren't just those in the executive suite. Unions are also demanding changes, to save members' jobs. In fact, innovation is happening more quickly in unionized organizations. There's a broad constituency growing against business as usual.

- "The question is no longer whether change in work organization will occur, but what changes will occur and who among the various stakeholders will benefit most. The answer depends on who the critical actors are in the process of organizational change and what their balance of power is."

You're in bed with the circus elephant. When the elephant rolls over, you notice. When the economy rolls over, you notice, too.

How All This Affects You

You don't have to be a futurist to see that all these changes are having a profound effect on people's lives. In fact, it would be quite easy to create a table that treats personal change in the same way as the preceding table showed organizational change.

	FROM . . .	TO . . .
Career	One	Several
Career path	Steadily upwards	Up, sideways, out...
Job security	Almost guaranteed	You could be out tomorrow
Relationship to employer	Like that of an indentured servant	Like that of a freelance contractor
Motivation	Status, ambition	Sanity, freedom, health, satisfaction

	FROM . . .	**TO . . .**
Education	Completed before starting a career	Continuous
Marriage	Stable	One in three will end in divorce
Division of labor	Man is primary breadwinner; woman is primary caregiver to children	All bets are off
Dream house	Split-level ranch house in suburbs	Renovated industrial loft in city; converted farm in country or in Tuscany
Relationship of home and work	Separate	Home may be primary or secondary work place
Retirement	At 65	This year, next year, sometime, never
Retirement lifestyle	Golf, travel	New forms of work, new adventures
Children	Leave home at 18	May not leave at all or may leave and come back
Children's lifestyle	A repeat of your own	Utterly unpredictable
Spiritual and community life	What you do in your spare time	Who you are

The rules are changing. While we don't know the new rules specifically, we do know their general shape. The new rules will require new skills for those who want to be more or less in charge of their lives. If you don't have the skills, you'll be less able to plan. You still may be able to dream, but there will be less chance of seeing those dreams with flesh on them. You simply won't have the money or the options.

The alternative to planning your escape to the circus of your choice is to find yourself at the mercy of other people's plans for you. And there's nothing more depressing than listening to someone muttering, "I could have been a contender." Unless it's being that person. Which leads us to a final table.

	WHERE I AM . . .	IN 10 YEARS I WANT . . .	TO GET THERE, I'LL . . .
Position	_____	_____	_____
Company type	_____	_____	_____
Prime mission	_____	_____	_____
Location	_____	_____	_____
Number of staff	_____	_____	_____
Salary (adjusted)	_____	_____	_____
Status	_____	_____	_____
House	_____	_____	_____
Car	_____	_____	_____
Marriage	_____	_____	_____
Children	_____	_____	_____
Vacations	_____	_____	_____
Happiness quotient	_____	_____	_____
Retirement plan	_____	_____	_____
Hobbies	_____	_____	_____
Spiritual life	_____	_____	_____
Community life	_____	_____	_____
Health, fitness	_____	_____	_____

Yes, it's the same exercise you went through before. But this time, we're looking at your daydreams. Or are we? And we've added a column: "To get there I'll . . ."

The rest of this book is about filling in that final column. First, however, you may want to stop right here, make no changes in your life, make no decisions. Let's just examine that possibility for a moment.

THE CONSEQUENCES OF DECIDING
NOT TO RUN AWAY TO THE CIRCUS

Deciding not to decide is a decision. And, like any other decision, it should be examined with the same beady eyes you'd turn on any decision to join the circus, become a bush pilot, or open an organic cotton mill. Some of the results of deciding not to decide, letting things roll on, include:

1. Putting your life and career decisions in someone else's hands. If you don't define your future, it's likely someone else will. And how much do you trust them?

2. You've decided not to find how high is up. You've decided that this is as good as it can possibly get and that no decision could make it any better. Congratulations: this is the best day of the rest of your life. Because if you're not going to change, this is it.

3. By deciding not to change anything, you are cutting yourself off from tools and techniques, know-how, and people you may need when those other folks decide to change your life for you. You've decided not to learn more about getting a new job, networking with new people, or exposing yourself to new knowledge. It's likely that if they're going to make a decision about your future, it'll be because your job, your contacts, or your knowledge is out of date.

4. By deciding not to run away, you may have decided to become a stone bore. If you have nothing new to talk about, people have nothing new to listen to. If you have nothing to become enthusiastic about, you will lack passion. And sooner or later, you will be kicked out of the car pool.

3

stealing the corporations' secrets

In which you will find out that:

1. You are a business, whether you realize it or not. Behave like one and draw up a business plan.

2. Organizations don't enjoy changing any more than you do, but they know that change is the only guarantee of survival.

3. Sometimes change finds you; sometimes you have to go out and hunt it down.

I have a cottage overlooking a lake in Northern Ontario—rocky shores, pines, misty mornings, quiet (if you don't mind the loons), large fire-

> Don't expect toothpicks to pry you out of steel traps.
>
> —TOM PETERS

place, big fridge, fat couches, and an off switch for the phone and fax. Most of the time I go up there to play Marti of the Primal Forest and discourse with the woodland rodents. It's the circus I run away to on spare weekends.

29

On some weekends however, it becomes part of my business, a place where corporate transformations of large businesses are planned. Through the years I have found myself increasingly inviting CEOs and their spouses to the cottage to talk about change because I realized that, when you start talking about any kind of change, it's hard to keep the discussion within tidy limits and that these CEOs, to a greater or lesser extent, were their companies and their companies were them (in the same way that the family farm is the farmer). Corporate change has a tendency to spill over into people's lives, starting with the CEO. So it was not surprising that quite often the CEO of a corporation was a person who wanted to change not just the company but also his or her own life: Both existed in parallel.

Some of these executives zero in on changing their companies. Some zero in on changing their lives. Same thing, really. Ego and vision and a lust for satisfaction intertwine. Over all the years of change management work, we've found you have to change yourself to change the company (this dismays a few people when I tell them). And, if you change your own life, I've found, your company, your family, and everything else will change anyway. We can focus on the company or we can focus on you, the individual, but many of the same things apply. The boundaries between work and home are blurring these days.

That's true, not just for CEOs, but for CAOs, CFOs, VPs, executive directors, managers, trainees, receptionists, union leaders, union members, and the cleaning staff. That shouldn't be a surprise. After the death of the lifelong job and the birth of the professionally transient, we are all essentially our own corporation, each of us an entity that goes through everything a corporation does. We individually grow, acquire, downsize, merge, and restructure. We give these processes different names when we're talking about individuals, but we experience change just as organizations do.

If you're a person who puts up vinyl siding, you already know you're your own business. You know your income depends on lifestyles and weather and economic conditions. If you're a CFO at a multinational or the person who packs the bags at the grocery store, you should look at yourself and your situation in the same way because what you're doing is subject to the same influences. What's inflicted on General Motors is inflicted on the USA.

The prime benefit of considering yourself a business is that you stop considering yourself an employee. Employees—even if they call themselves that—are over. So are many employers in the traditional sense.

Another benefit is that you are entitled to borrow the best practices of business. In fact, you have to. You must plan like a business and execute those plans with as much energy as you would if they were business plans handed to you by a demanding superior. You must devote to the change in your life the amount of time and effort you put into business.

Give your personal life the energy and thought that you'd give it if it were a small business, and you will achieve what you want much more quickly—even if you stay within your present company. If this seems too cold and calculating a way of dealing with daydreams, then you don't really want those daydreams to come true.

Acting as though your business life were a business in itself, distinct from the larger business of whatever organization you're working for at the moment, makes sense. In a world where change is a constant, you have to think of yourself as a separate entity. Make yourself more competitive, invest in yourself, and make new strategic alliances for the business that is you.

You are a company, and your company is you. Even if you're one of the diminishing percentage of us getting a regular paycheck, you're your own business: YouInc. Remember it always.

For some people, the idea of applying business logic to personal life turns out to be something of a mental hurdle. It makes them uncomfortable. It doesn't seem suitable. Like wearing rubber boots to a tea party, it's just not done. We forget that individuals have always stolen good ideas and techniques from business, such as computers, answering machines, financial planning, automated production (look at all those machines in your kitchen), the concept of team labor, and the Internet.

It's extraordinary how unprofessional some professional people are about their personal lives. I know a corporate lawyer who can drive a hard bargain when she's sitting at a boardroom table and charging her client in six-minute increments. But on her own time, she's putty in the hands of a real estate agent and routinely pays too much for the houses she's lived in. I know an office manager who is a pitbull about keeping costs down when it comes to supplies and furniture but who can't keep to her own grocery budget. I've met a developer who has a twenty-year plan for a particular area, knows where the school will be built in five years and where the shopping center will be needed in fifteen years, yet who can't somehow wrap his mind around the idea of putting money away for retirement.

I can't help thinking that this mindset is the reason why a happily married couple I know is very reluctant to describe how they first met because they were introduced through a computer dating agency. They have found that some of their acquaintances find this matter-of-fact approach to choosing a life partner too unromantic—even a bit shocking. It would, I suppose, have been more romantic to have left this aspect of their lives in the hands of chance and random events. But if they had, they might still be two single lonely hearts.

A number of the people I've interviewed stumbled on to the right environment by chance. Similarly, Albert Schweitzer changed his life because someone had left a magazine open to an article about Africa on a library table one day. Hollywood hopefuls are probably still hanging around Schwab's drugstore wearing tight sweaters hoping to be discovered by chance, like Lana Turner. And the North American trade in lottery tickets runs to the billions with millions hoping fate will take them by the scruff of the neck and redecorate the way they live.

For most of us, however, chance needs a helping hand. In our over-programmed lives, there isn't much room for chance between our jobs, our family responsibilities, and our mortgage payments. Who has time to hang around libraries or drugstores on the off-chance that our destiny is waiting there for us? And who's really willing to leave fate to the long, long odds of a lottery?

Companies don't have time to wait for chance, either. A few lucky companies may have stumbled onto a brilliant innovation or located an undiscovered genius lurking in the mailroom, but the best companies deliberately create new opportunities for growth and consciously reinvent themselves. Some of them have hired my company to help. Our job is to do what chance would do eventually, given time. As some wise person once said, "Planning is what you resort to when chance breaks down."

So here's what I intend to do: I'm going to explain some of the lessons we've learned in helping organizations change and suggest ways you can apply them to your own life. We've found that a lot of what works for ThemInc. works equally well for YouInc.

One of the first lessons should be that if, as Tom Peters suggests, we are in a steel trap, we need more than a toothpick to get us out. A lot of the toothpicks advocated in most personal change books seem disturbingly thin. We are advised to go away by ourselves for a while. We are told that we should treat ourselves better and give ourselves a nice treat during our quiet time every day. We are told to try new kinds of tea, exercise, change reading patterns, look ourselves in the mirror and tell ourselves that we have some good qualities. The idea seems to be that we're somehow consoling ourselves for failure, patting ourselves on our slumped backs and saying, "There, there. It's going to be all right. I love you just the way you are. Have a cup of Lemon Zinger." I'm a little more aggressive about my life than that. After all, why use a personal change toothpick when you can put the full force of an industrial-strength corporate change crowbar behind your dreams? Leverage is what it's all about.

WHY DO COMPANIES CHANGE?
IT'S USUALLY BECAUSE THEY'VE BEEN BATTERED

When I started my career, organizational change was not well established as a part of management consulting. There was no methodology for change, no rules, and not many case histories to go by. The people within the companies had not developed them. What organizations had developed were policies and procedures designed to stop change dead before it messed with the ways things had always been done. People said:

> "Change costs money."

> "Change is disruptive. It upsets people and lowers their productivity."

> "Changing something implies that the people here have been doing it wrong all along."

"If it ain't broke, don't fix it" was the motto of most corporations. So when "it" started breaking to the extent that people could no longer deny it—breaking technologically, demographically, economically, and in just about in every other way you can think of—there were few people around who knew how to fix it. "It" had never been broken in recent memory and the skill of what it took to put things right had to be learned all over again.

Corporations, whipped by their shareholders, learned the skills first. The lessons were rough. Among the first of those lessons was that the CEO can't change a company by sending a rousing memo, changing the company slogan to "Quality Is our Creed," and making every Friday dress down day. That was simply like changing the color of your Edsel.

After a certain amount of failure and stress, corporations learned that there were some more profound things you had to do if you were actually going to make a difference in the organization. At my company, we learned these things by listening to people at literally hundreds of companies. We also were better equipped than most corporations to consider what was really going on. We knew human behavior. Additionally, we had the outside perspective, and if you really want to know your country, it's best to ask a traveler from a far land.

My company has worked to change companies like Hostess Frito-Lay, Pepsi-Cola, Campbell Soup, Aetna Life and Casualty, Royal Insurance, Continental Insurance, IBM, Kraft-Jacobs Suchard, Ciba Vision, and army officers of the Czech Republic. All these companies and organizations needed, and wanted, to change. Globalization, technology, demographic shifts, and increasing competition kicked them into transforming the way they see and do things. Think about Chrysler fifteen years ago and then think about Chrysler now. Or about Harley-Davidson. Or about your bank, your phone company, or your corner store. They've transformed.

We know that the primary reason corporations change is not because economic or demographic seers forecast that change is necessary. Change also doesn't often come because something can be done more efficiently or humanely. Nor do organizations change for the greater good of the public or to decrease their impact on the planet's ability to sustain itself.

Organizations change because the pain of staying the same became greater than the pain involved in change.

Think of an organization you know that has gone through profound change. Then, think about why they did it. Was it because of the common good, altruism, great financial forecasting, or superb forward planning? Or was it because their backs were pushed so hard against the wall they had no choice? Was it a true interest in efficiency? Or was it the fact that their bankers were tapping their nervous fingers on the boardroom table? Was it an honest interest in their customers' welfare? Or the fact they were losing market share to Taiwan or a nationally franchised competitor? Nine times out of ten, it was because the pain of staying the same became greater than the pain involved in change.

That's the first lesson you have to learn if you want to run away to the circus: *People change because the pain of staying the same becomes greater than the pain involved in change.* You're not going to leave your job, town, or social attachments until the pain of staying there is more than the pain of packing your bag and heading down the road.

It's the reason you picked up this book. You're feeling pain. You think you want to change. You can plan the change. You can even, with the help of facts and figures like the ones we've given you, forecast the need to change. However, because you're like most of the race, you're not actually going to make any huge personal transformation until the pain comes and inflicts change upon you. This is not because you're unambitious, cowardly, or stupid, it's because, like most of planet, you don't change roads until you're kicked off the road you're on.

That's what happened to Paul Beaver.

UP THE CREEK WITHOUT ALMOST ANYTHING

In writing a book about personal change I knew I had to get case histories. Therefore, I created a questionnaire with the help of my colleagues. It was a three-page document with questions grouped around the following topics:

> Sometimes in the course of our lives we enter unknown territory for the first time and recognize with a jolt that at last we have come to the true place.
>
> —E. ANNIE PROULX

1. What was the specific pain that caused you to change?

2. What did you find was the greatest impediment to change?

3. Was your family supportive? In what ways did this manifest itself?

4. If you left your job, what was the reaction of your colleagues?

5. What, if any, regrets do you have?

6. What were the financial implications?

The questionnaire was not necessary. I abandoned it after the first phone call. Ask a person who has changed his or her life about what the change meant and all you have to do is hang on to the receiver. They love the fact they've changed and, quite rightly, are enthralled with their story. They make it sound like the best thing that ever happened, the nicest thing anyone could ever do for themselves. Their responses went far beyond the questions I planned to ask and took our discussions into much more interesting territory that anything I could have anticipated.

Paul Beaver was one of the earliest to prove that to me. He'd grown up in Upper Musquodoboit (pronounced Musk-a-da-bit), Nova Scotia. The plumbing was out the back door and down a trail. The lighting was kerosene—a Tom Sawyer boyhood in a colder part of the continent. You could expect to grow up fishing for cod or jollying a tractor on a small hardscrabble acreage.

He didn't. Instead he got a Ph.D. in Biology at the University of Chicago and then taught for a year at Purdue. Things got better. He became an assistant professor, studying evolutionary behavioral patterns in animals in the Biology Department at the University of Washington in Seattle. Then things got even better. He married and had two children, Spencer and Gwendolyn. This was paradise on the Pacific, five time zones away from Nova Scotia. At this point, he could legitimately look forward to getting tenure at the university (a job for life) and watching his kids grow.

Instead of that, the pain happened.

1. Paul didn't get tenure.

2. His wife took the kids "and ran off with a truck driver. I guess she thought she'd married some loser."

3. His field was sufficiently rarefied that he couldn't find a suitable replacement position.

"I felt bitter," Paul confided. "I felt that the world just wasn't being fair to me. Here I was working hard, trying to be a good father, and then I didn't have a career, my wife or kids."

A member of his thesis committee offered him a temporary consulting position with the Brookfield Zoo. The zoo was in the process of building Tropic World, a huge, multimillion-dollar indoor display. It would recreate the jungles of Africa, Southeast Asia, and the Amazon with gorillas, hippos, plants, the works. Paul's job was to fly down to the western Amazon region, known to biologists as the green paradise of the Amazon, on an expedition seeking out birds and plants.

Down there he became friendly with native Peruvians, living in their villages. He noticed they had far more problems than he did. But he also noticed that they "woke every morning smiling and laughing, happy about the miracle of life. They didn't expect it to be fair. This was an inspiration. It made me take a long look at my life and realize how I was wasting this precious miracle in feeling bitter about what had happened to me. It gave me a personal philosophy and a deeper insight into what it takes to be happy and really enjoy life."

But it wasn't just that the people were attractive. The western Amazon interested him immensely. "It made an immediate impression on me. As a biologist I loved the variety of plants—nearly half of the world's plants are in the Amazon. And it was wonderful to see monkeys in their natural forest—fascinating for a biologist to be in such a place."

The trip changed his life. "I didn't want to leave. I became so emotionally attached to the Amazon I just wanted to stay."

He remembered a tour guide he had met on a whitewater rafting trip on the Wenatchee River back in Washington State. "He told me his life story. He used to be a teacher. Then he quit his job and started out the rafting company. He said he'd been happy ever since. It made quite an impression on me. I though, well, why not? Why not take whatever risk it takes?"

He started methodically, the way an assistant professor would. He looked into the tourism industry.

"When people think of the Amazon, the mind conjures up a wilderness where one can have the greatest adventure of anywhere in the world. Even the word *Amazon* carries a kind of mysterious sound to it." Most of the existing tourist accommodations, however, were in secondary growth forest, comfortably close to the city. The alternative was nice, safe cruises up the river. But there was absolutely nothing that brought people deep into the forest, into the green jungles and cloud forest mountains he loved.

Start-up capital was small. Almost the only equipment he needed to invest in were machetes. He conducted a word-of-mouth campaign among friends, promising them jungle survival tours. He did seminars at nature centers, universities, colleges, hiking clubs, and libraries.

What he was offering was frighteningly simple. You took your machete and built the lean-to that would be your accommodations: The branches of the forest are your structural members, the vines hold them together, the water-shedding palm leaves are your roof. The resin in the trees burns like gasoline, or you can put it into a stream and paralyze the fish for your meal. The Yarina plant gives you fresh water. There are coconuts. You burn termite nests to repel the mosquitoes.

It wasn't a tenured position. "My mother cried. She thought this was kind of crazy. I had steady pay. I had medical insurance. As it's turned out I've been at it fifteen years and it's been the steadiest job I've ever known." What former colleagues thought "was a bit embarrassing: 'Paul is leaving to follow his dream.' I never thought of it like that. Each step along the way it seemed like the logical thing to do."

Things have gone beyond the grab-your-knife-and-take-to-the-trees stage. There's a lodge. There are staff. There are canoes and motorboats, a generator to recharge batteries, and camping gear so you don't have to build your own lean-to. There are tablecloths at dinner, float plane expeditions, and chilled wine. There's an office in Florida. There's a mention in the book *Buzzworm's Guide to Eco-Travel* that he offers one of the best 100 trips in the world. There's also a new wife, Dolores, and a third child.

But the basic lure is the same for Paul and for the people he introduces to the region. "There's no place in the world like the Amazon. The orchids and bromeliads, parrots and macaws, the curious monkeys. A lot of times people are kind of amazed by the whole thing. But if you take it step by step, it's not all that amazing. I've never felt threatened in the Amazon. I've had fewer run-ins with poisonous snakes than I have with crazy drivers in North America. Camping out is a snap. There's nothing hard to it. I like to work up a sweat and blaze a trail and carry a heavy pack. I feel for me, as an owner and a North American employing sixty Peruvians, I have to set the standard on how I want people to work. So when my employees see the bossman busting his butt, working up a sweat, it's going to inspire them to work hard. I like to work hard. There's no stress involved. When you're working for someone else—that's stressful. Working in an office up in Washington trying to get tenure—that was stressful to me.

"I feel very fortunate to have this life. Sometimes I think, 'Why me?' It's a gift to be able to earn one's living enjoying something so much.

"I save myself for the specialty expeditions, the ones that push exploration to the limit. I'm in it for the fun of it. Many of the tourists who go with me now have been on one of the lodge trips. I enjoy sharing an adventure with them."

What happened to BeaverCo.?

Change that's inflicted on you is not necessarily bad. For Paul Beaver, it turned out to be very much the opposite. He found a world he did not know, a job he hadn't imagined, a company that's unique, a new wife, and a child. That's an experience others have shared.

You could look at Paul Beaver's story and say, "Well, all that's about is some guy who got popped out of his job and fell into a new situation. That's all very nice and romantic in sort of an Indiana Jones kind of way, but according to the annual reports I read, that sort of thing doesn't happen to corporations. They make change: It isn't inflicted on them."

Let me reiterate: most corporations only wish they made change in advance of, rather than in response to, pain. Did General Motors lead the way to smaller, higher quality, more fuel-efficient, safer cars? They wish. In fact, each of those cards was dealt to them. Smaller was dealt them partly by the economy and partly by demographics. Fuel efficiency was dealt by the oil crisis. Safer was dealt to them by the federal government. Higher quality was dealt to them by the Japanese and the Germans. They read each card as it was dealt and wept. They wanted nothing more than not to have to make those changes, just as Paul Beaver reacted when his job disappeared and his wife walked.

IBM had Apple and Compaq inflicted on it: individuals took over computers from the MIS department and made them personal. America's pork farmers had Weight Watchers inflicted on them and had to invent a thinner pig, something their forefathers would never have understood. The Post Office got hit with FedEx and fax machines. Reynolds Tobacco did not decide to invent the cleaner smoking, low-tar cigarette: the Surgeon General motivated the public to inflict the change. A pill-poisoning maniac inflicted change on the whole pharmaceuticals packaging industry. And the numbers of things that are still being inflicted on the corporations and on YouInc. are growing. Technology hasn't stopped evolving and speeding up the pace of life. Trade barriers are falling faster than ever. Competition is growing, and your next competitor may be eight time zones away. Government will not stop tinkering: Washington or Brussels or Moscow will be visiting new regulations on you.

Of course Paul Beaver had change inflicted on him. In his book *The End of Work*, Jeremy Rifkin states that, in the global economy, 800 million people are unemployed or underemployed because of computers, robots, and telecommunications advances. It's happened to more than 4 million

> People change when they are forced to change, when they get a pink slip, when their spouse asks for a divorce, when they are at a low point and feel that they have nothing much to lose by changing. Most people aren't very good at changing proactively.
>
> —REBECCA MADDOX, PRESIDENT AND FOUNDER, CAPITAL ROSE

North Americans in the past decade. It's happened to every company I've talked to. That means you have think about the fact that you are going to have change inflicted on you. You may not decide to run away and join the circus—you may be driven away and have to join one.

It's best if you can decide which one for yourself, that is, define your own changes and your own terms. Paul Beaver's story sounds exotic and unlikely because of it unusual locale. Not many people find a new life in the rain forest. But lots of people fall in love with a place and then find a way to stay there. I have met quite a few people who have fallen in love with the far North and have made a new life for themselves in Baffin Island or Alaska. It's not everybody's cup of latte, but for certain people the life of the North is liberating and exhilarating. Other people have fallen in love with Alice Springs or Lisbon or Srinagar or Albuquerque. For them, the right geographical location makes all the other pieces in the puzzle fall into place.

As my friend with the career planning books would have said, Paul Beaver found his place in the world—quite literally. He stumbled across it at first, but he recognized it when he saw it. The rest was a matter of working out the details.

But we're not all Paul Beavers. Many of us are solidly rooted in communities that mean a lot to us and that we don't want to abandon, yet still we feel out of sorts. That's because geographical location is only one of many aspects of our environment and it may not be the one that needs to change. Millions of tourists go on vacation to beautiful places every year, and plenty of them fantasize about staying on forever, but they don't. I sometimes dream about renovating a seventeenth-century farmhouse in Tuscany, but I don't suppose I will.

UP THE ORGANIZATION? OR DOWN THE HALL?

The amount of change required to impel change differs from organization to organization and from person to person. I need just a slight twinge to send me scurrying to the dentist, whimpering; you may need an impacted wisdom tooth before you'll book an appointment. Pain thresholds vary at work, too. Getting a harsh memo from a supervisor may be enough to make some people clean out their desks. For others the pain required to change jobs may not be noticeable until after a demotion, ten years of ceaseless boredom, and being allotted a parking space in the farthest corner of the farthest lot.

There's another kind of pain I should mention, and that's the ache of a missed opportunity. Your present situation might be swell or even above average. But if the sweet enticements that change offers you are much better than what you have now, you may begin to feel the pangs presented by a possible missed opportunity. It's the difference between running to get away from something and running toward something you desperately want.

For example, suppose you are a successful lawyer. You are offered a chance to run for a seat in Congress. Both situations are good, but one is better. The pain of remaining a successful lawyer might be greater than the pain of missing the opportunity to become Mr. Smith goes to Washington. You choose and you change.

Successful change doesn't necessarily, or even often, mean a move to the Amazon, to an ashram, or from courtroom to Congress. It doesn't necessarily mean changing companies, careers, or spouses or saying you're going down to the corner to pick up the newspaper and ending up in a white linen suit at a waterfront bar in the Bight of Benin. It can be, and often is, as simple as getting rid of a truly bad tie and suddenly being happy with the rest of the outfit. You don't have to change saddles to get rid of the burr.

Lani Berger simply moved down the hall.

She'd been trained as an accountant. "My father died when I was a teenager and there were two uncles who were accountants and thought it was a good idea: steady work, good income, respectable profession, portable skill. Like most people about twenty years old I didn't know really what I wanted to do except that I wanted some security. The uncles arranged the tuition and I took the courses. I was good at it. I'm careful. I'm methodical. I could pack stacks and stacks of tax law into my head. I graduated in the top 10 percent.

"Took a month off. Went to California. Looked at the ocean. Came back here and got the job."

Here is Indiana. The job was in the accounting department of a large, old, and respected packaged goods manufacturer owned by a large, old, and respected family that had been putting their products into packages and selling them to all of America ever since the end of the First World War. I have some on my kitchen shelf. The product is an icon.

The situation was good. "This was more than just okay, this was fine. Young woman, first job. There's an apartment to decorate, clothes to buy. You can buy a car, you can take vacations, and you can pretend you're moving right along. Every so often you get a larger desk which you can brag about. They give you business cards you can show your Mom. And the people I worked with were good. Accountants are not dull. Ever been to an accountants' convention? They can misbehave as well as anyone. Plus, of course, we know how to make it tax deductible.

"The problem was that I felt I was starting to measure out my life. Every three months you have the quarterly reports. Every year you have the annual report. I'd look out from my office and the trees would be changing color and I'd say to myself, 'Ah, yes: third quarter.' I started relating to events that way. A friend would have a baby, and I'd keep track of the age by saying, 'Yes, she was born in the second quarter, 1992.'

"That wasn't the problem, and it was a while before I figured out what the problem was for me. What we did in my part of my department was report on things. You'd come to the end of the month or the quarter and you'd send a report up to the fourth floor. They'd move the line on the profit graph up or down. I didn't make the line move up or down, I simply reported it. It was sort of like doing play by play on some sort of snail that moved four times a year.

"The job involved a lot of skill, a lot of attention, and lot of know-how. But still, you were only reporting what had happened; not making it happen.

"I guess I did the traditional thing. I decided that I'd round things out a little for myself by going to night school. Continuing education. I'd been reading about pottery in some magazine and I did that. Thirteen week course: one quarter. Then I took a more advanced course and I started to fool around. Once you knew the techniques, they expected you to be creative. What I did was started making these pots that looked like my business. They had graphs on them and charts. I started thinking about them and I started making coffee mugs for the people at work. The guy doing the Nielsen reports would get a coffee cup with a Nielsen report on it; the woman who did the in-house travel arrangements would get one with an expense account voucher on it with all the expenses disallowed.

"People started asking me for these mugs at work. I did a coffee pot with five spouts on it and five handles for the five top guys in the department who were always arguing about whose responsibility things were. None of them could say anything because then people would figure the joke was on that person in particular.

"A woman comes into my office one day, and she looks at me strangely for a minute. She introduced herself and says she's head of New Product Development. She asks if I want to spend a half day down in her department fooling around. She's cleared it with my department.

"I went down there for half the day. They have all kinds of new products they've been trying to develop for the company. Some are working—but about 90 percent of all new products fail. There's a lot of imitation: every company in the country comes out with low-fat cheese at the same time, and there's not enough room for them all.

"She pushes a product at me and asks what do I think of that? And then she slides another one across the desk and I'd say something. We got laughing. That's how it went for the half day.

"Two months later she comes into my office and she's got a jar. It was made the way we'd been saying it could be made. They tried the product in a test market in New England. It failed—most new packaged goods products fail—but she asked if I wanted a transfer to her department."

Lani's present situation was good. The promised situation seemed better. The pain of remaining the same became greater than the pain of changing.

"We've had successes since I moved there: more than average. We're beating the average pretty well because I can bring a little accounting to the job and keep track of profitability and suggest some ideas. My uncles don't quite get it, but I'm happier, making things happen."

I've heard many stories like that. You don't have to move countries, get a divorce, or even change companies to make an enormous difference.

Corporations can change without moving head offices or operations. They can create an entirely new environment without leaving a community (in fact, the ones that do leave often lose more than they gain). The same is true of most of us.

Whether we stay put or move, we have to leave something behind. Paul left not only the United States, but also his academic ambitions and a certain way of life that went with them. He had to learn a new language and a new work style. You may have to shed some baggage, too, and pick up new skills and attitudes, even though you may be in the same house or the same office ten years from now.

Alas, I can't offer you an all-expenses-paid trip to the environment of your dreams. What I can do, however, is give you some tools that may help you look at your life in a new way and grope forward to your second life.

WHERE DOES IT HURT?

There are some things you run to. There are some things you're aching to run away from. A lot us concentrate on the destination and are in a state of denial about what's making us want to take the trip. It's important to do an inventory of what's ailing you so you don't end up with the same problem again. If your main problem is the faceless bureaucracy you deal with, you don't want to make a change that puts you back in another jungle of cubicles. If your problem is the disorganization of your present place, you want to identify that so you can find something where the lines are straighter and more carefully marked. If you're troubled by the need to keep making a fat income, you're not going to want to move to another situation where you're required to have a Mercedes.

It's hard to diagnose these things at a distance. With corporations, it can take days or weeks of down-and-dirty meetings to find out what's really hurting. But the exercise below can get you thinking. I've listed some common complaints translated into the realm of personal experience. Think them over: How much are they hurting you?

WHERE DOES IT HURT?

	A LITTLE	A LOT	LIKE AN IMPACTED WISDOM TOOTH
The running-away factors:			
Can't take the financial pressure	_____	_____	_____
Can't take the pressure from my spouse	_____	_____	_____
Can't take the family pressure	_____	_____	_____
Can't take the stress at work	_____	_____	_____
Don't like my kind of work	_____	_____	_____
Don't like my industry	_____	_____	_____
Don't like my company	_____	_____	_____

	A LITTLE	A LOT	LIKE AN IMPACTED WISDOM TOOTH
Don't like my boss	_____	_____	_____
Don't like my co-workers	_____	_____	_____
Don't like the people who work for me	_____	_____	_____
Don't like my customers	_____	_____	_____
Don't like all the travel I have to do	_____	_____	_____
Don't like my neighborhood	_____	_____	_____
Don't like this city/town	_____	_____	_____
Don't like this state	_____	_____	_____
Don't like my home	_____	_____	_____

The running-toward factors:

	A LITTLE	A LOT	LIKE AN IMPACTED WISDOM TOOTH
I want to work on my own	_____	_____	_____
I want to be part of a team	_____	_____	_____
I want a more secure job	_____	_____	_____
I want a more entrepreneurial job	_____	_____	_____
I want to use different skills	_____	_____	_____
I want to learn something new	_____	_____	_____
I want more travel	_____	_____	_____
I want more challenge	_____	_____	_____
I want more calm	_____	_____	_____
I want to be told what to do	_____	_____	_____
I want to be in charge	_____	_____	_____
I want a life	_____	_____	_____

If you know your pain, you're halfway to a cure. We'll be getting more and more into the causes of pain and possible cures later in the book. Each of those pains and each of those pain relievers define what kind of circus you should be aiming yourself toward and suggest which road to the circus will be easiest.

AFTER THE PAIN STOPS

From Paul Beaver's mountaintop lodge in Choctomal, it's a short trip to Gran Vilya. Gran Vilya is pre-Inca: 20,000 buildings now in ruins above a gorge more than a mile deep. This city in the clouds was rediscovered in 1985. It's empty. The people (a few thousand years ago) decided to change. Or, according to which scientists you believe, they had change inflicted on them. Possibly, there was the pain of an epidemic, a meteorite crash, the failure of their agricultural land, or displacement by other and fiercer peoples. Whatever happened to them, it made them leave behind a huge city.

> Who built Thebes of the seven gates?
> In the book the kings are named,
> But who hauled the rock?
> And Babylon, many times demolished,
> Who raised it again? In what houses
> Of gold-glittering Lima did the builders
> live?
> Where, when the Great Wall of China was
> finally done,
> Did the masons go?
> —BERTOLT BRECHT

Change means pain because it means letting go of something. That something may be a place, a comfortable rut, an outgrown ambition, a certain status, or familiar people. Some baggage you may get to take with you, but likely you'll have to leave more behind. Companies have to leave behind former successes and large investments in those successes to find new ones. They find the process wrenching, but rewarding if they follow through. What do you have to leave behind? And how much would you miss it if you did?

4

what kind of circus did you have in mind?

In which you will learn:

1. That if you can't dream it, you can't do it.

2. That you'll need more than one dream to make a new life for yourself.

3. How corporations dream up new products—a process you can use to reinvent yourself.

4. The rules of brainstorming.

This may come as a surprise, but before you can do your hard-headed business planning, you have to dream. Corporations know this. Top performers know this. If you can't dream it, you can't do it. If you can't fantasize about the joys of producing the world's best turkey sausages, you're never going to succeed in making them. If you can't

All I can see as I look back is a picture of myself going about my daily affairs in a half-dream state, sometimes discontented but never trying to find out why, vaguely making the best of things, rarely looking ahead except casually, almost as a game dreaming of what I would like to happen, but never seriously thinking how I could set about to make it happen.

—JOANNA FIELD

conceive of winning the America's Cup, it won't happen. If you can't daydream about being a daring young thing on the flying trapeze in the circus, you'll end up in the audience.

There's another thing: Dreams are mirrors of the pain that causes our hunger for change. When you're bothered by cold feet, you dream of tropical beaches. When you're ground down by a humdrum life, you may daydream of carving ships' figureheads in Maine. If you're afflicted by unending telephone calls, e-mails, and faxes, you daydream of herding sheep in the Pyrenees.

For most of us, daydreams are unlikely to be a direct A-to-B route to a second life. But it's worth paying attention to them because they tell you a lot about what you want. A company can't do what it doesn't dream. Neither can you. A company that dreams of producing the perfect luxury automobiles isn't going to do a great job of turning out subway cars. A person who dreams of a cleaner, greener land isn't going to do a great job of running a company that produces toxic chemicals.

You might as well confess right here that you do daydream because research shows that the average North American adult spends over a third of his or her waking hours in the act. Moreover, daydreaming by mid-life executives is apparently increasing, according to at least one researcher working in this area. Most of the content is fairly enjoyable but mundane. You're fantasizing about just what you should have said to that technolust-ravaged nerd from MIS if that important meeting were held over again. You think about what you'll do on the weekend if the weather's good or whether your new car should be practical and roomy or sporty and red.

Some of your daydreaming is less mundane. It's about chucking the job and the family and running away to Pago Pago or about selling everything and opening a clapboard inn in some Norman Rockwell–designed town in Vermont. You dream about a second or third life—one in which you'd be more in control and where everything would be kinder and gentler.

Some of these second-life daydreams are quite elaborate. I've had a senior executive of a steel company tell me everything that would be on the menu of the restaurant he daydreamed of owning on the West Coast. He also could tell me the name and vintage of every bottle in the wine cellar. He could describe how the servers would be uniformed and what kind of training program they'd go through: "They won't give their names unless the diner asks," he said.

I've heard a man who owned a chain of eleven dry cleaning establishments tell me in detail about his dream farm: the crops, the equipment, how it could be done organically, what stores would buy the produce, and the college courses he'd have to take to make sure the idea was a success. He even had ideas for the design of the packaging for the tomatoes.

A woman in the same business as I am told me exactly how much it would cost to start the stuffed toy factory she daydreamed of setting up in the Caribbean and how she planned to capture her major market. She told me what the animals would be named. "The sheep will be called Fang," she said, "The kids I've talked to like the idea of a sheep called Fang."

I know a firefighter who has his woodworking shop all laid out. Now and then he upgrades the imaginary tools and moves them around. A waitress in Cleveland told me over breakfast about her beauty salon and the colors of the chairs. My hairdresser talks endlessly about his dream of an antique jewelry shop.

Most of us aren't so specific about our dreams. We don't take our daydreams seriously. We tell our kids not to waste time on daydreams. We use the word *daydreamer* as a pejorative. We certainly wouldn't think of using daydreaming as a business tool.

And we'd be dead wrong. Chairpersons of the board, product managers, CFOs, and CEOs dream, although they might not use that word for it. Most people would be surprised by their daydreams. They're not always about doubling the share price, about halving the workforce, or having the federal government ban imports of their competitors' products. Their fantasies are sometimes about, say, creating a product that consumers loved so much that they would hardly need to advertise or boosting morale with new work standards so high that employees would whistle as they came to work and keep whistling the whole day. Like you, many of them want blue skies and blue birds: products they can be proud of, the love of consumers, and a mutually beneficial relationship with their partners.

Shareholders, market analysts, and the people who collect taxes are usually at odds with these daydreams. Foreign competitors also get in the way. The CEO is just as frustrated as the trainee associate. It's difficult to arrange a long-range vision when the NYSE is looking at your quarterly reports, the Revenuers have you under continuous audit, and child laborers someplace you've never heard of are turning out a product that's a mirror image of yours for three-quarters the price.

Yet CEOs, presidents, and managers keep on daydreaming, and there are a significant number for whom it works. That shouldn't be surprising. After all, there are Olympic athletes whose coaches prescribe directed daydreams. If they can fantasize themselves clearing the bar at 19 feet, studies show that they are more likely to be able to do it. If they can summon up the mental image of themselves shooting and scoring, it's more likely to happen. In fact, a number of corporate studies show that companies that put more emphasis on their belief system are more successful than companies that pay attention only to the bottom line. They have a daydream that people—their own employees and their customers—can buy into with pride.

Adidas began by dreaming of making the world's best sports shoes. Alexander Graham Bell daydreamed about communications with the deaf and came up with the telephone (although it should be mentioned that in the end he regarded the thing as an intrusion and would usually refuse to answer). Wilbur and Orville Wright dreamt about flying, Henry Ford about a machine that would make life for farmers easier (he thought the future was in tractors), and Edison . . . well, Edison daydreamed about practically everything. And what was the name of the guy who had daydreams about a computer on every desk?

Daydreams can be just as much use to you. Not only do they define you, they're an engine that you can put to work.

I began this chapter with a quotation from a book by Joanna Field. Actually, that was her pen name; her real name was Marion Milner. In 1926 she felt dissatisfied with her life and started to keep a diary of the things that bothered her and made her happy. She listened to her own daydreams and fleeting thoughts, recorded them, and tried to make sense of them. "I began to have an idea of my life, not as the slow shaping of achievement to fit my preconceived purposes, but as the gradual discovery and growth of a purpose which I did not know," she wrote. As she thought about her daydreams, she began to reshape her life to make it more fulfilling. Then she became a psychoanalyst so that she could help others do the same. It's probably the best story I know about somebody using daydreams to create a second life. Her daydreams became part of her working assets. Her understanding of daydreams and of what they could mean turned into a lifelong career.

Most of us don't believe that our dreams are worth anything. We tell ourselves that this is, after all, a logical world and dreams are illogical. Instead, we should remember that dreams are something that differentiates us from the gray computers on our desks. We may even think that our dreams are a betrayal of those we love and those who depend on us. This is, in most cases, nonsense. If you opened up your dreams and welcomed in the people you love, you might find that your dreams are shared, admired, or at least understood.

We confine our dreams, fencing them in. We tell ourselves that, well, there are always vacations. And in the end there's always retirement. We console ourselves that we can do what we dream about in two weeks a year, or whatever time is left to us after we turn sixty-five.

As a matter of fact, you have a choice. You can keep thinking like that or you can change now or in the very near future. You can do more than you ever thought possible.

GETTING SERIOUS ABOUT YOUR DAYDREAMS

When corporations need to create new products, they usually hold a brainstorming session to drum up ideas and consider different options. You can do the same thing. I know. I held one myself not too long ago when I found myself daydreaming about changing the directions of my life and career. I needed to clarify my unfocused thoughts, hold my daydreams up to the daylight, and let other people comment on them.

I wanted to answer two questions. If you are your own business, what's your product? And is there a market for that product?

First, the product. Any new product is a tough sell. That's why one of the lessons that packaged goods companies have learned is not to become fixated on a single new product too early in the process. It's better to choose from a dozen—better still, five hundred—new ideas created during a brainstorming session than to consider only one or two. Putting together a bank of product ideas gives companies a smorgasbord of new product concepts to test. At the very least, it gives them something to test any one idea against. A one-horse race is no race. The strategy goes a long way toward preventing the considerable expense of new product failure. Besides, without this creative process, would today's America be reaping the benefits of air-cushioned running shoes, recyclable packaging, or banking by Internet?

This advice flies in the face of a lot of the literature on change that tells you to follow your passion or do what you love. If I'd followed my first passion, I'd probably be married to Dewey Horton in Ohio. Dewey's a nice enough person, Ohio's a nice enough state, and I have nothing against truck drivers, but I'm glad I messed around a little first. "Don't get married too soon," my mom said. That's true of second lives, too. Don't elope to the circus tomorrow morning. Mull over the options. Experiment.

> When you're trying to find a second life, it's important to take the time to look through all the windows, consider all the options before jumping into a decision. A lot of people can't take the uncertainty and they would rather make a decision, any decision, than wait and explore their options.
>
> —JOE BOWDEN, MANAGING PRINCIPAL, RIGHT MANAGEMENT CONSULTANTS, HOUSTON

The other reason you should check out what kind of product you're going to sell is that, like most people who have spent a certain amount of time in the work world and have been engaged in a variety of projects, you may have quite a few passions and multiple skill sets to match. The first passion that comes to mind may simply be the last thing you did that you really enjoyed. Remember that time five years ago when you were so excited about a project that the time seemed to fly and you seriously wondered if you could make a living doing nothing but that, before you got so bogged down in the new job the boss had given you that the idea got put on the back burner? Yeah, *that* project.

And remember ten years ago when you visited that place by the water and you thought how for only a few bucks you could add seven rooms and take the present boathouse and turn it into a meeting room and— presto!—you'd have one of the world's sweetest little executive conference centers? You got so excited about the idea that you started phoning the local real estate people and you invited an architect to lunch. You talked about nothing else for months.

Remember when you were going to be a fisherman/designer/medical researcher/whatever? You've had a lot of dreams in your life. If you thought about it, any one of them might have been worth grabbing, then or now.

If you have only one dream in current circulation, you likely don't have enough. It's like a company becoming fixated on one idea to the exclusion of all others. It limits its imagination and possibilities.

Second, take into account the market for your product. In the corporate world, people know that consumers want new products: they crave them. But they also know that if they come up with products that are *too* new, the consumers will stay away in droves. Consumers like stuff that makes immediate sense. Lemon-scented detergent evidently makes sense, although I've never understood why anyone would like to smell like a lemon. Lemon-scented chocolate bars do not appear to make consumer sense, although to me there's just as much logic in them.

Is the world ready for your daydream? You have to do a reality check. Do other people understand it? Do they want to deal with it, buy it, or recommend it to others? Ask them. Get several of them together and brainstorm.

THE HOWS AND WHYS OF BRAINSTORMING

The rules are simple. First, assemble a group of four to eight people. You could include your spouse, your best friend, somebody who has mentored you, the most creative person you know, two people half your age, a couple of people whose experience is diametrically different from your own, and someone you know who has actually changed his or her life dramatically.

Take these people someplace comfortable, out of their normal surroundings and away from phones. You want a solid five hours with them, preferably starting in the morning. I took my group to my cottage, but all you need is some place where you can tape up flip chart paper and shut off the phones.

Why so many people? Because ideas, like some other stuff, happen better in groups. The person half your age can build on an idea that the person whose experience is diametrically opposed to yours has had. Your spouse can build on the idea of the most creative person you know. Teddy, the fisherman from down the lake, can add to the idea Edna started. I've seen these groups work, and there's a marvelous synergy. It's like creating a LAN of human minds.

This isn't just me saying so. In *The Fifth Discipline*, Peter Senge quotes a physicist, David Bohm, on the importance of dialogue: "Our thought is incoherent and the resulting counterproductiveness lies at the root of the world's problems. . . . The purpose of dialogue is to reveal the incoherence of our thought."

Daydreams are incoherent, too; they are unfinished and fuzzy in the details. Just where are you going to find room for that workshop? How big is this ideal hotel of yours? Where do you plan to get the financing for this whitewater rafting excursion business? Simply taking that daydream and putting it into words makes an enormous difference to the clarity of your thinking. Answering questions such as, "Just how much money do you think you could make doing that?" or "What color are the walls?" or "When's the kick-off party and who's coming?" add even more detail and more ideas.

You may feel diffident about assembling such a group. Don't. First, they'll be flattered. Everybody enjoys being asked for advice (in my experience, lots of people don't even wait to be asked). What would your reaction be to someone asking you, "I want to open a golf pro shop. But it's got to be different. I want a lot of ideas from people who can really think about it. Could you come to a barbecue on Wednesday?" (A barbecue is as good as a meeting. Even if you're serving hot dogs.)

The second thing you'll find is that people actually will put forward good ideas. ("A pro shop with antique equipment? Great idea. We could have a department like that.") Those ideas will help enhance the sort of change you'd planned in any event. Furthermore, they may give you an entirely new way of looking at your passion. You may end up opening an art gallery instead of painting or running a Caribbean bar in your home town rather than in St. Thomas.

About 99 percent of the groups I've been to are the most fun the participants have had all week, maybe all month. They get to be creative. They get to talk about dreams and be involved in them. They get to meet new people.

It's important to stock up on supplies. The sessions I've participated in required at least 50 large sheets of paper (about two by three feet), masking tape, and markers. You need to keep track of the ideas and tape them up to the walls where everyone can see them.

All set? Good. Now the rules of the game.

1. **Set some objectives.** And keep those objectives within limits. We don't want to change the way you brush your teeth—just your environment. You know the kinds of things you're willing to give up and what the burrs under your saddle are. You know what kinds of things you're not willing to give up and what your passions are. So your objective should read something like this: Find a second life that gets me away from winters, away from 9 to 5, away from managing 82 people, and away from anyplace I have to wear a suit. I would like to stay in the marketing area because it fascinates me, I'd like to work in a small town, and I'd like to build equity for my retirement.

Sit there for a few minutes and you can think of a dozen ways to satisfy that objective in the next dozen minutes. They could be as far apart as opening an all-natural juice stand in Texas, starting private marketing seminars combined with vacations somewhere in Mexico, or founding a suntan lotion vending machine business in Puerto Rico. If you sit there for another few minutes, you can build a bunch more ideas on those basic three.

2. **Keep the ideas in headline form.** Because the ideas will come faster than you'd believe, you need to keep them to just a few words. Instead of saying, "I think you should open a really nice Northern Italian restaurant which, you know, serves thin-crust, wood-baked pizza buffet style in Sarasota, Florida, along with a good selection of moderately priced imported Italian reds," have the participants deliver the core of the concept: pizza joint. The details can be worked out later in the session. You want to get the maximum number of ideas, and that means putting them in the minimum number of words.

3. **There are no bad ideas, only incomplete ideas.** People who lead advanced brainstorming sessions and charge the price of a Caribbean vacation for a one-day session will tell you that. They know it's true from experience. That's because what might seem like a bad idea, say, farming, can be worked on until it's a successful idea like organizing farm holidays for tourists. If you write the word *farming* on the sheet of paper taped to the wall, later in the session you can take that original idea—its bucolic appeal and outdoorsiness—and apply it to your core competencies, which include organization and people relations. There are no bad ideas. Write them down, capture them, and build on them later.

4. **No one is allowed to be negative.** Imagine you're holding such a session during the Jurassic period. Your idea is the wheel. The woman who invented the wheel wasn't surrounded by people saying, "It's too complex a system" or "It'll never fly" or "I knew a guy who tried to round the corners off squares but it got all messy—labor costs, you know." I've seen the cave painting in France that recorded this particular meeting. The woman is

shown walking out of the cave, obviously thinking about the idea of inventing fire to burn the naysayers.

The brain cannot create and edit at the same time. Your car cannot go forward while remaining in park or being shifted into reverse. This is not cant, this is science—human science, anyway. Use creativity first, build on the ideas, and edit later. Hit anyone who starts a sentence with "But . . . "

5. **No war stories.** There will be one person in every group who would, unless restrained, go on about why he had the idea and where and when. "I remember I was in Lake Taos, back around '75, with Edna, and I noticed in the hotel bathroom—it was Harrah's—that there was a television set, about seven inches if you measured diagonally, not a big thing, but it wasn't that far from the throne. So I was sitting there for a while because of the density of the airline food I'd had the day before and decided to put the television on and what they were doing was televising those Keno games in color so that you could play in the privacy of your own washroom, so my suggestion is . . . "Enthralling, but cut to the chase: you could gamble on the commode with television. You want a lot of ideas and excitement; war stories cut down on both the number and the high of the experience. Ask for the story in ten words, twenty max.

6. **Be strange.** The farther the acorn falls from the tree, the higher the young oak will grow. If the objective you set is to become an artist, you need to consider ideas like new ways to paint limousines, landscape art, designer pumpkins, custom-painted computer covers, dream interpretations on canvas, opening an art gallery on the Internet, franchised art sections in florist's stores, the first Western gallery in Russia, the first exclusively Russian gallery in Chicago, packaged edible art, and painting with spray cheese.

I started this book after writing two other books: one on the dynamics of corporate change and the other on the costs and causes of corporate abuse. Then I used this system and ended up writing about running away and joining the circus. Strange? Not really. Other people, and other kinds of people, kicked me off the sort of academic/corporate track I was stuck on. Without them I wouldn't have opened myself up to the new experiences writing this book is delivering. I wouldn't have done the research, I wouldn't have met some really interesting people, I wouldn't have gotten the ideas, and I wouldn't have linked what is happening with corporate processes. Other people got enthusiastic about my plans, some more enthusiastic than I was. They made me more enthusiastic. I made them more enthusiastic. They started thinking and doing things in their lives, too, like a society of mutual benefit.

Okay, you're ready to start this part of the process. Assemble your group. Announce the rules and announce your objective to them. Or let them read this chapter and post the objective on one of those sheets of paper on the wall. Then let the ideas flow, and they almost invariably will. Usually, participants find the session more fun than "Let's Make a Deal" and more intriguing than "Oprah."

Eventually, after two-and-a-half to three hours, the group will slow down on creating different ideas. At that point, give them each a marker. You tell them they've got ten votes each. They can assign all ten of those votes to a single idea, a single vote to ten different ideas, or six votes to one and four votes to another. Let them walk around the room marking the number of votes on the pieces of paper on which you've written the ideas.

Then have some sandwiches and talk about something else for a half hour, such as the weather, the Dow, or the Chicago Bulls. Take a walk around the block.

Come back. Take the five ideas that received the most votes, start to build on them, and flesh them out. Set yourself a target: you're going to add at least fifteen sub-ideas to the simple ideas; that's three sub-ideas for each main idea. Take an hour to do that and then discuss the difficulties with each of the built-up ideas you've generated. Then you can open the bar and relax.

WHAT A DIFFERENCE A DAY MAKES

There will be two results from your day, and one of them will surprise you. First, you now have fifteen ideas that meet the objectives as you stated them. That might be fifteen ideas more than you started with, or fourteen more ideas than the one you had fixed on. One of those ideas might start to look more attractive than the one you thought you wanted. Any of those ideas might supply you with concepts you could bend or warp to fit your original concept. You have an idea bank you can steal from.

Second, you have involved your spouse, your mentor, and your best friend in the process. Suddenly, you're not one person standing alone: you have a team. They appreciate that you're putting thought into your second life, that you have goals, and that you're welcoming them to be a part of your change. You'll likely find them more understanding and supportive as you make your way toward your second life, even if it is running away to the circus.

You may be nervous about the process. It may seem too California to be considered. Tell people it's a process that's been adopted at one time or another by major telephone companies, insurance companies, packaged goods manufacturers, large airlines, and small entrepreneurs. All of those things are true, and most of those organizations have found the process valuable.

If anyone thinks the idea is stupid, agree. Say they don't have to come. You don't want them anyway. The people who think that what you are doing is right are the forward thinkers of some of our leading corporations.

If that assurance still doesn't make you feel comfortable, my advice is to practice it with one or two people in a limited time. Your spouse and your mentor would be good choices, but it's nice to have at least one natural crazy there. Lateral thinking is sometimes something we all need a model for. But, even in a group of two, keep to the rules. Otherwise, I cannot guarantee success.

THE BARRIER BETWEEN YOUR EARS

Some of you will look at the ideas that emerged and immediately start raising objections:

> "I don't have training in that."

> "I'm too old to start all over again."

> "My partner would never agree."

At this point in the process many executives in companies going through change start raising the same kind of objections. "We couldn't possibly do that because . . . "and out comes the usual litany of too expensive, too time-consuming, too hard, too risky, too weird. You wouldn't believe the grief I got in one company when all I suggested was that they hold an executive retreat at an isolated fishing lodge.

Resistance to change is normal. Change puts most people off-balance and makes them feel out of their depth. It doesn't matter that we're talking about moving you from a rut that doesn't fit you any more to a situation in which you will have room to grow: it's still change and it's scary. It's a lot easier on the nerves to be a competent money-loser than successful risk-taker. So I expect objections. I even expect that quite a few of them are valid and will have to be addressed. Later.

The biggest barrier to change is between people's ears. To put it another way, people have blinders on that prevent them from seeing a wider horizon. They screen things out far too soon. It's OK to have criteria (I want to stay in Boston, I want to stay at such-and-such a salary level), but they apply these criteria far too soon. Maybe a Boston job means an interview in Seattle. Maybe the right job has lower pay but better benefits. The time to apply criteria is when there is a real decision to make, not before.

—WARREN RADTKE, GROUP SENIOR VP (RETIRED), RIGHT MANAGEMENT CONSULTANTS, BOSTON

part two

getting ready to escape

5

how to be your own consultant

In which you will learn that:

1. Corporate change happens at three levels: the level of the organization as a whole, the level of groups within the organization, and the individual level.

2. In your business plan you too will need to consider your overall organizational goals, your relationship to different groups, and your individual needs.

Amateurs invent; professionals steal. It saves time, every professional knows that. Take one good workable idea and use it as often as you can. (This is probably why so many TV shows and movies look the same these days.)

What I am going to explain in this chapter is not so much a plan of action as a framework for thinking about your current situation and for identifying the elements of the circus you want to run away to. Like any good consultant, you are going to gather information, analyze it, and then come up with a practical proposal for change, which I hope you will begin to implement.

When management consultants are asked to work with a new com-pany, they begin by finding out everything they can about the company. They interview managers, pore over financial documents, talk to customers and suppliers, read internal memos and PR documents, and, if they are particularly sensible, hang out at the corporate gathering places and chat to the people who really make things happen.

This is not, or should not be, just random information gathering. The research is designed to dig out problems, threats, opportunities, areas of friction, strengths, weaknesses, and potential change agents.

You are now going to do the same thing with your own career. And to give you a head start, we are going to explain a framework that we have used successfully for a number of years.

To put it in a nutshell, we've realized that there are three levels at which organizational change occurs:

1. At the level of the organization as a whole.

2. At the level of groups within the organization (both official and unofficial).

3. At the level of the individual.

Change must occur at all three of these levels or the whole effort is likely to fail. You cannot change an organization by changing only one part of it. Think about it:

- You want to take your organization into the global economy, but your sales force won't budge from Cleveland. Is it going to work?

- You want to computerize the organization, but the union as a group has dug its heels in. Is it going to work?

- You want your PR department to start coming back from lunch occasionally, but you as boss are unwilling to set an example. Is it going to work?

Organizations, whether they're General Motors, Robin's Donut Shops, the League of Women Voters, a tribe of bushmen trying to bring down an antelope, or the people who immediately surround you when you go in your front door, operate on these three levels. If the three levels aren't harmonized and united and do not understand each other, no change gets made.

Based on this insight, we created a diagram, which we call the change triangle. Circuses have three rings, so we took the geometry of something with three corners. Most of what happens to us seems to happen in threes: plays have three acts, the juggler starts with three balls, "Friends" has three commercials interruptions, there are three meals a day, and three strikes and you're back in the dugout.

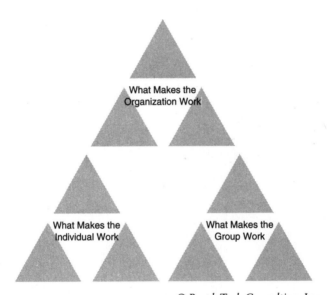

© *PeopleTech Consulting, Inc.*

This diagram started as a simple memory aid. It reminded us to look at all three areas of change when we were working with a particular organization. However, we found that the more we paid attention to the model in our work with companies, the more we succeeded. We could help companies change more rapidly, economically, and deeply. We could cut failure. We could turn visions into reality, something that a lot of Fortune 500 CEOs will tell you they've flunked at.

At each of the three levels, we also identified three broad areas for change:

1. At the organizational level, we looked at belief systems, performance drivers, and work processes.

2. At the group level, we considered group skills, group support for change, and the creation of healthy groups.

3. At the individual level, we had to remember to include individual buy-in for change, individual skills, and what we call individual response-ability.

When you put it all together, it looks like this:

Belief
Systems

What Makes the
Organization Work

Work
Processes

Performance
Drivers

Buy-In for
Change

Group
Skills

What Makes the
Individual Work

What Makes the
Group Work

Individual
Skills

Individual
Response-Ability

Group
Support
for Change

Healthy
Groups

© PeopleTech Consulting, Inc.

The model doesn't try to classify anything. It is not the magic solution to this or any other problem. It is simply a reminder of the different levels at which change takes place and a tool that helps us identify where change is needed inside the organization.

The triangle is our way of expressing how large organizations like ThemInc. work. We've also found, time and again, that it has a lot to do with how suborganizations within ThemInc. work, even at the level of the executive committee, which may number under a dozen people. That shouldn't surprise you. Companies are, as I said before, people. So are executive committees. And so is YouInc. The engines of change work on the same principles, even though it may take a V-12 engine to get ThemInc. to move, while all you need is a small, single cylinder motor with a pull starter.

In terms of change, there are two main things you can learn from ThemInc.'s hard-won lessons:

1. You can use the triangle to analyze where you are now and how each of the influences is contributing to your dissatisfaction.

2. You can use the triangle to gain perspective on each of the different levels and learn what you'll have to do to change the future of YouInc.

Perhaps it might help if I reworded the triangles a little, translated the management-speak, and made them more user-friendly:

© *PeopleTech Consulting, Inc.*

Relabeling the parts of the triangle does take a little of the voodoo out of it because it enables you to focus on where and how you fit into the context of the organization and the groups within it. Although it may appear to be all about you, it's more about how your environment suits you, not just how you suit your environment.

When I talk about your environment, I'm talking about people, not about office decor. You may feel oppressed by the beige broadloom or the gray cubicle walls, but if you dig a little deeper, you will find that they are simply the choices of the people in the organization. You may hate

> *Organizations don't learn and they don't*
> *see and they don't do anything.*
> *Organization is a concept, a shorthand;*
> *it's a name we give to a certain collec-*
> *tivity of people. . . . It is a useful abstrac-*
> *tion, for some purposes, but not for all.*
> *Abstractions, concepts, neither learn nor*
> *see; people do.*
>
> —PATRICIA PITCHER

the piece of technology you are required to work with, but it didn't clamber onto your desk all by itself. It was chosen, ordered, and installed by people who decided it fit into their idea of the organization. The triangle directs your attention to people in a structured way: the people you work for and with, the people who report to you, the people you consult, the people who look to you for answers, the people you attend meetings with, and the people who ride the elevator with you.

When I talk of organizational or corporate change, it was the people in that organization or corporation who made it happen, lived with it while it was happening, and reaped the benefits afterward. In your personal life this means parents, partners, children, and general hangers-on.

Unless you are an exceptional bully or a complete loner, you have to make change, not only in yourself, but also in those who sit around your table. For most of us the answer is to understand and enlist the whole of the company. To change the circus, you change all three rings. That's a heavier load than what you probably imagined, but it's the only way to make what you imagined possible. In the following nine chapters, we are going to look at the triangles one by one.

6

what you believe affects where you fit

In which you will find out:

1. That what you believe is more important than what you know.

2. That if your beliefs don't fit with the beliefs of the organization you work for, you will probably start daydreaming about running away to the circus.

3. How to zero in on what you believe.

In the first part of many annual reports, there's a vision statement that describes where a company wants to go. This may be followed by a mission statement that sums up the company's mandate, in other words, what the company actually does. These things, together with the value system of the company (which is seldom written down, but can be read from its culture) and the annual goals and objectives, are the keys to understanding the organization's belief system.

I have a friend who makes part of his living writing mission statements. It's quite remunerative because many organizations don't know quite where they are going and they are happy to pay someone to tell

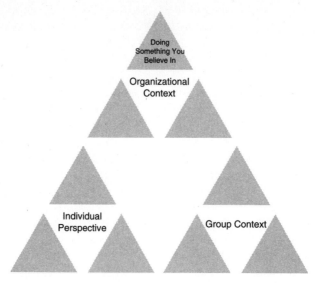

© *PeopleTech Consulting, Inc.*

them. Some days they say, "It's the bottom line, stupid," other days they cheer, "Strength through productivity" or chant "Lowest prices always" or "To serve and protect" or "Tomorrow's products today" or "We're Numero Uno in Niche." This is not to make fun of corporations: it's a tough world, and nobody has all the answers.

However, some companies have clear, concise, and understandable mission statements that don't change with the prevailing winds. They have a clear vision and a clear idea of what they need to do to get there. Even without reading the annual report, you could tell me what the Saturn car company's core belief is—or The Body Shop's or Benetton's or Nike's. You wouldn't have to interview the CEO: the mission is self-evident and obvious in everything they do, including advertising, product, distribution, and pricing.

Most companies don't have a coherent mission, let alone a clear vision. Pick any of the Fortune top 10. From their advertising, product, distribution, and pricing, could you formulate their mission in 25 words or less? I have seen mission statements that go on for three pages, promising everything to everyone and delivering very little to anyone. You could ask the CEOs of such companies to stand up and tell you what the corporate vision was, and they would probably be glad to, but I'm willing to bet from experience that the speech would change depending on when you asked. If you asked again in six months, you'd hear a different speech. If you asked in front of a different audience, you'd hear another speech entirely. If you asked another board member, you'd hear yet another speech. And, if you asked somebody at the bottom of the heap, you'd likely hear a resounding "Huh?" (I would be interested in playing the stock market some day with a strategy based solely on picking the firms with the shortest, simplest mission statements.)

The reason for having a mission statement is to help a company's people understand what is important and what customers can expect of them. A company with a complex or constantly changing mission confuses its employees. If one day it's "Bottom line," the employees will scamper to turn down the heat, crank out the sales, and cut the car allowances. If the next day it's "Innovation," the employees will hire creativity consultants, create design shops, and set up research labs. And if the next day it's "Quality," the employees will haul out the micrometers, stiffen the warranties, and call in the ISO 9000 inspectors. If this process continues for a sufficient number of days, the employees will end up exhausted and demoralized—unless they end up down the street working for a place that knows what it's trying to do. And we both know where the customers will end up.

You have a vision. If you are determined to reach that vision, you may need to draw up a mission statement. Those will be, *ipso facto*, YouInc.'s vision and mission statement. The place where you work has a mission statement that leads toward certain visions and precludes others. Are you a quality person in a bottom-line environment? Are you an innovator in a customer-is-always-right organization?

MATCHING YOUR BELIEF SYSTEMS IS MORE IMPORTANT THAN MATCHING YOUR SKILLS

Your belief systems are established early in life; you may adjust them here and there, but it's unlikely that they will change radically. The Jesuits used to say that if they could have care of a boy and a boy's education until he was seven years old, they'd have him for life. Miss Jean Brodie insisted, "Give me a girl at an impressionable age and she is mine forever." Radio station music directors claim music tastes don't change much after a person is seventeen, which is why you hear so many oldies stations on the dial and why you'll probably find yourself tripping over rap on the radio for the next twenty years.

By the time you're reading this, you're likely pretty much who you're going to be. In fact, according to some researchers, 30 percent of your

> *A lot of senior executives and CEOs don't believe that there is a life beyond winning at business. Change means looking at yourself, your beliefs, your relationships, and your attitude towards security. You have to ask yourself how much money is enough. You have to think about your core philosophy, about what it means to leave a legacy.*
>
> —CARL SAMUELS, BUSINESS LIFE TRANSITIONS, LOS ALAMITOS

behaviors are genetic, so unless you're going to do the difficult trick of changing your DNA, you're stuck with them. You may get fatter, you may learn new tricks, you may change your hair color, you may move to Aspen, but in your core beliefs, you're you. You're unlikely to become startlingly more ambitious, turn into a liar, or walk from a family you love.

So we're back to our original proposition: If you're not going to change yourself, you're going to have to change the world. The good news is that finding the right environment is easier because there are so many options to choose from. The work world comes in a dazzling assortment of forms these days, from 100,000-person, low-tech, regimented conglomerates that pound out the same widget month after month to one-person, high-tech virtual companies that shift their services every hour. There is a similar range of corporate belief systems—from the innovative to those that believe in tradition, from dollar-driven to community-conscious, from those that do everything in groups to those that celebrate the solitary. Some will give you the reassurance of a belief in regular routine; others will challenge you to go where no one has ever gone before and do what's never been done.

> *Corporations differ as much as species of animals. If someone who studies bears gets together with someone who studies beaver, they don't try to say that bears and beaver should live in the same habitat—but that's what we do with corporations when we apply standard approaches.*
>
> —HENRY MINTZBERG, PROFESSOR OF MANAGEMENT, MCGILL UNIVERSITY

No kidding. I've seen corporations that were bears and corporations that were beavers. I've seen corporate flamingoes, kangaroos, drunken buffalo, and vampires. When people call high-growth, start-up companies gazelles, I know just what they mean. I've even worked with a company that reminded me of Dr. Doolittle's Pushmi-Pullyu, the creature with two heads.

The bad news is that finding the right place for you may take a certain amount of trial and error. There are people with tidy minds whose vision of perfection would be to give you a test that would enable them to say, "You're a 158/A/C. You are precisely suited for Company W998, position 13C." However, it never works out because on the morning you took part seven of the test, you'd had too much coffee and that skewed part of the results. Also, in the time it took to classify the company into its particular slot, the company changed because it lost market share or took on a new major client.

Finding the right kind of place takes time, perseverance, and a certain amount of research. The effort is worth it, though. Ending up in a situation where your belief doesn't mate with the belief of the people you're working with is usually a recipe for disaster. Repeat to yourself ten times: *matching belief systems is more important than matching skills.*

You can find the circus you want. Take another look at the rough set of core beliefs you defined for yourself. Take out a few magazines and the local papers and browse, raising your eyes every so often to check back on the values you've worked out. Talk to friends, check the ads: do any of the companies or organizations match your beliefs? If freedom is your top priority, there are jobs that offer autonomy. If service to the community is what makes you tick, there are non-profit agencies. If money is what does it, there are more than enough companies that will match your interest in it.

FOLLOWING YOUR BELIEFS EQUALS
BELIEVING IN YOURSELF

Edie Lennon used to be a bureaucrat and a very senior one. You'd see her in newspaper photographs, five feet behind and just slightly to the right of that year's center of power. She'd usually have her lower lip tucked in behind her teeth and be looking at a point a mile beyond the camera. Her name never quite made the caption. Politicians and other bureaucrats used to phone her, but the media never got her number. She was famous at a certain level for her memoranda. She never gave speeches, but she'd written a number of key ones.

She was unmarried, her biological clock evidently being set on snooze. You would see her at interesting events with equally interesting men: fairly senior diplomats, entrepreneurs in emerging technology, and the occasional professor, providing he wasn't in a faculty that had anything to do with political science. She had a very subtle but very real power, she was successful in the quiet way that endears a bureaucrat to elected officials, and she seemed personally happy.

Now she runs a small factory that makes automobile seats and head-liners in a rust-belt town three hours' drive from the capital. Her government gray suits are gone. Her work clothes consist of jeans and the kind of T-shirts you get from oil companies when they're running a pro-motion. She likes to give quick tours of the factory, interrupting her spiel with fast and frequently profane conversations with the people operat-ing the machinery. They smile. She smiles. And I wonder if any of them could imagine this woman giving one of her genteel talks on the history of a state policy to a newly elected official.

"No office. Don't have one. This is management by continuous kib-itzing. Leadership by kidding around. It works. These people wouldn't know what to do with a memo if they got one. I do their performance evaluations with them on a napkin at Ray's Lunch, which is the only restaurant I've ever been in that actually has peanut butter sandwiches listed on the menu. In fact, I've developed a new dictum about perfor-mance evaluations: if you can't write the damn thing on the back of a napkin, it's probably too complicated for anybody to do anything about. Same with the marketing plan."

A lot of people blame the change on hormones. "She's just having an estrogen fit. We're thinking of it as sort of a sabbatical. She'll be back with the department soon," they say and they genuinely believe it. They obviously haven't seen her in her scuffed safety boots, taking lessons on how to run the plant forklift from a man in an NRA baseball cap.

The real reasons for the change are more complicated. "I don't like to decorate the rationale. It was essentially fairly primal. In government you get to pontificate about what industry should do. You write long policy papers on the subject: just-in-time, continuous improvement, global marketing, the rest of it. And you can spend your life believing that those papers are a real and a useful product. On the other hand, you can actu-ally go out and rub yourself up against the reality. What I thought in the end was that the reality would be a lot more fun. And it is." But there was more to it than that.

"I'd gone into government believing that I could do some good: make jobs happen and make jobs worthwhile. I was starry-eyed and passion-ate about that and I guess I'm still starry-eyed and passionate. Where I'd grown up there were too many people and too few jobs and I saw the effect on the kids I played with and on their parents. It was hard for many of them. Politicians used to wander around every four years and promise us that government could take care of this, kiss it all better. I grew up with that belief: I wanted to be in the government and make some good happen.

"I found that after a while that government—or at least the people within my particular department—didn't share my passion or whatever the hell it is. If you were to measure the bureaucrats' belief that they should have a job against the authenticity of their belief that they should do whatever it takes to create jobs for the voters, you'd find that most of them put staying in their comfortable offices ahead of the difficult and frustrating business of creating jobs. They might not say that. They might protest loudly if you accused them of it. But that's the truth.

"And so I found that I just didn't believe in government any more—or at least in my role in government. That was really what made it necessary to change. Otherwise, I wouldn't have believed in myself any more."

Some other changes made the big change possible: a medium-sized inheritance and a love affair with a 70-year-old cottage in the area. "It was sort of like God was coming around every day giving me a little poke in the arm, saying 'Why don't you try it, Edie, why don't you try it?' So what I did in the end was go to [a very senior bureaucrat] and ask his advice. He advised against it." She laughed. "But then who trusts the goddamn government these days?"

She looked around the factory. "These people here don't quite trust me yet. Most of them were unemployed and they don't think this is going to last. They think this is some kind of adventure for me. They're pretty accurate about the last part: it is. And it's about the most fun I've had in the last quarter century."

You could open a company, shed the suit, and do the things Edie Lennon is doing. You could take your professional knowledge and transplant it somewhere it would make a difference. You could "rub up against reality" as she puts it. You haven't done it yet.

How do you decide to make those changes? How do you decide on the particular changes you'd make? And how do you manage to make the changes? Don't answer yet.

YOUR VISION VS. YOUR VALUES

Edie Lennon went to work for the government because she thought that the government shared her belief system, which put job creation at the top of the agenda. However, the people she found didn't act as if job creation were their top priority. A lot of people have made similar mistakes. They join an organization thinking that the organization exists to fulfill a goal they see as important, only to find that what the organization said and did are two different things.

The fact of the matter is that what an organization says (in its vision or mission statement, annual report, press release, or political platform) may be at odds with its unwritten value system. Plenty of organizations include references to innovation in their mission statements, but when some bright spark comes forward with a neat new idea for solving a production bottleneck that requires shifting resources between departments, some companies that claim to value innovation may let the idea die rather than challenge the value of protecting departmental turf.

In many organizations, employees run up against an inherent contradiction between the stated missions and the unwritten value system. Nursing usually attracts people who value healing and caring, yet many hospitals put efficiency and institutional survival at the top of their list of values. The academic life sometimes attracts people who value teaching and who are sadly disillusioned when they go to work for universities that place a higher value on the ability to attract research grants.

Companies often parade their visions and mission statements when they recruit people. If the visions are borne out by the company's values, employees will stick around. If the two don't correspond, employees will either become cynical and unproductive or leave in search of a company that values what they value. A company that, day in and day out, values innovation will attract and keep the best innovators. Likewise, a company that values warm, soft cash will attract people with a similar fetish, and a company that values the good opinion of its customers will attract people who are willing to pay for top-notch service.

Companies use visions as a recruitment tool: they attract people with the same daydreams. What they sometimes forget is that values are a retention tool: companies keep the ones who share the corporate values.

> *If you're not willing to enthusiastically adopt the HP [Hewlett-Packard] Way, then you don't belong at HP. If you're not comfortable buying into Wal-Mart's fanatical dedication to its customers, then you don't belong at Wal-Mart. If you're not willing to be "Procterized," then you don't belong at Procter and Gamble. If you don't want to join the crusade for quality (even if you work in the cafeteria), then you don't*

*belong at Motorola and you certainly can't become a true
"Motorolan." If you question the right of individuals to make their
own decisions about what to buy (such as cigarettes), then you don't
belong at Philip Morris. If you're not comfortable with the Mormon-
influenced, clean-living, dedication-to-service atmosphere at Marriott,
then you'd better stay away. If you can't embrace the idea of "whole-
someness" and "magic" and "Pixie dust," and make yourself into a
clean-cut zealot, then you'd probably hate working at Disneyland.*

—JAMES C. COLLINS AND JERRY I. PORRAS

Exactly. You want to end up where you will be most comfortable. This means being with people who have similar values. Jeffrey E. Edwards, associate professor at the University of Michigan School of Business, says that the match or mismatch of values between a corporation and an employee is a better predictor of job stress levels than a mismatch between an employee's capabilities and the capabilities demanded by the corporation. If you're hired to do a job and you lack the skills, you're less stressed than if you're hired to do a job and don't share the beliefs of the person signing your paychecks. There's an emerging bunch of studies all pointing the same finger at the same problem.

Current hiring practices—the ones used by most companies—were developed in about 1917. The interviewer doesn't ask about your values, what satisfies you, or what makes you feel excited or happy. Interviewers ask what you can do. Most job candidates try to mirror the corporate priorities: they ask what the company wants done and then assess whether they can do it. In a lot of cases, especially in a tough job market, employees don't ask whether they as individuals actually value what the company wants done or whether they'll be comfortable with the way the company wants it done. Result? Stress, and the start of recurring daydreams about the circus.

You have to match your beliefs and your need for satisfaction with what's believed and needed corporately. That doesn't mean changing your beliefs. It means finding an organization that shares them.

This part of the change triangle is important because it's impossible to match beliefs when you have not defined your own. Most of us haven't: YouInc., like most corporations, does not have a clear belief system. As individuals we are as unready as the companies.

START WITH WHAT YOU BELIEVE (YOU *DO* KNOW WHAT YOU BELIEVE, DON'T YOU?)

Now you're probably shuffling from foot to foot wondering just what your belief system is. What's the mission statement for YouInc.?

This sounds like a huge, difficult assignment, summing up your deepest beliefs in one pithy sound bite. You can go the navel-gazing route, which some people find intensely satisfying and others find intensely tedious, or you can take a short cut and just do a bit of reminiscing. After all, the clues are in your past. Your history tells truths about you that you may not be able to articulate until you consider them.

Over the years, certain things have made you happy and some have left you cold. Collected and looked at with a bit of a jeweler's eye, what has made you feel good in the past is what is going to make you feel good in the future. Remember, the primary purpose of this book is not to change you, but to change your environment to make you feel satisfied.

But first, how do we define *satisfaction*? Well, there are different levels. Psychologist Abraham Maslow is regularly quoted about what he called his hierarchy of needs. These should be familiar to anyone who has ever taken a Psych 101 course. However, in case you were absent that day, I'm going to quote them here. The mass of persons have needs in approximately this order:

1. Physiological needs. This means water, food, and shelter. Try going without a couple of glasses of liquid a day for a few days and see how much you're interested in, say, becoming President. Of anything.

2. Safety needs. This means being reasonably assured that there's nothing under the bed that's going to get you when your lids drop or that you're not going to be downsized in the next outbreak of disappearances.

3. Social needs. You need to be accepted by your peers, by your superiors, and by your subordinates. Your dog understands the concept completely.

4. Self-esteem, your belief in your own value. Dear God, this one's been done to death on the afternoon talk shows and at parent-teacher meetings, but there it is. At the next parent-teacher meeting, when they tell you your child lacks self-esteem, haul off and quote Maslow by saying, "Peer acceptance really comes first, wouldn't you agree, Mrs. Hamish?"

5. Self-fulfillment or self-actualization. Some people confuse this with doing your own pottery, but it's more complicated. It means getting to do something you love.

Amazingly, sex doesn't enter the question. I guess Maslow would put it under social needs or self-esteem, depending on your current living situation.

The first two in the hierarchy are self-explanatory. It's the next three that are more interesting. Satisfying these needs will mean different things to different people.

The third, acceptance, depends on whose opinion you value. Some solitary or utterly self-absorbed people seem to skip this one completely. They apparently don't give a hoot if they're accepted or not. For the rest of us, acceptance may take the form of blending in or standing out. For some it comes from being considered helpful; for others it comes from being thought amusing, insightful, or decorative. Just what do your friends and family like about you, anyway? The answer may surprise you.

The fourth, self-esteem, is overhyped but necessary. It doesn't exist in a vacuum, which is why attempts to boost it without boosting creativity, skills, or knowledge at the same time are generally doomed to failure. So, what do you think you do well? Again, it's a question that's worth pausing for. When was the last time you asked yourself about it? Or do you— like the mass of us—keep spending your time kicking yourself about what you don't do well?

Self-fulfillment, the fifth need, is doing the things that make you feel most alive, most fully you. When was the last time you were enjoying what you were doing so much that you didn't notice time passing? What absorbs you so much that you never feel tired when you do it? These are your personal keys to self-fulfillment. The S&L branch manager doesn't consider the hours each month he devotes to building radio-controlled airplanes that important. It seems trivial. But it is the most self-fulfilling thing he does.

Another way to think about the hierarchy of needs is to consider the level at which your discontent emerges. If you are working in conditions that are physically or physiologically stressful, your idea of a change for the better is fairly straightforward: more heat, better lighting, less noise. If your work is dangerous or you are consumed with worries about security, then you have little time to spare to think about whether your peers accept you. If you are obsessed with the opinions of your boss or co-workers, you may lose track of your sense of self-esteem. And so forth.

A warning: Richard Farson, author of *Management of the Absurd*, has pointed out that when one set of needs is satisfied, discontent doesn't disappear, it just moves up a notch. If you need more quiet time at work and suddenly you get it, then your older and smaller problem with unpredictable work hours starts shouting louder. This is the theory of rising expectations: "It fuels the fire of revolution and change because it creates a discrepancy between what people have and what they now see is possible to have. That discrepancy is the source of discontent and the engine for change."

To get a sense of where you are and where your environment rubs you the wrong way, try the following test, which is based on some ideas from a colleague of mine, Barbara Moses, Ph.D., of BBM Human Resources.

IN THE PAST TEN YEARS, THIS HAS BEEN OF HOW MUCH IMPORTANCE TO ME? (1 IS LOWEST)

	1	2	3	4	5
Achieving things, being the best					
Beating the competition					
Being liked by others					
Being part of a team					
Being unique, different from others					
Challenges, doing tough things					
Change, lack of routine					
Community, local connections					
Craftsmanship					

	1	2	3	4	5
Creativity	——	——	——	——	——
Doing things my way	——	——	——	——	——
Doing a superb job for others	——	——	——	——	——
Doing things in my own time-frame	——	——	——	——	——
Earning others' respect	——	——	——	——	——
Education, acquiring knowledge	——	——	——	——	——
Efficiency, doing more with less	——	——	——	——	——
Entertainment, enjoying it/ providing it	——	——	——	——	——
Excitement, a go-go atmosphere	——	——	——	——	——
Fame	——	——	——	——	——
Family	——	——	——	——	——
Feeling good about myself	——	——	——	——	——
Fitness, health	——	——	——	——	——
Freedom	——	——	——	——	——
Friends	——	——	——	——	——
Fun	——	——	——	——	——
Getting my name in the paper	——	——	——	——	——
Hobbies, leisure pursuits	——	——	——	——	——
Home, making it attractive and comfortable	——	——	——	——	——
Honesty, being respected for it	——	——	——	——	——
Invention	——	——	——	——	——

	1	2	3	4	5
Innovation	___	___	___	___	___
Keeping up with the latest trends/fashions	___	___	___	___	___
Leadership, motivating others	___	___	___	___	___
Learning new skills	___	___	___	___	___
Leaving a legacy	___	___	___	___	___
Living where I want to live	___	___	___	___	___
Looking good	___	___	___	___	___
Love, romance, intimacy	___	___	___	___	___
Making decisions	___	___	___	___	___
Making money	___	___	___	___	___
Making plans	___	___	___	___	___
Making someone else feel good	___	___	___	___	___
Meeting new people	___	___	___	___	___
Organizing, creating order out of chaos	___	___	___	___	___
Peace and quiet	___	___	___	___	___
Political gamesmanship	___	___	___	___	___
Power, authority over others	___	___	___	___	___
Professionalism, doing it right	___	___	___	___	___
Quality of work or product	___	___	___	___	___
Recognition, reputation	___	___	___	___	___
Respect for the environment	___	___	___	___	___

	1	2	3	4	5
Saving money	___	___	___	___	___
Security	___	___	___	___	___
Serving other people	___	___	___	___	___
Solitude	___	___	___	___	___
Solving problems	___	___	___	___	___
Speed, doing things faster	___	___	___	___	___
Spending money	___	___	___	___	___
Spirituality	___	___	___	___	___
Sports	___	___	___	___	___
Status, prestige	___	___	___	___	___
Taking risks	___	___	___	___	___
Tradition, conservatism	___	___	___	___	___
Travel	___	___	___	___	___

Be brutally honest. You don't have to show it to anyone. If you really revel in status, power, and money, say so. The world has room for the likes of Donald Trump. Don't include community, education, and family just because it would please your mother or efficiency, solving problems, and being part of a team because it would impress your boss.

When you've finished, take a different color of pen. Mark in how well your current environment is delivering on the things you value (use *1* as the lowest).

Go over the list once more. Pick the three issues most important to you and rank them. Roughly speaking, those are the core of your value system. Do it again, picking the three issues most important to your environment and ranking them. (Don't rank your environment on the company's mission statement, but on your day-to-day experiences.) That's your company's core value system.

Be very careful about the rankings. Take the time to compare the ones you picked two at a time and put them in order. Those rankings may be the key to understanding how you do or do not fit into your current situation.

I stress this because of something that was pointed out by Larry Richard of Lawgistics, a counseling service for lawyers: "When a psychological need is met, it recedes and you don't think about it." That means if your current job delivers on one need, such as learning opportunities, you may take learning for granted as part of your work life. But if you leave that job to fulfill a different need, such as recognition, and you find the new job has few learning opportunities, you may be unhappier than you were before. Rankings are important. Grouping needs is also important. Take the time to get them right.

Okay, you've studied the list, picked your preferences, and compared them with your current workplace. How does YouInc.'s belief system match ThemInc.'s belief system? Are you a leader in an environment that demands you follow, a quiet person stuck in a go-go atmosphere, or someone who's deeply concerned about serving others in a place where the primary objective is merely shifting the product out the door? There has to be a mesh or there's a problem. If there's a big difference— a run-away-to-the-circus kind of difference—you have a further question to put to yourself. Is it easier to change yourself or to change your environment?

BELIEFS AND YOUR JOURNEY THROUGH LIFE

Where are you right now? If you are within hailing distance of midlife, the fit between what you believe and what you do may already be claiming your attention. According to a study carried out by the Association of Theological Schools, the age of theology students is rising, as professionals leave the business world to start second lives as ministers, priests, and rabbis. Many of these people are baby boomers who are searching for an element of meaning and spirituality that they somehow missed as they charged through university and corporate life.

For other people, the urge to express deep-seated beliefs may take the form of a vocation for environmental activism or community service. Whatever form it takes, it has to do with what Gail Sheehy calls "the feeding and crafting of the soul," which she refers to as "the real work of your Second Adulthood," a period that often starts as people enter their fifties.

Jennifer McNeil has worked as an office manager, theater administrator, and fund raiser for arts groups. "I always thought that what I was doing was benefiting the community, but gradually I started noticing certain contradictions. I worked for a fairly high-profile company that tried to match arts groups with corporate sponsorship. One of our clients was a group made up of handicapped adults who were trying to raise money for a permanent gallery to showcase their artwork. The retainer we charged them took a huge bite out of the money we raised, and we didn't raise as much as they'd hoped. I started to feel very uncomfortable about what I was doing. I left." Jennifer now runs a community arts group and lectures on art therapy.

> *The questions that people raise during transition are related to where they are in the lifecycle. Young people, for example, tend to focus on, "Where am I going? What do I want to be?" People in midlife are more inclined to ask, "What do I stand for?" People in their older years might ask, "What do I want to be my legacy?" Thinking about values helps people to see if there is a fit between their values and the work they are doing.*
>
> —LESLIE GORDON MAYER, PH.D., CONSULTING PSYCHOLOGIST

Sometimes you have to look beyond general belief systems at the underlying ethical foundations of your work. Is the work worth doing? Is the product beneficial to people? Will it last? Are the work processes non-exploitive and ecologically sound? Will you be able to look back on your work with pride twenty years from now?

Sharon McGavin, who went from being a senior vice-president at Ogilvy and Mather to chief development officer for the American Red Cross in greater New York, told a *Fortune* interviewer: "At the end of the day there is a feeling that this is all very, very worthwhile. . . . My children are proud of me." Denise Kuhlman, who left a job as a bankruptcy lawyer and applied for graduate school in psychology, said, "I have no intention of practicing law in the future. In my heart of hearts, I want to do things that are good for people."

What do you want in your heart of hearts? Have you listened to it lately? If you did, where might it lead you?

7

we're all driven

In which you will learn that:

1. Your environment has to provide the incentives that drive you to succeed.

2. The incentives need to be real and immediate enough to get your feet out of bed each morning.

3. Different things motivate different people.

4. You have to find a circus that will deliver a daily dose of whatever keeps you rolling.

We've talked about how your basic beliefs have to be expressed in your working and living environment and suggested that you're likely to feel very dissatisfied if they aren't. Beliefs are the foundation of who you are and the kind of work you do. In fact, they are so deeply embedded that you don't really think about them on a daily basis.

What does affect your daily life are more immediate things like incentives, feedback, and a sense of achievement (or, if you are in a more poisonous environment, fear, stress, and frustration). Good or bad, these things are called performance drivers in consultant-speak. Here we'll call

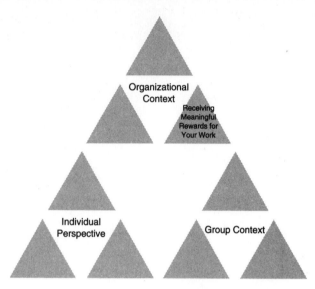

© PeopleTech Consulting, Inc.

them simply meaningful rewards. Whatever tag you hang on them, their presence drives you to push yourself and succeed and their absence drives you to despair and inertia.

> Our chief want in life is somebody who will make us do what we can.
>
> —RALPH WALDO EMERSON

We all need some fairly immediate gratification in our lives, a little daily incentive, a reason to swing our feet out of bed morning after morning. We need it like a circus dog needs a treat at the end of a trick, a child needs praise for taking out the garbage, or a salesperson needs a commission this month. Even CEOs work better when they know there will be big handfuls of stock options at the end of the year.

Rewards tie your day-to-day actions to your long-term goals. So whatever your circus ends up being, it'll also have to deliver the things that drive you to succeed on a daily or weekly basis.

THE CHALLENGE-OF-THE-WEEK FACTOR

Gordon Farnham had to go hunting for daily drivers to add some fairly immediate gratification to his retirement. He found he didn't have a reason to get out of bed in the morning, so he went looking for a new circus.

The retirement was well planned and well financed. There was a winter home on St. Simon's Island, Georgia, and a summer home in the Finger Lakes, both one-story buildings designed with the kind of conveniences that many retired people say they want. Both homes were located near hospitals that offered special facilities for the aging. Both had superior golf courses, good fishing, and adequate libraries.

"I'd done the research about cost-of-living, health care costs, average temperature in December, annual rainfall, and property taxes: all of that. I had about five file folders full of it. We'd visited about eight communities and made a very logical decision. I'm kind of a pain in the butt that way."

Before retirement, Farnham had been vice-president of what he describes as "an intentionally boring financial institution. We were the kind of place that didn't mess around with pork futures or shopping center mortgages. It's an old-money place where the clients tend to think in terms of generations rather than trying to make 20 percent a year in biotechnology stocks. They're happy with 8 percent, as long as it comes in year after year after year. God help you if it doesn't."

At his retirement at sixty, he actually got an inscribed gold watch. For tax reasons, there was still a place on the board, but it was clearly understood that he wouldn't offer "an excess of advice." The younger men taking over wanted to venture into more aggressive investments because that was what the younger clients were interested in. In short, Farnham was perfectly free to do absolutely nothing and had the money to enjoy it.

"We started with the mandatory cruise. I met three other men on the boat who had just retired and were taking the mandatory cruise. Evidently, the cruise lines call this 'the Mother market,' as in 'Mother, when we retire, I'm going to take you on a cruise.'

"Then we did the other retirement things. I tried fishing. I'd been fishing twice before in my life, both times on clients' boats where you didn't have to actually catch or clean the fish yourselves: there were people to do it for you. This was different.

"I researched everything: fish finders, water temperatures, boats, motors, migratory patterns. I bought all the toys: the reels, the electronics, the trolling motors, the lures. I watched the television shows: there are a surprising number of television shows about fishing.

"I hated fishing. It's cold and uncomfortable. The fish are perverse. And when you catch them, they're slippery and they're ugly and they smell. And those are just the pieces you're supposed to keep. I decided to leave the industry to the professionals." The fishing gear was sold.

Gardening came next. "It's all insects and root rot and dirty finger-nails and none of the books really tell you how to deal with those things correctly and efficiently."

Gardening was followed by photography. "I started seeing my whole life through a viewfinder. I thought I'd be satisfied by seeing the pictures. I wasn't. I've always hated other peoples' photo albums. I found I was bored by my own, too."

At that point Farnham undertook a very logical exercise: He tried to remember the last thing that he'd enjoyed doing. "It was odd. The last thing that had given me any kind of kick was planning and supervising the building of our two retirement houses. I didn't much like the life I was leading in them, but actually figuring out what made a good retire-ment house and then actually having it built in a way that made eco-nomic sense had excited me.

"I'd done a lot of research on passive heating and cooling, trying to cut down on the energy bills we'd have in retirement. You can actually use the sun to air-condition a house if you plan right. I'd also done research on what makes a house easier to use for people whose eyesight and agility aren't the best. Current houses don't make a lot of sense. Why do kitchen designers make cupboards so deep you can't reach the stuff at the back? Why aren't there seats in showers? Why not make stairs less steep and why not make them wider? I've got a remote control for my television. Why don't I have a remote control for my security system? I used to build houses in my mind while I was out in the garden. Maybe that's what happened to the herbaceous border."

Retired financial managers don't start developing houses specu-latively. They fish or garden or take up a hobby like photography. "When I started, I had difficulty explaining why I was doing what I was doing to my former colleagues. I think they thought that I'd lost my capital and was trying to put together an income. And it took a long time to explain the notion to my wife. I think she thought it was just another new hobby and I'd get over it."

After twenty-three houses, Gordon's wife Elizabeth is convinced that Farnham Homes is more than a hobby. "At first I thought, 'Well, at least it will keep him from hanging around the kitchen.' Then I got worried. It was becoming a kind of obsession with him. He'd walk around kick-ing cabinets and telling me how a logical person would redesign these so that retired people could use them more easily. And then he began to disappear for hours. I finally found out that he was out looking at land. Then one day he came in and told me that he'd bought some. Five months later he'd built the first house, which sold in about two weeks to a couple from New York. A week later, he was bullying the contractor about building the second house. Right now, he has three going up and two of them are pre-sold. He worries a lot but then he's always worried about anything he liked. And he's out the front door every morning by 6:30."

Gordon explains why. "The thing is, I've got a new reason to swing my feet out of the bed every morning. Every day is some kind of new contest, a new challenge. What kind of kitchen taps would a person with arthritis like to use? How the hell would you organize a bathroom cabinet for somebody whose sight is going? Even the garden: what in God's name can you plant on the ground that doesn't have to be mowed? How do you design guest rooms for grandchildren so they'll want to come but won't want to stay too long?

"In a lot of ways it's like my former job. There was a daily challenge—or at least a challenge of the week to keep you fresh. Like 'How do you have a person owning a company without really owning it for tax purposes?' or 'How do I get $13 million out of an African country where they've just slapped bans on the export of hard currency?'

"Those challenges were real to me. They weren't like gardening or photography. They were about real life or at least what I imagine real life to be. The sheer variety of them kept me going. There was something new every morning, something real that I could fix that no one else was fixing."

HOW COMPANIES USE PERFORMANCE DRIVERS TO MOTIVATE PEOPLE

Suppose a company believes in customer satisfaction. Because of that belief, it wants to cut the customer rejection rate of its sub-assemblies from 4 percent to 1 percent because this will slash its warranty costs from $10 million to $2 million a year and increase its return business. The company can do a number of things:

1. It can adopt a slogan like "Perfection Is the Vital Breath of Our Corporation's Life" and hang it in the lunch room.

2. It can send each employee on the line a memo.

3. It can announce a 5 percent bonus when the ultimate goal is met.

4. It can announce a 1 percent bonus each time the rejection rate goes down a point.

5. The president can come down to the assembly line, announce a 1 percent bonus in cash each time the rate goes down a point and a barbecue when the goal is halfway met. He also promises to let the people know how they're doing on a weekly basis because the project is important to the long-term mission.

Corporations have tried all these things. There are no prizes for figuring out which one works best. People will nod obligingly when you talk about short-term pain for long-term gain, but if you really want to get their attention, promise some short-term gain.

Immediate gratification isn't bad, it's human. It's why you reward yourself with a beer after mowing the lawn and why the diet plan people get the group together every week and cheer those who've reached their goals. Having a bottle of champagne after mowing the lawn all summer doesn't make it nor does getting a trophy after clocking in with your target weight after a year and a half. I knew a sales manager who covered the floor of the boardroom with ten-dollar bills, made the salespeople walk across them in their bare feet, and them promised the bundle to whoever showed up at the end of the week with the most sales. It seemed to work.

> An estimated twenty million Americans are staying in jobs they hate
> in order to keep their health insurance—when research indicates that
> career dissatisfaction is more likely than anything else to make them
> need to use it.
>
> —BARBARA BAILEY REINHOLD

I don't know about you, but I don't get up every morning and think to myself, "Great, I've still got health insurance." I need a more immediate incentive for doing something. Otherwise, I'd probably still be teaching in a university.

The challenge for the management consultant is that one person's performance driver may be another person's yawn. Believing I'm having fun may make me put in sixteen-hour days. On the other hand, you may prefer that the company say it in greenbacks. Believing they can save a life today may send rescue workers into a burning apartment block, but you may do it because you're intellectually interested in demonstrating the technology of fire retardants. You may take to the barricades because you hate the enemy; I may do it because of peer pressure. Good leaders realize this and try to assemble an array of performance drivers: loyalty, greed, belief in the common good, joy, thrills, a plaque, a memo, days off, a silver pin, a parking space closer to the door, a ride in a hot air balloon, a weekend in the Bahamas, or an invitation to come to work again tomorrow.

They also know there are two types of drivers. The first includes those that work on a person day after day: money, a chance to get ahead, or respect. The second type includes drivers that have only a transitory effect: the sales contest, the productivity award, or the plaque you get for meeting new quality targets. A dog almost always will run after a piece of sirloin tip. The same dog may be only temporarily affected by the female across the park. An employee may work because of peer respect that's expressed regularly. The same employee may perk up only temporarily because of the promise of a four-day weekend at Paradise Island.

Good leaders also realize several other things:

1. A performance driver that worked in the past won't necessarily work today. Free fondue dishes for a job well done may have stirred up the troops twenty years ago, but today you can't give the things away. Similarly, an earnest chat about job security worked during the recession, but get the same words out of your mouth today and people will simply glower at you resentfully. A teamwork incentive might work today where ten years ago it would have puzzled people.

2. The immediate rewards of a job should be refreshed every so often. A performance driver that's exciting today may be just background noise next quarter. Offering somebody a day off for meeting the biweekly quota will work—for a while. Gradually the biweekly day off becomes expected, a part of the employment package. You're not going to be able to take it away. It has become a birthright instead of an incentive.

3. Performance drivers work particularly well when they're tied to new goals or programs. They draw attention to the change. If

you have a new quality goal, you'll underscore the meaning of it if you give away Rolexes. If you have a new teamwork strategy, people will get the idea better when you give away Super Bowl tickets to teams that meet immediate objectives.

4. Performance drivers work best across a company if all the performers are motivated by the same thing. Savvy managers know how to recruit for this.

WHAT DRIVES YOU?

Just as you have to match your beliefs with those of your workplace, you have to make sure the environment you're headed toward provides the drivers that will make you do your best work. If you're motivated by the occasional hit of cash, don't head for a situation where the monetary rewards are due in twenty years. If what appeals to you are high fives from the group at quitting time, don't put yourself all alone in a tower at the end of the Internet with no one to talk to but your Pentium chip.

The trouble is that it's easy to kid yourself about what drives you. Young women in beauty pageants invariably express a fervent desire for world peace, but very few actually go on to work for peace-related organizations. In public, we are inclined to say things like "duty, honor, and country" when asked why we do what we do.

Right. And Sly Stallone is in it for the art.

What gets me out of bed in the morning? I'm excited by learning new things. One of my personal goals is never to repeat a day. I have a low boredom threshold. If you point me toward a new and interesting project, my mood improves, my reptile brain clicks on, and I start making strange chuffing noises. If you head me toward people who are excited about what they're doing, you'll hear the same noise amplified.

What drives you? I've devised and tested the nice short questionnaire on page 96. It's based, not on what you think you think or what it might be swell to tell others you think, but on your recent history. When was the last time you went the extra mile? The questionnaire works best if you begin by writing down what the incident was (for example, "The entire eastern MIS went down and we had the weekend to fix it" or "We had an offer from a major Japanese distributor and needed to find a way to readjust our operational systems to fill it") and then figure out what it was about the incident that did it for you (challenge? adversity? innovation?). Other words or phrases you might find handy include the following:

Greed

Fun

New situation

Deadline

Fear

Team spirit

Short-term gain

Pride

Control

Promotion

Proving myself

Comfort

Love

Praise from boss

Publicity

To get the job off my desk

Intellectual stimulation

Anything for a quiet life

Getting the better of Henry Divot just this one more time

QUESTIONNAIRE 1:
WHAT DRIVES YOU?

1. In the past three years, the thing that drove me to work the hardest two weeks was:

   _____

   _____

2. In the past three years, the thing that motivated me to work the hardest week was:

   _____

   _____

3. In the past three years, the thing that motivated me to work the hardest three days was:

   _____

   _____

4. In the past three years, the thing that motivated me to work the hardest day was:

   _____

   _____

If your answers came out "duty, honor, and country," I know a Marine recruiter who is anxious to meet you. After the psychological tests, she may let you into the Corps, where you'll be perfectly happy.

TOO MUCH WHIP, TOO LITTLE CARROT

Now we need to look at the other side of motivation, also known as disincentives. Over the last three years, what temporary conditions have had you downing tools, folding your arms, and refusing to do your best? These disincentives are important because they keep you from doing your best. Just ask the cart horse: too much whip is as bad as too little carrot.

Reduce the negative incident to a phrase or a word. Here are some handy ones:

Lack of recognition

Disorganization

Abuse

Fear

Jealousy

Utter boredom

Anxiety about failure

Too much work

Someone else being shafted

Lack of direction

A sense that the project was useless

Dislike of the person in charge

Knowing someone else would get the credit

No communication

Interference

Not enough help

Lack of financial support

Lack of management support

Not enough freedom

QUESTIONNAIRE 2:
WHAT DRIVES YOU CRAZY?

1. In the past three years, the incident that had me slowing down the most in a two-week period was:

_____

_____

2. In the past three years, the incident that had me slowing down the most for a three-day period was:

_____

_____

3. In the past three years, the thing that had me walk out of work in disgust for a day was:

_____

_____

All of this has a lot to do with what kind of circus you create for yourself. You may have a vision of yourself in a flannel shirt working as a fishing guide in northern Quebec, but if you respond best to sales contests, you're just not going to be happy. Your daydream of owning a bistro may give you a bunch of happy hours, but if your current performance drivers include having weekends off, you won't last long.

Your meaningful rewards have to mesh with what you're doing or what you're going to do. Otherwise, you'll end up just as cheerless—or cheerful—as you are now. Which means that you have to contrive your circus so it will deliver up a daily dose of whatever keeps you rolling.

HOW TO BE 2.7 TIMES HAPPIER
ON HALF THE SALARY

I know a man who ran a large hotel in a larger chain. He was very good at what he did. He understood the economics of the hospitality industry. He was a good leader of a diverse workforce. He had an eye for detail and noticed if there was no shampoo in room 2207. He was good at all those things, and the chain rewarded him very well. He dressed well, ate well, and traveled well. But even though the job was rewarding and he was good at it, he wasn't happy. Being paid a bunch, being in charge of a large organization, or answering to an appreciative head office wasn't why he'd gotten into the business.

He'd gone into the industry because he liked throwing parties, being a host, welcoming people, making them feel good, serving them something that was the best they'd ever tasted, and then showing them to a comfortable, attractive room. He would have liked to be a member of nineteenth-century aristocracy, throwing hunt balls and dinner parties and inviting people to his country estate for the weekend.

His performance drivers were at odds with his corporation's. Being host to 1,287 convention delegates and managing their conference rooms and coffee breaks and name tags while making sure the profit margin didn't sink below projections while at the same time carrying out union negotiations with 178 chambermaids just isn't the same as, for example, running a small resort in a small community in the Sunbelt. Which is what he does now.

He estimates his current income at half his former salary. He estimates his current workload at double that for the hotel chain. Some psychologist out there will doubtless have an objective measurement for happiness, but I don't at the moment. All I know is that I met him at the large hotel and I've stayed at the small resort. I would estimate that he is 2.7 times as happy as he was.

A lot of other things had to happen, and the road from the hotel chain to the small resort was bumpy at times. However, I believe that the primary cause of his happiness is that he aligned his performance drivers with those of his corporation, even though he had to start the corporation himself.

8

working at something you enjoy—or maybe you'd rather be a nail than a hammer

In which you will find out that:

1. How you work has a lot to do with how well you work.

2. If the way you're expected to work doesn't match your individual work style, it may be time for a change.

3. New work styles are emerging—with new opportunities and new dangers.

4. Corporations (and individuals) sometimes mistake change for progress.

5. Understanding your work style will help you find the right circus.

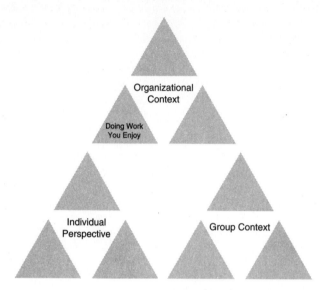

© *PeopleTech Consulting, Inc.*

Like beliefs and performance drivers, your organization's work processes have to fit your personal needs for you to be content. Work processes are about how you get the job done: for example, whether you prefer to work nine-to-five, whether you like to work by yourself up a telephone pole or in a committee room with everybody making notes, who you report to, and what your deadlines are. The idea is to make sure that the work processes that you get in your new circus are the ones that suit you best, the ones that work the way you enjoy.

Brian Trimble changed all of his work processes when he started his second life.

These days, Trimble is an infuriating man you'd love to meet at a party. His stories are amazing, joyous, and true. His successes, both personal and professional, are the kinds of things you wish were on your resume. His happiness and his zest for living in the moment are as infectious as the flu. He is in vibrant health for a

If you see a carpenter that's alive to his work, you'll notice that . . . he's not trying to get the nail down and out of the way so he can hurry up and get another one. Although he may be working fast, each lick is like a separate person that he's hitting with his hammer. It's like as though there's a separate friend of his that one moment. And when he gets out of it, here comes another one. Unique, all by itself.

—NICK LINDSAY, CARPENTER, FROM *WORKING*, BY STUDS TERKEL

fifty-three-year-old. And, toward the end of the party, you begin to suspect that in his spare time he builds suspension bridges out of recycled toxic waste for deprived Nepalese villagers and sings the "Ode to Joy" while he does it.

In the morning, you hate him. You hate him because he's living the kind of life you wanted. More than that: he took the kind of life you're feeling hemmed in by and transformed it into something a lot like your dreams if you could make them come true.

Before he made the transformation, he was an upper-middle executive in a communications company, one of those firms that own five television stations, a scattering of cable companies, and an interest in a satellite direct broadcast operation. He was in confident command of a dozen people who in turn were in command of more than 200 other people. His life was full of trips to the coast, speeches at industry conventions, large three-day strategy meetings, five telephone numbers, a large mortgage, evenings spent with the flavor-of-the-month software, an electronic daytimer kept up to date by a personal assistant, attractive stock options, his broker's number on his speed dialer, a small but growing folk art collection, three grown and starting-to-be-successful children, a wife who had a senior position in a growing MIS consultancy, a one-third share in a sailboat he seldom got a chance to use, and a blood-pressure problem he was keeping under control with a low-fat diet and a trainer-designed exercise program.

There's more. He had the respect of the people who worked for him and the considerable respect of his boss: the man was hoping he'd take over the company one day. His wife and children did more than just like him. Looking at his work from the outside, it seemed challenging, leading-edge, and innovative—all those words that the business magazines use.

In the movies when something's going this well, you just know that the music is suddenly going to get creepy and sinister, because fate is about to turn on the unsuspecting hero. For Trimble, it was a combination of things: a bad reading of an X-ray, the collapse of a savings and loan company, and two mergers that failed in a row. You don't need the precise details; most people hear stories like it every day.

"But it wasn't just those things. It wasn't even the combination of those things. It was those things combined with what had begun happening in my head," Trimble tells you.

He was working in his den at home one day and looked up to see the gardener driving the new riding mower he'd bought. "I wanted to be running the mower, instead of working on the new equipment strategy I was scheduled to present the next day."

A few days later he opened the scheduling window on his computer and found that everything was planned for the next two months. "Everything," he says "And there were appointments into the next year. There was a conference call scheduled eight months into the future. And I remember sitting there wishing that I could fast-forward through the whole schedule, just like you fast-forward through a video you've seen before. You know what's going to happen. All you want to do is check the end."

"I began imagining each of the VPs being the color his department was on the organization chart. Finance was gray. Marketing was purple. Operations was brown. Communications was yellow. Blend them together and you get a color much like manure.

"There was no synergy. Their work was their work. My work was my work. And everything was carved in stone: situation meetings at 8:00 on Thursdays, monthly reports on the last Tuesday of the month. Don't color outside the lines. It was a system, and it probably used to mean something. My problem was that I found I didn't want to work that way. I didn't mind the actual work, but I minded doing it that way."

He made a change. There are now eight charter sailboats in a hurricane hole in the Lesser Antilles. He works on them in the high winter season, doing make-and-mend chores for the people who charter them. Occasionally, he becomes a crew member. "Never captain, though. I don't want to have to be that competent any more." In spring the boats go north to the Chesapeake, chartered to the summer crowd there. His wife runs the computer that takes care of scheduling, inventories, and cash flow. There's a two-room house with a red tin roof overlooking the harbor. On the Chesapeake, they live aboard whatever boat they haven't rented.

Communications are expensive: they come in on a special direct-from-satellite version of cellular developed for sailors that runs about $5 a minute. There are no cars. The wardrobe fits in a duffel bag. Taxes still require an accountant ("This is a capital-intensive business"), but not much money. Blood pressure is slightly below normal, although the diet has gone by the boards (they don't stock much Metamucil in the islands).

"I know: it isn't reality," he says. "I've also been told it's pretty damned immature and shallow. Guy I used to work with even told me it was trite because I'd run away to sea. They come down south, charter from me for ten days and tell me that. The only solution I've come up with is to agree with them. I more than agree with them, I build on their arguments. It seems to help them."

Like Paul Beaver, Trimble made a massive change: his business, his hours, his place, what his family did, and what was in the fridge. That may be a symptom of the degree of pain he was experiencing. Many people I've spoken to have changed only one or two of those things and have gotten the same results. The changes are not as romantic as running away to sea but they've produced the same smiles.

THE NEW WORK PROCESSES: YOU'RE ALLOWED TO COLOR OUTSIDE THE LINES

Is there life after the organization chart? Bryan Trimble suggests that there is. In fact, despite what he says to the people who charter his boats, he is convinced that the only life worth living is way off the usual organization charts into undiscovered regions where there may be dragons. The only life for him, anyway.

Take another look at the chart on page 22. The organization chart at some companies is starting to look more like an abstract expressionist painting. Some companies don't bother with charts at all: for example, at companies like DreamWorks, Oticon, and CREO, nobody has a job title. These are companies? Why not? Coloring outside the lines is allowed in more and more places, encouraged in some, and mandatory at a few. It's those companies you would do well to watch.

Even the lines themselves are blurring, moving, or disappearing entirely. People are even having trouble figuring out what is a product and service and have to talk about "provices" and "serducts." It's hard to know where to color. Some jobs are evaporating; new jobs are being created. Lots of people make up their job descriptions as they go along. We're not just changing work processes, we're inventing new ones.

It's not just the organization chart that's transforming, it's the actual work that people are doing that is becoming more fluid, harder to describe, and difficult to pin down. What do people do all day? Sure there are still people clocking in at 8:59 A.M. to deal with paperwork at standard-issue desks. There are others who clock in at unpredictable hours (4:28 P.M., 5:43 A.M., 9:17 P.M.). They have no office and no desk— only a locker from which they take a basket of supplies to whatever space is available. They sit on a sofa, plug in a laptop, get a cappuccino from the kitchen, do some work, make some calls, stop for a while to play backgammon with a colleague while discussing a new product line, carry on a heated discussion with another colleague via e-mail, check out after three hours, and wander off to an art gallery to do some research on architectural photography for a new advertising campaign. This is work? Why not? A woman on a Mercury outboard assembly line used to put eight bolts into the engine. Now, she does 24 separate operations, guided by a computer program that she helped create. Then she signs the job she's put together. This is an assembly line? Again, why not?

Office designers are scrambling to keep up with the weird and wonderful work processes that are emerging. They collaborate with anthropologists, ergonomists, and psychologists trying to figure out what the process of work is nowadays and to create new and eclectic work settings to support individual needs and teamwork.

THE DANGERS OF THE NEW "FREEDOM"

For some people, productivity means getting away from anything that smacks of the traditional office with other people who distract you when you need to concentrate and who interrupt your work with their concerns. As Gil Gordon, a telecommuting consultant, says, "It's like the old saying that the hospital is a terrible place to get healthy. The office is a terrible place to do work." Well, certain kinds of work, anyway.

> The new physics [of work] is about balance—juggling many things in many states of development—and about integration—with your colleagues and their projects. Information is available anywhere; people no longer are tethered to their desks. As a consequence they go to the office for new reasons: to be with each other, to collaborate, to learn, to socialize.
>
> —CHARLES FISHMAN

Flextime, compressed work weeks, job sharing, and working from home part- or full-time are options at many companies. Modems, pagers, laptops, and cellular phones mean that you can make anything into an office: a restaurant table, a departure lounge, or a car.

There are dangers in all of this. One is that millions of us now commute down the hall to what used to be the den, too often by way of the fridge. You don't get to complain about the traffic any more, unless you happen to trip over the cat. Anecdotal evidence suggests that telecommuters moved home to have time for the family. Anecdotal evidence also suggests that most telecommuters still don't have time to walk the dog.

Fax machines and e-mail shrink time and add what is often artificial urgency to tasks we used to let ripen in the back of our minds for a day. If the client can send it to us in nanoseconds, we feel we have to respond at the same warp speed. Electronic communications turn the home or cottage business into some kind of hyper-kinetic pingpong game. (Fortunately, someone invented voice mail to slow it down. "Push 1 for limbo, push 2 for oblivion." Properly used, voice mail can decelerate work to an almost Caribbean pace.)

The net effect of all these changes is that despite the layering on of technology, the average North American management type is (a) working more and (b) earning less. We are producing better products and services. These products and services are closer to what the consumer wants and are available at a point that is closer to where and when the consumer wants them. We do more with less, we aim higher, and we are more responsive, but (a) and (b) are still true for a lot of us.

> The rise of work is not confined to a few, selective groups, but has affected the great majority of working Americans. Hours have risen for men as well as women, for those in the working class as well as professionals. They have grown for all marital statuses and income groups. The increase also spans a wide range of industries. Indeed, the shrinkage of leisure experienced by nearly all types of Americans has created a profound structural crisis of time.
>
> —JULIET SCHOR

Should we all sit down and weep? Not necessarily. Go back over all the things that have happened to us and reflect on them. What the re-engineers and the techies have delivered to us is a smorgasbord of new work processes. We don't have to be satisfied with the old industrial model. On the other hand, we should beware the temptations of technolust until we understand just what in heaven's name we're really after when we set out to find a work process that fits us.

NEW WORK PROCESSES: WORKING THE WAY YOU ENJOY

Consider those changes with care. Some of these changes you may like, some you may imagine you like, and some you know you don't. Quite a few people preferred the industrial model: tell us what to do and we'll march off and do it, no questions asked. We'd rather be nails than hammers; it's more comfy. "Give the electronic stuff to the techno-fetishists and leave me alone to install the lug nuts."

Personally, I love the way I can be "at my office" when I'm two thousand miles away. I can have my cake and diet, too. However, I know lots of people would find my situation unnerving.

You can choose your work style if you design your circus correctly. If your preferred work process involves teams, design it or choose it so that you get to work in a team. If it involves working nine to five instead of picking your own hours, make absolutely sure that that's what's on offer. If you prefer the guidance of a manager to being let loose on your own, make sure you're not head honcho. Your work processes have to align just as certainly as your belief systems and your performance drivers. Otherwise, you're adding to a pile of irritants that will turn into an avalanche.

How do you make sure your work processes match with whatever you're running away to? Look at the following table. Here we've listed some aspects of work processes. Feel free to add others that inspire you. Circle your preferred option in one color. Circle your company's preferred option in another.

	TRADITIONAL	NEWER OPTIONS	OR . . . ?
Hours	9 to 5, Monday to Friday	Flextime, compressed work week	When the spirit moves you
Location	Office, plant	Home, hotel, car	Sailboat, halfway up a mountain, Hong Kong
Contact	In meetings or by memos	By modem, cellphone, fax	You decide
Deadlines	Regular (weekly, monthly, quarterly)	Depends on the project	Some hourly, some every five years
Report to	Immediate superior	Project teams	Yourself

	TRADITIONAL	NEWER OPTIONS	OR . . . ?
Type of work	Analysis, production	Innovation, creation	Reinventing the world
Learning	In formal professional development seminars	During sabbaticals, corporate universities	During three-day weekends
Selling yourself	With a CV that lists work experience and education	Networking	Through Web sites, videos, project portfolios
Relationship to clients	The client requests a service, you supply it	Partnership through uncertainty	Working together
Job title	Look at your current business card	No title at all	President, You Inc.

What appeals to you? What is your current situation? Is there a match? Where are the major differences between you and your work environment? Are those conditions that you can expect to change within your present situation? And are those conditions you expect to achieve in the circus you're putting together for YouInc.?

Organizational and personal beliefs are the big picture, the dream. Performance drivers can be short, medium, or long term, ideally a combination of the three. Work processes, however, are the immediate, daily experiences of the rubber hitting the road, the hammer hitting the nail. If they don't suit you, it's more like a hammer repeatedly hitting your thumb. If that's how you feel, finding a second life is not simply a good idea, it's your duty to yourself.

Early in my life, I got a good lesson in the importance of being passionate about the things you choose to do. My mother decided that my brother and I should have piano lessons. My brother really hated it. He used to practice the piano while wearing his football helmet, as a way of signalling to my mother what he really wanted to do. One day my father said to him, "You really hate playing piano, don't you?" My brother said he couldn't take another minute of it. So my father got a chain, hooked it around the piano, hooked that to the tractor, and dragged the piano out into a field. Then he poured diesel fuel over the piano and set it on fire. "Go get your mother," my father said. It was his way of telling us that there is no point in doing things that you are not passionate about.

New Ointment, Same Fly?

Let me state an important caveat here because it's the kind of problem that will slither out from under your bed and night and mug you severely if you don't pay attention. *Do not mistake change for progress.* Corporations do this routinely, and you've seen them do it.

I recently found out about an interesting situation at a manufacturing company. Management had installed a new voice mail system. Tracking reports indicated that the sales function was spending 13 percent less time on the phone. They were happy with this apparent change in the work process. This was good: the sales people must be making more productive, proactive sales calls. What management was not happy with was the fact that sales figures were down 11 percent.

I went to the phone. I dialed sales. I was told to press a button. I was told to press another button. And another button. I complied with all three requests. I listened to some music from a radio station I would not voluntarily listen to. I was transferred to a recording of an audio commercial for their new product line. I was put in touch with a recording that asked me to leave a message because "your call is valuable to us." Right. In changing the work process for the sales force, they'd also changed the work process for the consumer. The sales department was spending 13 percent less time on the phone. The customer was spending twice as much.

I called a competitor's sales department. A salesperson answered personally, immediately. Any student in the class want to guess what was happening?

The human animal is easily confused. We call this *cognitive dissonance*, which sounds so official that we can all feel better about it. A lot of the confusion these days seems to be caused by mistaking change for progress. The chain of logic goes something like this: The wheel was technology. It made work easier. Voice mail is technology. It will make work easier. This is logic trap number one. Voice mail is easier, in a sense. It turns out that voice mail in this particular case was easier for the sales department. It got rid of those nasty noises coming from the beige plastic boxes with all the buttons and lights on the desks in their offices. It was not easier for the customer.

The customers' calls were "valuable to us." However, it turned out the customer's calls were more valuable to the customers than to the sales department. The customers started substituting a competitor's phone number when they made calls.

Writer/fruit picker/longshoreman Reg Theriault in *How to Tell When You're Tired* tells about a fellow worker who'd quit the backbreaking day labor environment that Reg had been involved in all his life and started a chicken farm. The chicken farm idea turned out to be less attractive than the man and his wife had imagined. He announced that he was getting out of it and buying cows instead. His wife was in favor: "She'll go for anything to get away from all that chickenshit."

Reg Theriault's point—for anyone who wasn't raised on a farm—was that the color and smell may be different, but what comes out of chickens and what comes out of cows is still manure. And you're still behind the shovel. There's change, but no progress. You're still using the same work process and still at the end of the same shovel.

> *After years of listening to me talk about the joys of boating, my stockbroker broke down and bought a cruiser. He loved it. The solitude of the ocean was the perfect escape from the stresses of civilization, he said. But he became uncomfortable when he went out of range of his VHF and cell phone, not to mention missing* Wall Street Week. *So he bought a single-sideband radio. It was downhill from then on. He became a communications junkie. He wanted everything on his boat that he had in his office, including instant landline hook-ups, and data and facsimile transmissions. He got it all—including the stress he was so anxious to leave behind.*
>
> —KEN ENGLERT

I have a number of friends, myself not least of them, who have made the same mistake. We get a laptop so we can work anywhere. We get a cellular phone to back up the laptop. We get a built-in fax and e-mail and v-mail. All of this is to make ourselves splendidly independent. We can go anywhere we want. We're free!

Except that, because my friends didn't match the change in technology with a change in work processes, they feel trapped, not free. They've added new demands on their time without re-examining the old ones. The chains to the office aren't as obvious because they're electron-thin. However, they are still chains. Instead of getting out of the office, my friends have found that the office is everywhere and they can't leave.

If Scrooge had given Bob Cratchit a computer, Cratchit would still be chained to his desk, keyboarding in his fingerless mittens and feeling sorry for himself on Christmas Eve. You have to change the actual work processes, not just the equipment.

Dress-down Fridays don't change a company's work processes. All they do is change the clothes—and only on Fridays. Instead of one dress code, there are now two. In the next change, there will be three dress codes a week. (I'm sure this is all being promoted by the fashion mafia. They want you to have three wardrobes.) But even if Scrooge had let Cratchit wear jeans on Fridays, he'd still be Scrooge and Cratchit would still be Crachit—same shovel, different poop; different ointment, same fly.

To avoid being fooled by the wrong changes, you have to go back to the first principles of changing your work process. Define what work process has given you the most satisfaction in the past. Get as close to that work process as possible. You cannot satisfy yourself 100 percent, but from my experience you can get a lot closer.

Designing Your Work Process at Your Circus

Check the work process chart on pages 108–109 and then fill in the one below. As with previous exercises, it's always best to validate your answers against your own personal history. It's neat to imagine that you'd like to have no fixed hours at all. But think back to a point where you didn't have any and remember how you felt about it. It's nice to imagine life without a boss, but bring to mind activities in which you've been bossless. Was it all that much fun? Do you really want to forge ahead without some direction? Or do you want a different kind of boss, one more in tune with your beliefs, drivers, and work processes?

Be careful what you wish for. You may end up getting it and then hating it.

	WHAT YOU HAVE NOW	WHAT YOU WANT	WHAT THE DREAM OFFERS
Hours	_____	_____	_____
Location	_____	_____	_____
Report to	_____	_____	_____

	WHAT YOU HAVE NOW	**WHAT YOU WANT**	**WHAT THE DREAM OFFERS**
Deadlines	_____	_____	_____
Type of work	_____	_____	_____
Learning	_____	_____	_____
Selling yourself	_____	_____	_____
Relationship to clients	_____	_____	_____
Job title	_____	_____	_____

A FURTHER CONSIDERATION:
DO YOU WANT TO GET PHYSICAL?

Maybe you also should think about what your life is doing to your body. Do you spend too much time in front of a computer? What's that doing to your eyes, back, and carpal tunnels? How's the air in the building you work in? What sort of food are you eating when you don't have time for proper meals? Do you find yourself getting headaches or stomachaches on a regular basis?

I exercise. You probably do, too. On the stationary bike, the treadmill, and the stair machine, we probably pump out enough kilowattage to power a small town in Minnesota during a hard winter. If we hooked all the people who do the same thing onto the national power grid, we could probably stop global warming.

It does us good, no doubt, but we still treat exercise as something separate from work, something extra that we have to squeeze into our schedules. We build up tension at the office and release it at the gym. But what if we found ways to get physical at work? What would that do for our stressful lives?

Take a minute and think of five physical activities you've enjoyed lately. Those five activities could include biking in a park, full-contact gardening, skating, square dancing, renovating the attic, washing the car, or Zen archery. Now, ask yourself:

- How many of these activities are almost purely physical?

- How many are much more physical than what you're doing now?

- Would you do something like that for money?

- Are you creative enough to find a way to do it?

A friend of mine produces commercials and short documentaries. This is creative work ("How do we best show the role of peasant in France in the twelfth century?") and work that demands negotiating skills. ("What do you mean digital editing costs $150 an hour?") Most of the work demands that he sits in a chair looking at a person or screen. What he does voluntarily—slowly and for no pay—is haul rocks, mix concrete, and drudge on his knees to build himself a cobblestone driveway at his place in the country. He will do this happily for eight hours a day. He will come up the driveway whistling. This physical work suits him, at least for the weekend.

My gynecologist digs ponds by hand in an area of alluvial till (he taught me the term). That's a different work process. To my mind the digging is as valuable to him as advising on birthing procedures.

I have a relative who used to manage a department store. He took up making tables. He starts by cutting down the trees. He finds a considerable comfort in combing the intellectual creativity with the cardiovascular benefits of turning pine into a harvest table.

Reg Theriault, quoted earlier, talks about the physical laborer's envy of the white-collar workers' clean, white shirts and the fact that they can go home after seven hours' work while he and his shift moved 158-pound sacks of coffee from the bottom of a freighter's hold. He had three things to say about this.

> As someone who has spent over 20 years as a social worker, school counselor, and therapist in private practice, I have earned the right to ask some basic questions about myself and my profession. . . . I'm tired of sitting and listening, and even active modes of therapy feel constraining. Oddly, some of my best sessions occur when I go out and play ball with adolescent clients, or take a walk in the park with adults who tolerate my need for physical relief. I don't know how Freud and his colleagues did it, but I find all this sitting really maddening. I keep thinking I should use my hands to build a house, my heart to help build a community . . . .
>
> —GEORGE D. COHEN, THERAPIST, SAN DIEGO

First, because Reg had had some schooling, he knew that "a college education doesn't make the bags any lighter." The degree didn't change the work process. Second, he really had no envy for the white-collar workers. In his opinion they were as badly off as he was. Third, when those in charge put an ad in the paper asking for people to work at the job of unloading ships, more than 30 percent of the applicants came from white-collar jobs. The highest percentage of applications came from schoolteachers.

Reg is someone I'd like to meet. For thirty years he did physical work: building melon cartons, strapping down containers, and unloading trucks. Then he sat down and wrote a book, another different work process.

After thirty years or even twenty, a lot of the people I've met want to get off their chairs and play in the mud. I know group product managers who muck out the stalls in the stables at 6:00 on a gray Saturday morning. When someone meets them in the dawn hours, they cry, "Isn't the air marvelous?"

Well, it is. The air is not full of opinions or messages and has been scrubbed clean of questions. The lines of communications are clear except on the days when they steam a bit. Who's in charge is the person who wants to see the job done right. Most of us like physical activity, and it's at least as valid a human activity as debating politics and usually more productive. We golf, garden, and spend extraordinary amounts of money for special shoes that help us to lose at tennis more convincingly. However, most people reject the thought of doing something more physical when they're considering a change in career paths. We pay to use our muscles, but we won't use our muscles for pay. My advice is to consider the option. The right environment for you might be pitching hay instead of pitching clients.

Go back and take another look at that list of five activities you've enjoyed lately. Are you sure there isn't a circus lurking in one of them?

9

there's no such animal as a one-person circus

In which you will find out that:

1. Unless you are planning to become a full-time hermit, you will have to work with other people.

2. You need people to advise you, coach you, serve as your mentor, and fill in the gaps in your knowledge.

3. If you're smart, you will choose who those people will be.

4. If you're even smarter, you also will deal with your "invisible" board of directors.

5. You are part of a network, a web of professional relationships, a fact that will affect your circus.

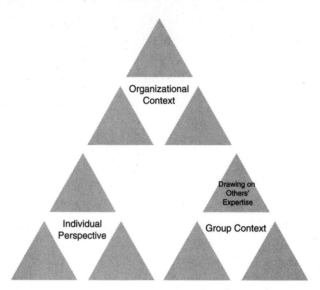

© PeopleTech Consulting, Inc.

I spend a certain amount of my time working alone, upstairs at home or in a den overlooking the pine woods when I'm at the cottage. At home in the city, there's no one else here except the cleaning person twice a week and the gardener occasionally. At the cottage there are the loons and a rumored bear I've never actually seen. Being alone is important to me. I accomplish things I couldn't in a busy office and I accomplish quite different kinds of things from those I would do in a corporate environment.

However, it takes a lot of people to keep me working in my splendid solitude. I have an energetic and efficient executive assistant at our head office. I have a researcher on call. There's someone else who makes my travel arrangements (she knows the second-best hotel in Istanbul and how to get from Manhattan to Oshkosh without spending even a minute in Detroit). Someone else straightens out my computer problems. There's an accountant, a team of five I work with on business strategy, several teams I work with in client service, and a

> *Collaboration is called for when an individual's charm, charisma, authority or expertise just isn't enough to get the job done. Real challenges rarely lend themselves to routine dispatch. If they did, they wouldn't be real challenges.*
>
> —MICHAEL SCHRAGE

solid board of directors. Checking my fax log, it takes about 35 people, most of whom I am in touch with weekly, to keep me working alone.

Even a Basque shepherd has to interact with a group of people. Thoreau used to abandon Walden Pond every so often to hit the bars in town and, after a year and a half, he vacated the premises completely. You need folks—as anyone who has tried to make an office in a lonely attic will tell you.

But being who you are, you have particular ways you want to deal with them, just as you have your own beliefs, your own performance drivers, and your own preferred work processes. Choosing the way you fit in with specific groups is just as important as ensuring that you fit into the overall organizational context. That's something we've found over and over in the corporate world. If you can't get along with the clown, the lady on the trapeze, and the sword swallower, you won't enjoy working at the circus. If the strong man is having the sulks, the lion tamer is screaming for bigger billing, and the circus bookkeeper isn't with the program, you might as well fold the tent.

The next three chapters look at the part of the change triangle called group interaction:

- This chapter tells you why you need a team whether you're going to grow zucchinis in the country or start your own consulting firm. It also helps you figure out what kind of team you'll need.

- Chapter 10 tells you how to get your team's support. You can have the most talented team around, but if they think you're headed in the wrong direction, you're not going anywhere. I direct your attention to the example of football coaches who have failed to inspire their folks as well as the example of a number of corporations that have stumbled over the inert bodies of their own employees by not telling them where the bus was going and why.

- Chapter 11 is about the care and feeding of a team. You can't plant a zucchini and not water the thing. Even hybrid seeds being turned out by genetic engineers need a little love. Likely you've been part of a team that was set up, forgotten, and languished to death. It could have been in a corporation, in a school, at a volunteer organization. Whatever and wherever it was, you don't want to repeat the experience in your circus.

All three are lessons corporations still have much to learn about. That's why you keep hearing things like this from your partner, cousin, and neighbor:

> "Head office hasn't a clue what's going on around here."

> "If there were any more politics around here, we'd be the Republican Party."

> "MIS doesn't even know what business we're in."

> "He would have read the writing on the wall but he was scared about being stabbed in the back."

> "I'm surrounded by fools and incompetents."

> "Don't you just dread those Monday morning meetings we have to go to?"

> "If the marketing department didn't exist, there'd be no reason to invent them."

Sound familiar? It doesn't have to be that way, and it won't be if you select your circus team carefully and look after it properly.

Now, I don't want to stir up any false expectations. Team building is a messy business. The rigid triangle representing the various aspects of group behavior here is merely symbolic. Out in the real world there are no straight lines, the cells aren't neatly compartmentalized, and their corners are dented because in the real world you're dealing with real people instead of androids. The healthiness of a team affects how you build that team's skills or choose members for their skills. Their support of change can be improved, but also depends to a large extent on selection. Their skills will improve and become more accessible if their morale is high. And so on. Nothing happens in isolation. Nevertheless, you still have to check off the points:

1. Have you put together the right team with the right skills?

2. Do they support and understand where you're going?

3. Do you know how to keep them healthy, happy, and working together?

WILLIAM GOTTLIEB'S BOARD OF DIRECTORS

"I'm boring," he says. "I could name you maybe half-a-dozen people who've changed their life with no plan at all. They just walked up to the edge of the canyon and stepped off like Wile E. Coyote in the Roadrunner cartoons. A year or so later you find out that they've opened an art gallery, they have a business restoring antique cars, they've opened up a daycare center, they sell solar water heaters in a building center.

"Doing that sort of thing—walking up to the edge of the canyon and then suddenly, whoosh! taking one more step—that would drive me crazy. I have to plan things. When I'm making Sunday dinner I write down the time everything has to go in so that there are no conflicts and I check it all with my wife. When I'm going on a business trip I have a permanent inventory of what should go in the suitcase: so many shirts per day, deodorant, photocopies of my credit cards. I'm boring. Probably it's because my parents were theater producers and we were always in a different city and in a different house. Being anal was my form of adolescent rebellion."

William Gottlieb is anything but boring. He's just more organized than everyone else. "Other people drive me nuts. They just do things. Just go and do them. I have to check with other people."

Checking is a simple word for a very smart thing that Bill does. When he's checking, he's not looking for sympathy, permission, or off-the-cuff comment. He's looking for expert help, informed opinion, and raw ideas. You don't pick these up off the street, in a bar, or, necessarily, from your brother-in-law.

Eleven years ago, he was in women's fashion, a family business he got into through a different part of his family. "It was making me crazy. First they wanted it high, and then they wanted it low. Then they decided they wanted anti-fashion—everyone was dressing in black jeans and black T-shirts. Then the economy told them customers didn't want any clothes at all. In the meantime the stores are expanding and contracting like blowfish. They'd shift their payables to 120 and 180 days. Then they'd stop paying altogether and wondering if I'd like a lessee department or would I rather get out of the business altogether?

"Keeping up with all this was making me extremely nervous. First we moved the production to Kentucky. Then we moved it to Thailand. Then we contracted it out because we figured someone else should take the risk of owning the actual machinery and dealing with the workforce and we would stick to the design and sales, thank you very much. That's what we know and that's what we'll do. Stick to what you know. It sounded like a good idea at the time.

"I've got five investors to take care of. They're all like-minded people. They all made their money going from city to city selling fashion goods out of trunks in hotel rooms. When we started, we figured this for a good idea. We were all basically sales guys who came from the same place.

"When the ship hit the sand, I found myself in a room with five guys with the same experience. We all stood around trying to sell each other solutions. Ever see five sales guys trying to sell each other something all at the same time? It is not productive.

"Each of these guys has the same experience. Maybe each of them had twenty years in the business. But between the five of them, you don't have a hundred years' experience. You have twenty years of experience repeated five times. Actually, what you had there was maybe ten years of experience repeated ten times. We were sticking to what we knew, but it turned out we didn't know a whole hell of a lot, excuse the expression.

"We had no breadth of experience. The experience might have been deep but it wasn't wide. We didn't really know finance except what the accountants and the factors and the stores told us. We didn't know vast amounts about production, especially the new machinery they've got these days, except what our contractors were letting us know. And as for designing, we're depending on what we're feeling in the pricking of our thumbs and what some 23-year-old kids with a college degree and a tattoo around his belly button is telling us.

"You get five sales guys together and you don't have a team. What you've got is a bunch of five guys grousing about sales. It's fun in a way being able to trade war stories, but it isn't going to get you anywhere.

"So the economy and I decided I should go into a different business. This was a decision that the IRS smiled upon. They figured it would be good if I made some income again. There was also general agreement among family members."

The business he went into—and we're going to disguise this heavily—was model boats. It was very much a niche market. It was a market where the retailers were amateurs in the best sense. Most of them were in it because they got personal satisfaction from talking about the hobby and all the esoterica that goes with it. The consumers were similarly enthralled. They were as connected to their hobby as any Internet junkie. The fashion quotient was low. A model of an 1842 clipper will still be a model of an 1842 clipper in ten years. The hemlines, at least in the classic part of the model boat market, don't go up and down. What sells today will sell tomorrow.

There were other attractions. The sector lacked marketing expertise. To a large extent the industry was a group of people making a living from a much-loved hobby. Bill thought he could add concepts like value-added, toll-free customer and retailer support lines, add-on sales, guarantees, and the model boater's version of the fashion show.

It was also a big enough market. Almost any niche market in North America with its 300 million consumers can support you handsomely. "One-third of one percent of that market is still a million people. If you get 10 percent of them to buy something worth ten dollars from you in a year, you have a million dollars. Our boat kits go for from $99 to $429. It's a business. The thing was, not many people in it had realized that it was. They thought it was a hobby."

He had a natural interest in the hobby. For many years, he'd hidden away in a spare bedroom building galleons, paddle-wheelers, and freighters. "Three hours every Sunday and at least half an hour every weekday. It's better than Scotch to settle you down. Besides, I'm a little diabetic. Anyway, where else is a guy like me going to get to be a pirate captain? You know how satisfying it is making little tiny people walk off little tiny planks? Especially when they look like head buyers?"

The typical salesperson's reaction to the opportunity would have been to hire five other salespeople and hit the road flogging. "But I'd already been there. Wasn't the answer. I didn't figure out what the answer was till I got the question right."

The question was, what makes a business successful? Bill says, "I looked at businesses outside fashion. The good ones—the ones that work—don't just have a buyer. They have a buyer and a marketing guy and someone who can work up the numbers and someone who can pick locations. They have a board of directors, and at the good companies, the board of directors isn't made up entirely of relatives and old friends. They're people who can come to the table and bring a lot of different kinds of experience.

"What do I know about building boats? I know how to stick them together. I know a few guys at hobby shops I like to talk to. And I know how to sell things. What I don't know is how to make them, how to package them, how to do the numbers, and a lot of other things.

"So a year before I make the change, I form a board of directors. There's my accountant who has tried for years to keep me out of trouble and who's very creative at it and who cares about me. There is my lawyer, who admittedly is my wife's cousin, but who's a good lawyer anyway. There are two hobby shop owners: one from Jersey and one from down south. There's a young fellow who's won some awards for packaging, and there's a person from one of the Eastern trade missions who's anxious to increase his country's exports and who builds model boats himself. Most of them wouldn't mind a little investment, especially because it's something they love."

"We're all flattered to be in the same room with each other. They're excited about something new—except for the accountant, and it's his job not to get excited. So instead of just getting sales advice, I'm getting advice on manufacturing, on in-store display, on guarantees, on cash flows. A lot of good ideas, a lot of energy. What you want is a team."

TEN CLOWNS DON'T MAKE A CIRCUS

Despite a lot of management hype about the joys of teamwork, working with other people can be frustrating, annoying, and counterproductive, even at the circus. The Ringling Brothers held grudges against each other. Mr. Barnum and Mr. Bailey enjoyed gossiping about each other's inadequacies. The crowd at the original Circus Maximus seldom agreed about which act got thumbs up and which act got the terminal thumbs down. In short, even at the circus, people want to run away—probably to a nice, calm management accountancy firm.

You need to work with a group because running a silk flower shop or one-person computer consultancy demands a variety of skills, some of which you may not have. For example, this book, in a very real sense, was written by a group. We had a researcher, an interviewer, someone to sweat the details, and someone who actually could use a computer, not to mention all the skilled people at the publishing house who helped design, manufacture, promote, and sell the book: in short, a team, different people with different skill sets.

Even if you want to move to a different position within the same organization, you are still going to need a team. If you've got an idea for a new product or service, you don't get ten folks from operations together to make it click. Companies have learned that putting ten chartered accountants full-time on a project to carve the lean from the mean may be a good exercise in accountancy, but it isn't good management any more. You get one person from sales, one from distribution, and one from customer service. That may sound obvious, but in too many companies, it isn't.

The reason is fairly understandable. We like to talk to people who talk the same talk, walk the same walk, and share the same values. Inviting someone from the eighth floor or the shop floor makes us uncomfortable. They use different jargon. They dress differently. Their priorities are going to seem somewhat skewed. Get used to it. The group you'll be working with will not be clones of yourself. They'd be useless if they were. You need the diversity and, if you're like most people engaged in creating change, you'll come to relish it. Good groups or teams reinforce each other, cheer each other on, and make whole new kinds of work possible that aren't possible for an individual with one skill set and one mindset.

So your particular circus has to hire more than just a bunch of clowns. You need a barker, a trapeze artist, a lion tamer, somebody to put up posters and sell tickets, and a guy to follow the elephants with a shovel. Otherwise, as Bill would say, "If all you've got is ten clowns, that puts you on the sidewalk with the mimes instead of putting you under the big top."

BUILDING A TEAM: HOW TO GET GROUP EXPERTISE

Let's start with a fairly common dream: running a Bob Newhart–style bed and breakfast. I confess to having had it myself: serving freshly roasted coffee and freshly baked croissants to bright, interesting travelers who've spent the night as paying guests at my cozy Queen Anne house in New England overlooking the mill pond, etc. Don't tell me that the same dream hasn't flashed across your mind at one time, even for a second.

You'd need a team. You could canvass your current colleagues and friends and put together some kind of group, but the lessons learned in aerospace development or button-making or whatever you've been doing up to now don't necessarily apply to what you need to run an inn. Management experience, however profound, is not uniformly applicable to all kinds of work. Any number of conglomerates have proven that just because you're good at selling soft drinks, for example, you may not be terrific at selling fast food.

To find out about what kind of team is needed to run an inn, you have to talk to real live innkeepers. You know this is a practical idea because you've probably met someone who has tried to get into the same business as you or do the same job you're in now and you've seen them fall on some part of their anatomy because they didn't ask enough questions of people who were already doing it well. If they'd talked to you first, you could have told them how to avoid some of the painfully obvious mistakes they made.

There are plenty of Bob Newhart wannabes who have come to grief because they didn't talk to a successful innkeeper, because they put their questions to motel operators instead of innkeepers, or because they quizzed failing innkeepers who, after all, have more time to give advice.

Your task is straightforward:

1. Go find some successful innkeepers. They'd be the ones who've spent ten years in the business and have a sign outside that says "No vacancy." One-half dozen isn't too many; the more you ask, the more you'll find out. Keep notes.

2. Tell them that you want to talk to them and make an appointment. Buy them lunch if possible. If somebody came to you and set out the same proposition, you'd react well and openly.

3. Your first question is, "Who do you rely on most to give you solid advice?" The answer may be the bank, the local real estate guru, the person who runs the local tourist board, another innkeeper, the guests, or Aunt Dora.

4. Your second question is, "Who do you rely on secondly?"

5. The third question is, "Who do rely on thirdly?" and so on.

This process is so obvious that almost nobody does it. The corporations that do carry out this kind of research refer to it as a "best practices inventory" or words to that effect. At the end of the process, you should have a workable consensus on the mix of skills and personalities you'll need on your team. You'll have more than that: you'll also have in your Rolodex the names and numbers of advisers who know you, who appreciate what you're going through, and who will be available to give advice when the bed-and-breakfast bug bites.

Some may cringe at this prescription: "It'll let everybody know what I'm doing!" I'll remind you of the Soviet's secret laboratories. By keeping everything hush-hush they kept more information out than they were keeping in.

CREATING A BOARD OF DIRECTORS FOR YOUINC.

Today's corporations have an array of teams. One's busy on marketing, even though the team might include an accountant, someone from the factory, and a product designer. There'll be a team for installing the Six Sigma or TQM training program, which in addition to the human relations director also will include representatives from the union, distribution, and MIS. There'll be a team working on long-term strategic positioning. Sitting around the table from the CEO there may be a consultant, a demographer, an economist, and three representatives from the company's suppliers. Having more than one task often means having more than one team.

I have a personal board of directors. It's different from my corporation's board because I have some personal goals that diverge from those of the corporation I work with. More than one task, more than one team. Even if you're joining a circus, you may have personal goals that diverge from the circus's. Nobody is one-dimensional. You have work goals and personal goals in everything from your finances to your health to your golfing handicap. Any of all of these areas might benefit from some advice.

My company has a corporate board to help track and predict what is going on in the business. I have a personal board to help me with what's happening in my individual career. I need somebody who is a bit more cautious than I am to rein in my wilder impulses and somebody who is just a bit crazier to egg me on when I get stale. That's true even if I'm not going to change jobs, but simply trying to grow within my current one. Anything that adds brains, prudence, or imagination to your own ideas and creativity is a big help.

On my personal board is a chief financial officer to help me tiptoe through the subsections of the tax acts and guide me in my personal investments. This is in contrast to the CFO who acts on the corporate board to do what's right for the organization as a whole. There is a marketing specialist, who helped me package my particular skills and target them at the right people in the right way. There is a head of research, who helps me find trends before anyone else does. There is me. And there is someone else as chair. I make a lousy chair. I tend to take over meetings and I need someone to whack me back into place and get the best out of the other people. Some people call board members like mine coaches or mentors. I see it as something broader than that.

I stole my terms of reference for my board from someone else. Those terms include the fact that the board, not me, gets to decide when they'll meet and what they'll do. They also decide what tasks I have to take on myself to get to the agreed-upon goal. I asked for a one-year commitment from these people. They've hung on a lot longer because they're having fun and because they're finding the ideas they get from participating help fuel their own dreams.

We formalized the idea at an insurance company called The Co-operators. Almost everyone there has a mentoring team that supports them inside the company like a personal board of advisers. They can bounce their ideas off people who represent a whole cross-section of the company rather than ricocheting them off the same old departmental coffee klatch. That helps the company by exposing their people to the widest possible view of the corporate horizon. It helps individuals find their dreams without necessarily leaving the company. At another company where we did something similar, a woman moved from the payroll department to running a resort within the organization. She stayed in the circus but she changed rings.

SELECTING BOARD MEMBERS

The checklists below should help you highlight the kind of help you need from a team, whether it's personal or corporate. The business planning list helps whether you're staying in your current organization or setting up your own tent. Either way, you may need help on strategy, training, or marketing to help adjust your environment to fit you. If you want to go from an introverted accounting department to an extroverted sales job, you'll want the kind of backup that mentors in sales, marketing, advertising, and distribution can give you. If you'd like to trade in your cubicle for the sometimes bittersweet joys of telecommuting, you're going to want help in strategy, human resources, and communications.

When you look at the personal planning list, it's important to remember that you're not trying to change yourself, you're simply trying to get new skill sets that will enable you to adapt easily to the kind of environment you want for yourself.

	EXTREMELY IMPORTANT	**VERY IMPORTANT**	**I KNOW ABOUT THIS STUFF**	**UNIMPORTANT**
Business planning				
Research	_____	_____	_____	_____
Strategy	_____	_____	_____	_____
Initial financing	_____	_____	_____	_____
Ongoing financing	_____	_____	_____	_____
Real estate	_____	_____	_____	_____
Human resources	_____	_____	_____	_____
Training	_____	_____	_____	_____
Communications	_____	_____	_____	_____
Dealing with suppliers	_____	_____	_____	_____
R&D	_____	_____	_____	_____
Information technology	_____	_____	_____	_____
Production	_____	_____	_____	_____
Quality control	_____	_____	_____	_____
Distribution	_____	_____	_____	_____
Marketing	_____	_____	_____	_____
Advertising	_____	_____	_____	_____
Sales	_____	_____	_____	_____
Personal planning				
Personal strategy	_____	_____	_____	_____
Mentoring to succeed in my present job	_____	_____	_____	_____

	EXTREMELY IMPORTANT	VERY IMPORTANT	I KNOW ABOUT THIS STUFF	UNIMPORTANT
Financial planning	_____	_____	_____	_____
Research	_____	_____	_____	_____
Vocational consultation	_____	_____	_____	_____
Relocation assistance	_____	_____	_____	_____
Training for new skills	_____	_____	_____	_____
Networking	_____	_____	_____	_____
Marketing myself	_____	_____	_____	_____
Physical fitness	_____	_____	_____	_____

THE BOARD OF DIRECTORS YOU DON'T SEE

Richard Chagnon of Right Management Consultants in Philadelphia is a delightful and intelligent consultant. A former Catholic priest, he's an insightful man as well, with a wealth of experience in counseling. When I talked to him about strategic alliances or boards of directors for MeInc., he mentioned what he calls a meditative council. It's an interesting idea.

His experience is that most of us already have a mental board of directors or a mental web. That mental group is made up of parents, former teachers, former bosses, mentors, rivals, friends, enemies, and relatives. They don't have to be at our meetings for their voices to be heard because, whenever we make a decision, we'll hear their voices whether we want to or not.

If we plan a new career, we will hear our parents comment on it. If we buy a new suit, we'll hear our co-workers comment on it. If we buy a new car, we'll hear our neighbors comment on it. If we talk about our plans to start a fishing lure company, we'll hear them all in chorus, singing the song they usually sing:

"We've never done anything like that in our family."

"If that's what would make you happy, dear, you go right ahead."

"Fishing's a stupid sport."

"Do you really mean that or are you just fantasizing?"

"What's the matter, are you now too good for us?"

Richard's point is that we must manage our invisible board as professionally as we would manage a real one. This, fortunately, is easy. You don't have to fire a mental member. All you have to do when you hear the voice is to say that he or she is not contributing, smile, and tune out. You can even replace a negative person with someone you respect and admire. For example: If I were Jackie (a former mentor and a remarkably wise person), what would I do? Even then, however, you are not bound to abide by what you hear. As racing driver A. J. Foyt (who was never a priest and is not usually a counselor) once advised, "Listen to everyone, but do what you want."

SOURCING YOUR TEAM MEMBERS: THE NETWORK

If your company doesn't have a formalized system in place for mentoring or exchanging ideas, you may have to set up one of your own. People do it all the time. It's called networking.

The bad, greedy 1980s did a lot of damage to the word *networking*. It started out as a perfectly simple term for keeping informed by keeping in touch with people and ended up as a euphemism for using people as you clawed your way up the corporate ladder. These days when you say the word *networking* to someone, the person invariably looks at her watch and says that she's needed on the phone to Houston. In fact, I've started to use the word to break up conversations I don't want to continue. Works every time.

> *A lot of people network only when they have a problem to solve. This is like my sons at college, who call me only when they have a problem, the solution to which is my checking account. Networking really means keeping in touch with your contacts on a regular basis, even if there is no immediate reason for calling or getting together. Find out what is on other people's plates, look for ways to solve other people's problems, don't just call when you have a problem you want them to help you solve.*
>
> —LEE LINDEMAN, VICE-PRESIDENT AND DIRECTOR, CAREER MANAGEMENT SERVICES, RIGHT ASSOCIATES, BOSTON

Networking too often refers to people who want things from you, people who never gave you the time of day when they were on the way up, but who, on the way out, down, or in circles, suddenly want to become your best friend. At least until they've got where they are going.

But without fail every career counselor I've talked to has mentioned the vital importance of networking as a way to find second lives. They brought it up so often that I began to listen. And after listening, I found myself starting to network more. And I found the networking starting to have success. Don't you hate it when conventional wisdom is right?

> Networking is extremely important. Officially we say that informal networks provide 80 percent of the important contacts and formal networks the other 20 percent, but unofficially, I think that 80 percent is an underestimate.
>
> —JUDY BARTON, MANAGING DIRECTOR, RIGHT MANAGEMENT CONSULTANTS, TAMPA

There's a right and wrong way to network. There are ineffective techniques and effective ones. Dr. David Blank, a psychologist in Boca Raton, spends a lot of time helping people network. "Some people try to do their networking from an office, making calls and generating a lot of correspondence. They don't get out enough to see other people and places.

"A big opportunity that many people overlook are conferences. All sorts of organizations hold conferences, often in the fall. These are ideal places to meet people, not during the daytime sessions, but between 4 P.M. and midnight, when the really important exchanges occur."

If getting out from behind your desk and asking other people for help makes you want to run screaming into the night, remember that people are flattered when you seek them out and even more flattered when you ask them for something. Give them a chance to talk about what they are good at. When you ask for advice, most people will fall about with delight, like my dog when I scratch his belly. We're talking serious ego gratification. There may be some people who are simply too busy to help or who don't have the expertise you thought they did, but by and large, you will find that putting together a board of directors is not as daunting as it sounds. All you have to do is start.

It might take the form of job shadowing, information interviews, or even apprenticeships. A friend of a friend who had a rather dull job in sales once simply walked into the office of the organization's research librarian, whom she had long envied, and said, "I want to do what you do. I want to enjoy my work the way you seem to enjoy your work. I want to be your understudy so that when you're ready to do something else, I can replace you." Although her chosen mentor was a little surprised, she also was flattered and agreed to give her some coaching. My friend also took some evening classes in information technology to round out her education. When her mentor took a job at another company, she moved into the librarian's office. She is now coaching a new understudy and stays in touch with her mentor.

Can someone who is opening a shoe repair outlet network? Moneysworth & Best did. They tugged the sleeves of real estate experts, shoe companies, marketing people, and more. I just opened the Yellow Pages section for the city I'm writing in today: they have four locations here. I also phoned their head office and found that they had more than 70 outlets across the continent and were also getting heavily into selling their shoe care products in outlets that weren't their own.

The message is that networking, forming a team, getting yourself a board of directors or a group of mentors, and mingling with good people from a bunch of different disciplines isn't valuable just for people in suits.

NETWORKING, THE WEBBED ORGANIZATION, AND YOU

Before we leave the subject of networking, there's one more lesson from the corporate world that is worth stealing: the idea of partnerships. When you go looking for the advice, feedback, and support you need to propel yourself out of a rut into something new, we've found that you need to go beyond the traditional sources and look at all the people who affect what you do.

Corporations have started to learn this lesson. Before the recession/ global competitiveness crunch/technological revolution, most organizations had boxy organization charts like the one on the next page.

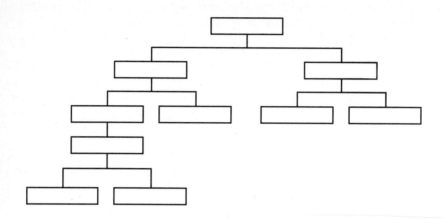

After tottering on the edge of chaos, organizations knew that the last chance to put themselves on firmer ground was to take a larger view of their organization. The recession/competitiveness/technology chaos told them, definitively, that they did not exist in the lofty solitude they'd previously enjoyed. Consumers, suppliers, governments, and competitors were making decisions for the organization, rudely ignoring the fact that they weren't on the chart. Sony could make decisions for Motorola even though they weren't on Motorola's chart. Customers could start buying all sorts of different soups even though they weren't on Campbell's chart. People who owned lots of oil in Arabia could dictate the size of Chevys, Chryslers, and Fords, even though their names were not on the Big Three's charts in Detroit.

The corporations had a choice. Either they could ignore this phenomenon and carry on in splendid isolation or they could devise a chart that reflected what was really going on. There were numerous companies that coughed once or twice and said that they thought the unions were part of their chart. Some companies suddenly came right out with it, smiled, and said that they'd known their consumers had been on their chart all along, it's just that their org chart didn't show them clearly. The new charts looked like the following.

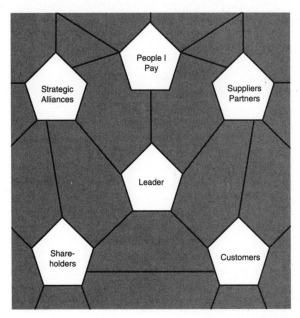

© *PeopleTech Consulting, Inc.*

What this chart says is that organizations depend on suppliers, customers, strategic alliances, employees, and shareholders. You get more from a supplier, say, by forging a long-term relationship than by beating down the price of every delivery of components. You get more out of customers if, instead of selling them a toaster, you say to them, "I want to be your small appliance manufacturer for life" and then behaving as though you meant it. You get more from your employees if you tell them the truth. Your job is to provide real leadership, and real leadership consists of something other than bullying. Of course, all this had been true all along, but the chaos made the thing clearer.

You don't have to run your own business to use this model. You already know that you'll get better work from subordinates by creating a long-term relationship instead of constantly beating them upside the head to meet impossible deadlines. You'll get the respect and support of your colleagues in other departments if you provide them with a useful service rather than the minimum required in your job description. And you'll get better work from everyone if everyone has a clear understanding of how they're getting continuing value from you. If the people around you don't see how you're benefiting them by doing what you do, you're headed for trouble. Just because you get a regular paycheck doesn't mean you don't have to think strategically. Get your internal contacts up to date and keep them up to date.

The Japanese have known all this for a long time. Although their industries fight it out on home turf, when it comes to selling abroad, they form alliances with their largest competitors because they know that their largest competitor can be their greatest ally.

Think of this web of relationships as networking on a corporate scale. Now, how are you going to apply this idea to your circus?

- Who will be the suppliers and partners—external or internal— for your circus? Who sells you the peanuts and the greasepaint and rents you the field to put up your tent? How can you have mutually beneficial relationships with these people? My advice is to think of what's in it for them, that is, what would be their job perks if this were a job. Fame? Respect? The advantage of sharing knowledge with you? Or just money (which is seldom good enough)?

- Who are your shareholders? Your circus may not be a public company, but there are people who have at least part of their future happiness or cash invested in it. Those people include your family, your bank, the mortgage company, your suppliers, the people who depend on you for what you're supplying, and a long list of others. These shareholders do not necessarily need a hard cash dividend. Again think of what job perks you'd offer if this were a job. Can you offer them travel, a title, intelligence, a chance to meet people, excitement, or ego gratification?

- Who are your customers? Who's buying what you're selling? Who's going to watch the show? The people who market professional basketball realized that, if basketball were all they were selling, they wouldn't have as many people coming as often. So they introduced cheerleaders, music, entertainment, and a lot of other things that don't put a ball through a hoop and, in doing so, widened their audience. Are people going to come to see just you, just juggling? Or are you going to offer them more? If you're in research, are you also going to offer interpretation and service development ideas? If you're in production, are you also going to offer to recycle waste, improve quality, or add features? How does this benefit you? Does it get you more respect, more travel, or more security? Are any of those in line with the kind of fit you're after? Be relentless or find somebody who can help you be relentless. Consider it as an above-college-level marketing/advertising/sales/promotion problem. Is the marketing/advertising/sales/promotion plan you're going to be able to come up with better than what's already in the market?

• What are your strategic alliances? The first place to look is among the ranks of your competitors, the people in the same business as you or with the same title as you. What can two circuses do together that one circus can't? Can they share advertising, get together to do a better deal with the farmer who rents the field, get bulk rates on peanuts, share information on which towns have poor attendance for circuses? The CEO of a television network once told me, "We don't hear about openness among peers. There is still too much protecting of turf. In the future, we'll move beyond peers sharing information openly to a point where we'll see companies sharing with minority partners." Sharing the bailing bucket with the people in the same boat seems like a solid idea. The idea works within the organization as well. If you're in sales and are competing with marketing and advertising for dollars, what can you put together with the other departments to create a win-win-win solution? Share employees? Commission common research? Integrate computer functions? And how will that solution benefit you in terms of getting the environment you want for yourself? Would it make your position less stressful? Would it cut your work hours? Would it give you more time to be more creative?

Spend a day or two thinking about it. Who is going to be your competition? How can you act together with them to make things better for the consumer and better for both of your organizations? Car rental companies used to imagine they were in competition with transit companies. Now they see that there's considerable synergy. The transit user is a prime market for a rental car. For transit companies, a person who is renting a car often is not a person who abandons transit to buy a car.

• And how about the people you control? By this point, you've
started to define what you really want out of your second life.
What's in it for them? Will they be as satisfied as you want to be?
How can you improve that? If you're thinking of working on a
beach or a mountaintop, how will that work for them? Do they
get more authority, clearer lines of communication, more
defined and finite responsibilities, a title, or more recognition?
MacDonald's has an employee of the month. Wal-Mart calls
their people "associates." Any number of companies have profit
sharing. What are you going to do?

The web is not as static as the old organization chart used to
be. It can be a temporary structure responding to a temporary
opportunity. You may have two webs for two clearly defined purposes. Or a dozen. The only things that should not change are
the equality of the power relationships and the webbing that
holds it together, that is, the idea of mutual benefit.

The term *mutual benefit* is the key. In choosing your personal or corporate board, you should be looking to see how
membership on your board benefits that board member. In the
beginning, you're looking for people with the skills you need to
get the job done. In the long term, however, you are choosing
them for their mindsets. Will they interact well with each other?
Will they have opportunities to learn from each other while you
learn from them?

Mutual benefit can nudge the group closer together.
Corporations know this. That's why a car maker may have a
banker, a union leader, and an ecologist on the board. The
banker gives advice but also gets to loan money. The union
leader can state his or her members' views to the board but also
can go to the members and cushion surprises that might have
hurt him/her politically. The ecologist can give the board guidance but also can get an education in the art of the possible. In
all cases, there's a recognizable mutual benefit. Everybody's back
gets scratched.

10

ganging up on change

In which you will find out that:

1. People who are going through what you are going through can support your change.

2. Even a single buddy can prop up your morale when you embark on a second life.

3. Certain people should be avoided at all costs when you are trying something new with your life.

4. Maybe you need some professional help.

Sometimes getting to your circus means joining a group headed in the same direction or, as a woman I know would describe it, joining a gang. "We all have gangs," says Penny Deal, although she doesn't look as though she'd know what a gang was. I'd like to have a quilt made of the labels from her wardrobe. It would be interesting to sleep under an Armani-Gucci-Chanel.

> *Shared visions compel courage so naturally that people don't even realize the extent of their courage.*
>
> —PETER SENG

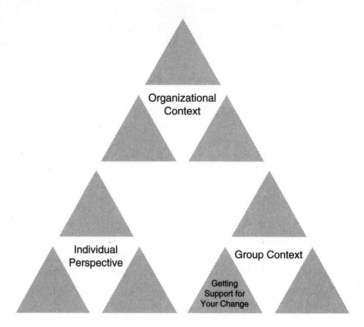

© PeopleTech Consulting, Inc.

But listen to her: "I used to belong to a gang when I was a kid. There were about eight or so of us. It wasn't really a *gang* gang. No leather jackets, knives, none of that: not the way some of the girl gangs are these days. We were vicious, but we used our mouths. And we were tough. We didn't wear those skirts with the poodles on them. No twin sets. We smoked. And we inhaled."

Ms. Deal moves large amounts of money in a variety of financial instruments from one place to another, like from Guernsey to Monaco to the Isle of Man. My understanding is that she does this for large and respected organizations, making a small profit on each movement. She makes many small profits a year on substantial sums. That is the limit of my understanding.

"You grow up and you understand that most things are gangs. Journalism is all about gangs: that's why they call it pack journalism. Lawyers are divided up into several gangs, and you can practically tell which gang they're in by what kind of suits they're wearing. Fashion designers and their groupies are a gang. Think of a group and then think of a gang. What makes doctors different from the Crips? Doctors wear gang colors. Doctors protect their turf. Doctors have a secret gang language. Everybody in the gang benefits. Shriners are a gang." (Come to think of it, I belonged to a gang as a kid in Ohio. We called it 4-H.)

"Gangs can be a force for good. Think of Weight Watchers. That's typical gang behavior. They run in packs. They speak code language. They bond. They have some disrespect for people outside the gang. They have territory." Psychiatrists would call this *pack behavior* and explain that there's an alpha animal in each pack, whether it's dogs or people losing pounds. "That's a pretty good gang. They support each other, like Gamblers Anonymous or Rotarians.

"As a group they've figured out how they can do things that they couldn't do as individuals. Just like a gang. Just like the men I meet down at the athletic club. They wouldn't be buffing their butts if they didn't have twenty other guys in the gym to impress. Doing it on their own, they'd be lifting lighter weights for fewer sets. When I walk by, they tuck in their gut. When I leave the room, their waist goes up four inches."

Gangs let you do what you can't do yourself. Gangs exist for mutual benefit.

Ms. Deal wanted to change part of her life. She was a little bored with moving large sums around, even though according to the evidence, she's good at it. Probably Wayne Newton is tired of singing Wayne Newton songs. I hope he's tired of it, anyway.

"But I wanted a part-time new life. So I remembered when I'd last had some fun. The gang was fun. You could make a little noise. You could act out a little. I like to think of it as an early form of feminism. I also wanted to do something as different from this as possible. Something I could see.

"Children's clothing. There was a lot to recommend it. First of all, children are natural gang members. They like to dress as part of a gang even when they're four, five, or six. Take them out of their gang clothes and they'll kick you in the ankle because that's what the rest of the gang is wearing. Same thing if you take off a Shriner's fez. So I could form a gang which sold gang clothes to gang members. Second, it had to do with children and I don't have any. Third, I like clothes.

"Now, in order for me to do this part time, I had to form a gang. We'd all change a little, and together we'd accomplish a lot. With a gang, you spread the amount of change around; you're not doing all the change yourself.

"Of course, I had to pick my gang carefully. In this business I've hired quite a few stars. When you hire a star, you get a star, which is nice, but what you need is a team. I wanted people who could support each other, build on each other's talents. The whole had to be more than the sum of its parts.

"I was looking for people like myself. People who'd been successful. But people who were multidimensional and who, like me, felt that their work was using only one dimension.

"I talked to all sorts of people, sounding them out, seeing where they were in their lives—how much energy they had left over from their jobs, how many other commitments they had. Not everyone was interested. But when I asked, 'Do you want to help me start a children's clothing line, part time? do something new?' several people said 'yes.'

"Seven people said yes. All successful. All a bit bored and wanting a completely new kind of challenge. I took them all to lunch and talked about the idea generally. I looked to see who got enthusiastic and who started talking with her hands. You can't always trust what comes out of people's mouths, but when they start talking with their hands . . .

"Then I waited a couple of months and I phoned them up again. And casually, I asked if any of them had ever had lunch with each other after the first meeting. Five of them had. That was my gang.

"One of them knew finance, one knew production, one was dynamite with retail—that sort of thing. None had ever done children's clothing before. That didn't matter. This kind of team knew how to shift focus, shift talents. I'd rather have the part-time advice of somebody who knows what they're talking about than the full-time advice of a dolt. And if I have a gang of them? They get along; they complement each other." She raises her eyebrows.

"It's working. Slowly. Three test markets, one small catalog. I can go into some neighborhoods and see five-, six-, seven-year-old gangs growing, all wearing our stuff. We're losing money. That's to be expected at this date. We won't lose money for long.

"And we're having fun. We're acting out. We all like the change. We all needed some change in our lives. It's a lot more interesting than redecorating the living room one more time. And this way we get to egg each other on, keep each other motivated and fresh.

"We're going to be the first clothing advertiser on early-morning cartoon television. Wait for it."

Penny Deal didn't change her entire life. She simply arranged to spend part of it at the circus, taking some friends along to keep herself focused. They benefit; she benefits. According to at least one colleague, the decision's been good: "She comes back from those meetings energized. She's enthusiastic. She has new ideas. She's bouncing. And she's easier to work with. I think things she learned working with that group helped her work with the group we have here. Or 'gang,' as she calls it."

YOU NEED A FRIEND

Change is too often lonely. The antidote to that loneliness is to find or create a group that is going through a similar kind of change and do it together. This is not exactly the same thing as your personal board of directors, although there may be some overlap. Boards of directors can help with advice and support in many ways, but they are not necessarily wrestling with change

> Do it yourself, but don't do it alone.
>
> —REBECCA MADDOX

themselves. They can coach you from the sidelines, but they aren't out there getting dirty themselves.

I've already mentioned Weight Watchers and Gamblers Anonymous. There are dozens of other examples. Women experiencing their first pregnancy need to talk to other pregnant women about the changes they are undergoing. People who have recently moved to a foreign country seek out other expats who will show them the ropes and understand the culture shock they feel. Parents with disabled children, the recently bereaved, the outplaced, and those who have been diagnosed with cancer all turn to others who have gone through the same situation to help them find their way.

Do these parallels suggest a level of trauma associated with major change? Yes, they do. They should. Even when you are following your dream, running away to a circus that excites you, you will have moments, maybe days, weeks, or months, when you feel that you have done the wrong thing, made the biggest mistake you have ever made. You will stumble around in your own personal wilderness at some point. This is when you need somebody who may have no particular advice to give, but who will listen sympathetically and provide tea, gin, or whatever the occasion calls for during the dark night of the soul.

Rebecca Maddox, the founder and president of Capital Rose, knows all about this, so much so that she wrote a wonderful book for women considering entrepreneurship called *Inc. Your Dreams*. (Men can learn a lot from it, too.)

Maddox believes that change is ultimately positive and necessary, but she doesn't sugarcoat the realities. In an interview, she was refreshingly candid: "I think we've overdosed on change lately. The only thing more overrated is natural childbirth. Books are full of the joys of change, but change is difficult. When I went through significant change in my life, I found the experience bittersweet and often painful. The emotional ramifications continued for a long time."

Family members may be all you need, but for many of us, our families have too much at stake to be dispassionate listeners. They have demands on you and may not be patient enough to wait as you sort through all the options facing you. They may be more interested in the outcome of your change and anxious to hurry you through the process. Thus, you need a gang.

FORMING A GANG

A gang by definition is a society of mutual need. Unfortunately, there is no foolproof way of putting a gang together. You don't decide on a gang all by yourself. Sometimes the gang decides on you. Butch Cassidy knew that. But I can offer some hints on finding a gang.

First, you have to make sure there is mutual need. You have to have something to offer as well as something you want. If you're going to ask, say, a tax expert to be on your team, what do you give that person in return? You're allowed to say it in greenbacks, but there might be a more effective and more bonding way.

Second, be prepared to start small and be fairly casual at first. You don't have to go out and take over the world. Invite a few people over and suggest, "Could we all start with a common goal of sometime, somehow finding a way to build equity for the time when we're no longer working?" When you see how people respond, you will find out how the group works together, who has the great ideas, and who does the actual follow-through. You should date before you go steady.

Third, ask someone else's opinion about how the group is performing as a group. Everyone has a blind spot and may not notice problems—or progress. I once felt that a group I was in was going round in circles, until someone pointed out to me that over the course of six months we'd developed a common language for talking about problems and that this was the essential prerequisite for the changes we needed to make. It was an important achievement, but I was focused on something else and nearly missed it.

Fourth, take time to choose people. You've already listed your own skills and the skills your circus will require. If you subtract the first from the second, you'll know what skills the group has to deliver to get what you want done. Take it seriously.

Fifth, give it time. You are not going to know all your problems or all your opportunities on day one. Your choice of a gang on day one won't be your choice of a gang on day 365. Be patient, be flexible, and be prepared to listen.

THE BUDDY SYSTEM: A GANG OF TWO

Maybe you can't handle a gang. Maybe a gang can't handle you. Maybe you're the kind of person who makes things happen with just one or two other people. Analyze your past. But I'd guess the very least you need is a buddy, however simple your aim seems.

Kids learning to swim have to have buddies so they won't drown. Adults learning to change need buddies to keep them from drowning, too.

Sam Morgenstern found his buddy at a professional development course. After a few too many years as the deputy registrar for a professional association of architects, he decided to attend one of the courses sponsored by the association. The title of the course was "Dynamic Presentation Skills." Sam made very few presentations, but he was considering a career change and felt that the course might give him more confidence when he went for job interviews.

"I don't remember much about the course or the speaker, really," he told me. "But in the first coffee break I started chatting to one of the other participants, a guy called Chris. He was a member of the association and he, too, was thinking about a career change. In a sense, we couldn't have been more different. He was an architect and he wanted to get into furniture design. My background was in accounting, and I was toying with the idea of using my skills in a new area, maybe a computer company. But we both wanted to do something different. That was what we had in common.

"We stayed in touch. I went to all sorts of interviews, most of them dead ends, and he made furniture in his garage that none of the furniture manufacturers seemed to like. For about a year we used to get together and compare the bruises on our respective egos and cheer each other up. I bought one of his tables. He asked me to give him a hand with his taxes. But mostly we just spent a few hours each month drinking beer and telling each other to keep trying when nobody else seemed to think we could ever do anything different.

"I had the first breakthrough, when I got a new job at a software company. It wasn't a great job, but with the experience I got there, I eventually found something that I liked a lot better. Chris was encouraged. He thought my good luck would mean good luck for him too, and I guess it did. He eventually found a manufacturer who liked his designs and put a couple into production. He kept up his regular job and did furniture design on the side for several months until he was ready to move into it full-time.

> What you primarily need is not advice, although that may occasionally be useful, but rather to put into words your dilemmas and your feelings so that you can fully understand what is going on. Beware of the listener who "knows exactly what you ought to do," but also be suspicious if you find yourself explaining away your listener's reactions if they don't happen to fit with yours—especially if several people have reacted the same way to what you say.
>
> —WILLIAM BRIDGES

"We still get together a couple of times a year to compare notes. He sold me some more of his furniture, and I still give him accounting advice for his three-person company of designers and prototype builders. Our conversations are probably less intense now that we've more or less found what we were looking for. But during the period of searching, we were buddies in the wilderness together, looking for the oasis, propping each other up, urging each other to keep going, talking about how great it would be when we finally had what we wanted. Without Chris, I think I would have given up."

Buddies are the people to whom you can confess doubts, crazy ideas, and emotions. To your personal board of directors you might say, "I've got to learn to market myself and I'm not sure where to start." To your gang or your buddy you can say, "Marketing myself is one of the hardest things I've ever had to do. It's like going to job interviews every day of my life. I feel I'm constantly being judged and it's stressful." And the buddy nods and agrees that it is stressful and that you're pretty brave to keep doing it.

To your personal board of directors you might say, "Do you think I'm offering too many services and that I'm not being clear about what my core business is? How do I stick to certain central services if it means turning away potential business?" To your gang or your buddy you can let your hair down: "I feel a need to be all things to all people, and it's probably bad for my business. But I'm not yet confident enough to turn people down, even if they are asking things that aren't really central to my business. Has anyone else felt like that when they were starting out?" Your buddy knows exactly what you mean.

Buddies see us through the tough times. And we do the same for them. This is the great thing about buddies: The struggles we endure, the self-doubt we experience, and the pitfalls we tumble into are shared. It's like the camaraderie of soldiers in wartime. Many of the veterans I've met have had some horrific experiences, but they remember that they went through them shoulder to shoulder with their comrades and that got them through. During the grimmest stages of personal change, the chance to compare notes with a fellow sufferer may be what gets you through.

The buddy relationship is, or should be, mutually beneficial. You get a shoulder to cry on and a pat on the back. Your buddy should get the same if the relationship's working. If it's not working, you'll find your buddy doing a lot of call screening.

WARNING! BEWARE BASSETT BUDDIES

Pick your buddies carefully. The kind of people you must avoid at all costs are the kind I call *bassetts*. Like the low-slung dog of the same name, they droop, seem perpetually sad, and move slowly, if at all. They sigh a lot. Things will never work out. It's been tried before and it failed. Or it's been tried before and been a success, but it won't work this time. Or it's the wrong time in the moon or business cycle. One U.S. President was said to have kept one of these naysayers on staff just so he could say in speeches, "Some senior advisers warned me about taking this direction, but I say the American people deserve vision . . ."

Bassetts can infect you with contact melancholia. They will add on to your stories of self-doubt and anxiety. They will take your feeling that you are out on a limb and make you feel you are out on a frail twig.

You've no doubt worked with a bassett or two. They spend more time looking for problems than looking for solutions. If you've got more than one, they will one-up each other by creating disaster scenarios that are just over the horizon. As they leave a meeting at which you have spelled out a new idea and they have demolished it, they lay a soft hand on your shoulder and say, "Tough break, kid, but it just wouldn't have worked out." You know the type.

In a business sense, you may occasionally need the bassett's advice, although you don't want one in your gang or on your board of directors.

Go to the person alone and get the problems laid out for you. Then take the problems back to the board and find solutions. If the bassett says, "The return on equity will be too low," assemble your board and say, "How can we improve the ROI?" You'll get answers:

> "We can cut the investment by . . ."

> "We can raise the return by . . ."

> Or even: "Hell, you weren't going into this thing because you wanted ROI, were you?"

And for heaven's sake: Don't be your own bassett. You can't afford the energy.

Maybe You Need a Professional Buddy

If you have canvassed all of your friends and associates and you can't find anyone with gang or buddy material, consider looking for a professional counselor. Take your time and choose carefully. This person can make the difference between successful and nearly successful change.

Don't just take the first name in the Yellow Pages. Get recommendations from friends and associates. If you know any human resources professionals, ask them. Here are some things to bear in mind:

1. You are probably looking for someone who is older than you. Ideally that person has had a career or three before turning to counseling, maybe even in a field similar to your own.

2. You need a peer you can respect (otherwise, you won't listen and that's a waste of your money and the counselor's time). If you are a senior VP, you want to talk to someone who has had a senior position in business and knows what you do without your having to explain mundane details.

3. You need a good personality fit. You must like the counselor. You must feel able to talk freely to that person. You may even find yourself talking about personal details, so pick someone you feel you can trust.

Judy Barton, a career counselor in Tampa, helps people through the pain of being fired. I can imagine telling her my life story. She would listen. She would understand. She'd make an ideal buddy. She's had other jobs, lost them or left them, made changes in her life, dealt with bereavement, illness, and childbirth. She keeps a large box of Kleenex and a jar of chocolate chip cookies in her office. She knows when to be bracing (she calls it "slap therapy") and when to be sympathetic ("lap time"). She puts her home number on her business card. She's there when you are still reeling from the news that you have two hours to clean out your desk. The first thing she usually says to people is, "I'm your good news." She doesn't want you to find just any old job and will counsel you not to jump into anything too soon. She's there to help you find your circus.

You need your own Judy Barton. If you don't have a Judy Barton among your friends, maybe you should go out and hire one.

11

work is social: healthy groups

In which you will find out:

1. That unhealthy teams are worse than no teams at all.

2. How to tell if your team isn't working well.

3. That too much communication is as bad as too little.

4. That leaving the rat race behind for life as a telecommuter may not be all it's cracked up to be.

A primary method of avoiding malaria is to drain the swamp. A primary method of avoiding lung cancer is to avoid tobacco. A primary method of avoiding arteriosclerosis is to avoid fat. Much of the secret in maintaining a healthy group—your board of directors, your gang, or perhaps the other members of the circus—is to avoid what makes groups unhealthy.

> *Nothing is as invisible as the obvious.*
>
> —RICHARD FARSON

"Works productively with others" isn't just something that fourth grade teachers write on report cards. It's also what makes the world go

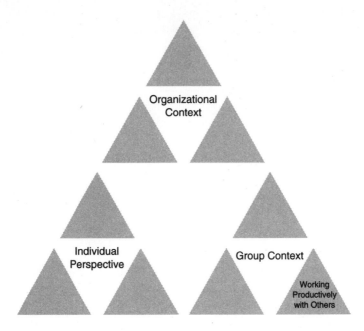

Organizational
Context

Individual
Perspective

Group Context

Working
Productively
with Others

© PeopleTech Consulting, Inc.

around. Unfortunately, and you've seen this for yourself, working productively with others isn't as common as the average person's ability to diagnose world politics. That's why organizations spend a lot of corporate time getting groups to work well together. My company has tried to help. Along the way, we've developed a list of common group ailments.

SYMPTOMS OF UNHEALTHY GROUPS

Read the following section before you go into a meeting with your gang. Is your group or gang experiencing any of these symptoms?

- **No clarity of purpose.** The members don't quite know why they're getting together every Tuesday (other than the fact that they always get together on Tuesday) or the members gather at cross purposes. This is the Project Gargantua Task Force: one member is coming to make sure he can slough off all responsibility, another is going to take all the credit, and another is coming because it's a good place to network about the Project Bizzaro task force. This is an unhealthy group. In twenty-five words or less, write your team's objective on a white board or have it silkscreened on a T-shirt. "It's the economy, stupid" had an admirable brevity, although it could have been more definitive. What's the primary purpose of your group?

- **No open discourse.** The guy from marketing is playing Mr. Secret about the fall plans, the distribution person keeps saying she'll get back to the group pretty soon about costs, and the person from the head office is being coy about almost everything. The purpose of such a group is clear: to slow the speed of information dissemination to a rate that serves the people back in marketing, distribution, or the head office. This kind of corporate constipation can be cleared up if there's more clarity of purpose and if the group is responsible for results. An example of a major corporation making a group responsible for results was General Electric CEO "Neutron" Jack Welch's decision to make promotions and bonuses for employees dependent on group success. Discourse opened up fairly quickly. You may not have that kind of carrot to put in front of your team, but peer pressure and constant reminders can do wonders.

- **No crisp decision making.** Groups can be very good at avoiding decisions. Put two managers in a room with me, I can get them to espouse three opinions. Part of the cure is to state, right up front, the purpose of the get-together. That's not a bad thing to write on your white board either.

- **No mutual respect.** The man from food preparation doesn't think the head waiter's job has anything to do with his and not much to do with the success of the restaurant. The head waiter regards the waiters as infinitely replaceable. The boss is regarded by just about everyone as a deep-pocketed amateur. As team leader you have to increase their respect for each other. Cite their accomplishments to each other. Don't leave anybody out. If you show respect for each of them, you'll find the others coming along. And make sure they understand each others' problems. You don't want a whine tasting, but it's useful for each of them to briefly state their three main roadblocks. It not only puts them on the table for discussion, but it also increases respect. After all, don't you always respect someone smart enough to ask for your opinions?

Depressingly familiar problems, aren't they? If they constitute some of the reasons you want to leave your current situation, then make sure they don't rear their ugly little heads in your new circus. Let's look at the causes of these ailments.

SOME GROUPS ARE SICK AT BIRTH: GENETIC CAUSES OF UNHEALTHY GROUPS

"In your absence, we appointed you to be our representative to the committee. Congratulations."

You've been a member of a committee that doesn't work. In fact the number of committees that don't work is large enough that the word *committee* has fallen into disuse. It deserves to: it is so misused and abused that it needs a quiet corner of a remote room to lie down until it recovers.

These days we use other words for committees: task forces, project teams, flying squads, and groups. Unfortunately, most of these words stand for the same old dysfunctional groupings that make otherwise sociable people believe mistakenly that they would be happier working from home.

The original idea behind a committee was to enrich a decision by bringing together a variety of talent. Unfortunately, committees (even those that are called task forces or project teams) are sometimes put together for quite different reasons:

1. Management wants to say it consulted the troops, so it sets up a group of folks it can point to and say, "We consulted them." Then management goes its own sweet way. Result: the group becomes demoralized.

2. Somebody wants a team so they have someone else to blame—or a whole group of people to spread the blame around. They want a say, but they don't want responsibility. Unofficially, these people are known as "bunch quitters."

3. Somebody wants a team as a forum for views that wouldn't be listened to anywhere else.

4. Somebody wants a committee so that he or she can grab the glory. If you've seen it happen, you've also seen the results:

individual members of the team become secretive. They won't bring out their best ideas. In fact, they might start bringing out their worst and then writing a dissenting report. I've been in that board room at least three times and it isn't pretty.

Not only are committees and work groups created for the wrong reasons, but organizations often tend to label a group of people a team or a committee when in fact they are just a collection of people who are brought together at regular intervals. Somebody wants a team because they've just finished a management book, and the management books say teams are the way the world's going and you have to have one.

Horsefeathers. Giving a group a name like *team* or *task force* doesn't make it so, any more than calling the four people in your car pool *The Beatles* helps you sing. A real team has to have real team responsibilities and real team authority. William Whyte spotted this years ago and wrote about it in his book, *The Organization Man*. He called it false collectivization.

Think about it when you put your board of directors together for YouInc. Are they just a bunch of people in a room together or do they actually have some way to work together, some common ground for discussing issues? Are they achieving results through interaction, or is the outcome simply the sum of individual contributions and no more?

GROUP DYNAMICS, AND WHY YOU WANT TO RUN AWAY TO THE CIRCUS

Take a long, hard look at your current job and think about the groups, committees, and teams that you are part of. Are they dysfunctional? Are they the reason you keeping staring out of the window and dreaming about life under the big top? The solution to dysfunctional work groupings is not necessarily solitude. The solution is better work groups.

Whether you are working with five people in a start-up company, on your own with an informal board of directors, or trying to move to a new position in your company, you have to think long and hard about group culture. And that means thinking about meetings.

I knew a thoughtful executive who kept track of the meetings he attended in his daybook for three months. He rated each meeting according to its usefulness. "After three months, I found that perhaps a quarter of the meetings I was asked to be at were useful or moderately useful." Given his job as a senior vice-president, he couldn't refuse to go

> *Man was born free and everywhere he is in meetings.*
>
> —JEAN-JACQUES ROUSSEAU,
> SLIGHTLY UPDATED

to meetings. He reached for the only sane solution: he stopped keeping his ratings book.

Based on an informal survey of people I've talked to, I have concluded that 67.3 percent of people who leave the corporate world for a one-person business or a start-up do so because they can't take the meetings any more. The comments I quoted at the beginning of this book had a lot to do with meetings. Meetings can make even enjoyable jobs feel like gerbil wheels and can sap energy, enthusiasm, and productivity faster than it takes to say, "The chair recognizes Harriet Percival."

Most of the people we've talked about so far still attend meetings on a regular basis. Paul Beaver has to go to meetings at Amazonia Expeditions, although he has a much better view from the window than most people. Edie Lennon holds her meetings at Ray's Lunch and writes the minutes on a paper napkins, but they are still meetings. Gordon Farnham spends his days meeting with contractors, real-estate agents, and prospective buyers, although he's usually on a building site when he does so and the meetings seldom last longer than the five minutes it takes to decide to widen a door or raise a window. Bryan Trimble attends very few meetings, many of them with just his wife and his accountant, but they are still meetings. William Gottlieb has his board of directors.

What they find different about the meetings they go to now, compared with the meetings in their first life, is that they know why they are there and what they want to happen. Not one of them has to go to a meeting just because it is Tuesday and the group always meets on Tuesday. They have some choice and control over the number and kind of meetings they attend. They call a meeting when they need to solve problems, drum up business, or exchange ideas. It makes for healthier groups. They do not attend meetings with the primary purpose of impressing other people. There are no PowerPoint presentations, no colored charts, and very little paper. Dress code is casual, language is informal, the surroundings are functional, and the location is convenient. They have learned the wisdom articulated by Peter Drucker: "One can either work or meet. One cannot do both at the same time."

Thinking about meetings and healthy groups is one way to assess your current situation and plan your future circus. How much meeting is enough for you? Can you do it by e-mail, fax, or modem or are you going to have to show up in person? How often? How formally? Where? Who else will be there and how do you feel about them?

There's a technique to be stolen from the reflective vice-president I wrote about. Diagnose the meetings you attend. Keep a diary for a few weeks and note:

- The number of meetings you attended.

- How long they lasted.

- Whether you emerged with a clearer sense of what needed to be done.

- Whether the matter could have been handled just as well in five minutes over the phone.

How many meetings does your circus need to function? And how many will it take to stop it functioning altogether?

One way to cut down the number of meetings you call is to get tough about the people you're inviting. Sure it's nice to see Bob and Carol and Ted and Alice all together, but maybe a one-on-one with Alice plus a quick note to Bob, Carol, and Ted would get the job done faster and get you more information from the one person who really matters. It'd free up Bob, Carol, and Ted's time, too.

Another useful exercise is to identify meeting junkies, the people for whom the meeting is the job. They float from boardroom to boardroom in a White Rabbit fashion, glancing at their watches and flipping through their pocket diaries. All these people do is go to meetings, drop in five redundant sentences, nod convincingly, make three notes, and hurry off to disappear down the rabbit hole of yet another gathering. To them, meetings are an easy way to make a living. They fill up hours and hours and hours they would otherwise have to fill with productive work.

A third way is to add up the hourly fees of those who attend. Seven people at $80 an hour is $560 an hour. Whoever said talk is cheap wasn't thinking about business meetings. Is it worth it? How could you cut that bill in half? Would YouInc. pay that much money for this kind of result? (It's tempting to imagine what would happen to the Great American meeting if the same people who carry around clipboards and stopwatches on the production line started clicking their watches during the product distribution meeting in Room 3-B.)

I think organizations could learn from YouInc. just as much as the other way around. I believe that as more and more people start up their own businesses and contract their services to corporations, the pressure will be on to make sure that meetings serve a definite purpose and don't waste time. People paid by the hour or on a straight salary don't care as much as people who are paid by the project or by results or people who don't have others to cover for them when they're stuck in a committee room. This is a healthy development.

The Overcommunication Issue: How to Bludgeon a Group to Death

Meetings are related to another problem: overcommunication in many workplaces. If you are scrutinizing your environment as a prelude to finding a better fitting one, look at the amount of information you have to deal with in your work and try to assess how much of it is valuable and how much is deadweight.

A 1997 survey of Fortune 1000 companies conducted for Pitney Bowes by researchers at San Jose State University found that seven out of ten people were overwhelmed by the volume of information they had to deal with every day. The average number of messages sent and received each day by the people in the survey was 178—by pager, fax, e-mail, telephone, and Post-it note. Many people complained that the communications gridlock meant that the only time they could do real work was in the evenings and on weekends. Office hours were simply spent handling the deluge of messages.

My report of the survey says nothing about the content of the messages, but judging by the stuff that comes through my office, a lot of those messages are redundant, irrelevant, or advertising. As for surfing the Net, I can find more usable information more quickly in the year-old magazines in my dentist's waiting room.

I won't ask you to count the messages you deal with every day because that would just add to your daily chores, but you should reflect on how communication and overcommunication affect how you feel about your work environment and your personal productivity.

Janet Addison is executive director of a charitable organization that raises money for research in tropical medicine. "I remember the days when I would come to work and check my in basket. That was it. Pink telephone message slips, memos, and mail (what they now call snail mail)—it all went in there, and it never took much more than a half hour at the beginning of the day to deal with it. Now I have to check my voice mail, fire up the computer, and check the e-mail, check the fax machine, and then go through my in basket for stuff. I weed out the bulletin board stuff (co-workers selling kittens or looking for apartments) and the stuff that gets duplicated (lawyers always send you a fax and follow it with a snail mail copy) and stuff that gets circulated but doesn't actually have to be read, and I'm left with the actual business stuff and a few personal messages and, by the time I'm through with that, it's time for lunch. I seem to be doing less and less real work each day."

Many people feel they have no control over the forms of communication they use and no way to stem the flood of messages. Designing your own circus may involve taking control and creating some filters to get rid of unwanted communication while you get your work done.

How Overcommunication Kills Teamwork

Think about an organization with unhealthy communications practices that you've been in or watched. Or, if you've spent the last ten years on a desert island, ask someone else. The results of unhealthy groups include:

- **Slow decisions.** Slow decisions cost money. Deferring a decision on location can cost you another month's interest on money, for example. Slow decisions also increase stomach acidity levels. And they take the joy out of things. There's no fun in taking the trip if you end up in a mud hole every hundred feet. Remember, you speed things up by keeping the group on track and expecting a result from every get-together. Haste makes waste has been dumped in favor of just-in-time decisions. Stick to the schedule, unless there's a very good reason not to. And if there's a very good reason, get a tight schedule for dealing with it.

- **Mind bog.** Overcommunication overloads the synapses and confuses people about what the real issues are. That means they get less time to spend on real issues, which means your primary purposes aren't being served. In meetings, if it's not necessary to say something, it's necessary not to say it. Edit for your group. This book was edited. Lots of lovely interesting stuff ended up on the floor because it was getting in the way of the main message.

- **Increased politics.** When you get groups picking sides, you've at least halved the potential effectiveness of that group. Clarity of purpose helps edge out the politicians.

- **Decreased participation.** Ever noticed that informal groups work better than formal groups? A sports and social committee gets stuff done faster, has better ideas, and works in a more joyous atmosphere than a plans and procedures committee. More people come and the contribution level is higher. It pays to reflect on the reasons. First, the sports and social committee has a clear mandate—to plan the company picnic. Second, everybody's more or less equal. No one department has a monopoly on fun. Third, discourse is clear. Nobody says, "global vertical integration." Fourth, there's less information overload. It'd be a strange company where 81-page reports with color pie charts were distributed in advance of a confab on an event featuring three-legged races.

This leads to a question: how close can you make your team meeting to a sports and social meeting?

IS THE ALTERNATIVE TO WORKING WITH AN UNHEALTHY GROUP WORKING FROM HOME?

Dr. David Blank believes that some people try working from home just because they are reacting to the stress of corporate life, not because they really think they would prefer to work on their own. They seize the chance to work from home, assuming that anything would be better than the situation they are in, but they quickly find out that they have solved the wrong problem.

Judging by the failed telecommuters I've talked with, people often think that they want less interaction with others when it's simply that they need better quality interaction, or interaction in a different form.

Dora Sieber, a former editor in a publishing house, used to sit through editorial meetings that took up most of her Thursday mornings. "I used to wake up on Thursday mornings with a faint headache. We'd sit there in a room from which the oxygen was gradually withdrawn, talking about the same projects, week after week, repeating things for whoever had missed the meeting the previous week, answering the same questions over and over. Once in a while we'd have an interesting discussion about new or possible acquisitions, but by that time most of us were faint with hunger or lack of air and it generally petered out quickly.

"At first I thought perhaps I was just an introspective sort of person who worked best on my own, and I considered becoming a freelance editor, but that wasn't it at all. Good in-house editors aren't shy, retiring types who are happiest when they are alone with a manuscript and a blue pencil. They are rather like counselors or coaches in some ways. They deal with authors with touchy egos, people who prefer to communicate in writing rather than in person, creative people who keep strange hours. They do not lack people skills and they are good at talking about ideas. They have to sell those ideas to other people in the publishing house. They can work alone and they can work with others. What was getting me down was the fact that the meetings were dysfunctional and there were no opportunities in my job for genuine teamwork.

"I would have been miserable as a freelance editor because the life is too solitary. It took me some time to figure out how to use my skills, but after a few false starts, I realized that I was good at coaching other people to write more effectively. I left the publishing company and started my own corporate training business, specializing in business communication skills. I now go to two kinds of meetings: planning meetings with one or two other people, at which we talk about communication problems and figure out how to create training that will solve those problems, and the seminars themselves, at which I put on my coaching hat and make sure that I keep people awake with different activities, a combination of group and individual work, and lots of freewheeling discussion. The hours fly by."

> In the workplace, home office, sales floor, service kiosk, home—we will be "talking" to programs that are beginning to look surprisingly alike: all full of animated pictures we are supposed to pick, like push-buttons on a toddler's toy. The toy is supposed to please us. Somehow, it is supposed to replace the satisfactions of transacting meaning with a mature human being, in the confusion of natural language, together, in a room, at a touching distance.
>
> —ELLEN ULLMAN,
> COMPUTER PROGRAMMER

Don't make the mistake of assuming that, because you hate your office environment, you will hate all office environments or that, because you hate the meetings you attend, you therefore will hate all meetings. For many people, work is their community, even more than their neighborhood at home. It's where they plug into the world. Working at home feels like being unplugged. No gossip. No way to see your coworker's latest holiday photographs or another example of Dave's strange collection of ties. No politics or speculation about what's really happening in the corner office. Nobody bringing in donuts. No background noise of telephones and photocopiers and talk. No buzz. Just you and your work, day after day.

Adjusting your Environment to Suit How You Work with Groups

"It's lonely at the middle," Maria di Norcia says ruefully. "And since I'm the kind of person who tends to say yes to things without thinking them through, I had to find out the hard way."

Maria does corporate communications for a financial company. We are squeezed into her office, which is bulging with books, magazines, and piles of paper. There are two large bulletin boards covered with clippings, jotted notes, and photographs. Her computer workstation is almost invisible beneath a layer of Post-it notes. I'm afraid to put down my coffee cup in case I lose it, but I am quite sure that Maria knows exactly where everything is in that office.

"A few years ago I was administrative assistant for the head of communications. Among other things, I worked on the company newsletter and did some photo research for a quarterly journal that was distributed to our clients and customers. What I was doing wasn't particularly creative or fulfilling, so I thought I might as well upgrade my skills in desktop publishing. I figured that at least I could improve the look of the newsletter, which we did entirely in-house, whereas the journal was laid out by a professional designer.

"I went on some courses and spent hours poring over those manuals that are written by geeks in some strange language that only vaguely resembles English. I learned what the software could do and then I took some more courses about effective design and layout. The newsletters started to look as good as the journal, and after a while, my boss asked if I'd like to take on the design of the journal as well. We figured that the money we saved by bringing the design work in-house could be used to buy illustrations and cartoons to make our publications more attractive. It seemed like a good idea at the time.

"After a while other people came to me to get stuff designed. I spent more and more time doing desktop work, and other stuff sort of faded away. Work became just me and my workstation, hour after hour. So I wasn't particularly surprised when my boss suggested I should consider working from home. They were expanding the marketing department and they wanted my space. They figured I could do my design work anywhere and come in to the office for occasional meetings. I had a fairly long commute, so I said yes. This, too, seemed like a good idea at the time.

"My husband and I cleared out the spare bedroom and turned it into a home office. The company paid for some rewiring and moved in my workstation.

"What a disaster. I was climbing the walls after six weeks, but it took me another six weeks to admit that the whole experiment was a failure. The isolation was awful. At the office, I'd assumed that I was spending most of my days just working at the computer, but it turned out I'd spent a lot of time talking to people, even if it was just discussing possible photographs for journal covers or chatting with people on my breaks.

"I went in to see my boss and said that I would be prepared to do anything, as long as I could do it in the office. She hemmed and hawed and said she'd see what she could do, but she didn't sound very positive. My old space was now being used by another department. Everyone was happy with my work and wanted me to keep doing it. I felt like a victim of my own success. I quite liked the design work, but it wasn't taking me in a direction I wanted to go. I wanted to do more writing.

"My husband and I talked it over. He suggested that since I'd got myself into this mess by taking extra training, maybe I could take extra training to get out.

"So for about a year, I stuck with the telecommuting, but I took courses in communications, editing, writing, even radio production. I wrote for a local weekly for a while and then I started writing a newsletter for my husband's business—he's an acoustical engineer. I was working practically around the clock, but I was desperate. Once I had a portfolio of writing, I started applying for communications jobs.

"I got offers from a couple of places, but nothing that was quite right. Then the communications officer at my company applied for maternity leave. I jumped at the chance. I was going to get that job, and nothing was going to stop me. It was kind of funny—I was wildly overprepared for the interview. New suit, impressive portfolio, examples of my work coming out of my ears. I even went for coaching in interview skills. But the thing that probably clinched it was that I had already started coaching another employee in desktop design skills and he was able to take on the work I'd been doing.

"The day I moved back to the office was wonderful. Because I'd felt so isolated at home, I went out of my way to talk to people. I hardly ever used my phone or e-mail for internal communications: I went to see people in person. The effect was the same as networking, but at the time, I was just celebrating not being on my own.

"I knew I had six months to figure out a way to stay. I had to make myself indispensable. So I offered to work on the annual report, which everyone else hated and avoided like the plague, and I created a new monthly pamphlet called "Required Reading," which was quick summaries of current articles in financial journals and related books, the stuff that nobody has time to track down and read in full. And I did tons of interviews for the journal, partly to learn more about the company, partly to make myself more visible. I made sure I got to know someone in each department.

"It worked. When Shauna came back from maternity leave, they reorganized the department, and I stayed on. With Shauna back, it felt strange at first having only one job to do instead of doing two. I was so used to doing several things at once that I put together a self-help course in effective business writing for other people in the company and promoted that.

"When the time came for me to go on maternity leave, my job was secure. This time, staying at home wasn't so awful, because I knew it was only temporary and, anyway, with twins you're never really alone."

When you go looking for the right work environment, when and how and how often you see people is crucial. Maria found that the desktop design work she did closed off opportunities to interact with people and that writing and interviewing opened them up again. Even when she was doing design work full time at the office, she was still part of the office community. Working from home was convenient, but it only took a few weeks for her to figure out that the commute was worth the trouble, just to be part of the group at work.

Of course, there are plenty of people who prefer to be solitary when they work and find offices too noisy and jangling. Many people need peace and quiet to do their best work, whether it's writing computer code or reading blueprints. For some people, telecommuting works just fine. But unless you're a hermit by nature, it works best when you find other ways to stay in touch with a community of people. The trick is finding the right community, determining your needs, and matching it with the right circus.

12

are you qualified for your dream?

In which you will find out that:

1. Your dream must have some basis in reality—your reality.

2. It's a good idea to understand why you like what you like.

3. You may need to acquire new skills that fit your dream.

The change triangle sorts change into three areas. The first was the organizational context or corporate culture. Corporate cultures can be read, after you know what to look for. You can get a handle on the different types of cor-

> We all have to be our own product managers. We have to pack our own parachutes, nobody else can do it for us.
>
> —GIL WETZEL, GROUP EVP, EASTERN REGION, RIGHT MANAGEMENT CONSULTANTS, PHILADELPHIA

porate cultures at Apple, at Shanghai Truck Company Number 13, at

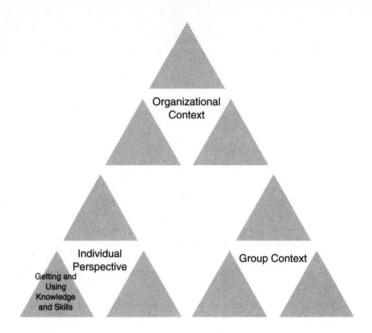

© *PeopleTech Consulting, Inc.*

St. Jude's Hospital, or at Ferdinand's Live Bait and Sushi simply by standing at the front gate as the employees arrive. Look at their faces, look at their transportation, look at what they're carrying, look at their clothes, and watch how they relate to each other, if they do. And having read the culture, you can tell whether or not it's a culture that would help you work or make you feel like a square peg in a round hole.

The second area identified in the change triangle was group behavior. It reflects values shared by a smaller number of people. Those values may be shaped partly by the organizational framework, but they can and do vary wildly within individual companies. The product group in New Haven behaves differently from the product group in Wyoming, which differs from the product group in Berlin. In the same way, a group from the legal department is going to differ from a group created within sales. The groups you are part of can determine whether you experience satisfaction or frustration in your work.

The third section of the triangle, individual behaviors, deals with the one-person-at-a-time factors that have tripped up more change efforts than I like to think about. This is where dreams meet reality. The collision of the ideal and the actual is often noisy, one on one, in your face, up close and personal—all those things most people find hardest.

But it has to happen. It's time to expose your dreams to the harsh light of day. Do they fit reality—yours, your family's, and the market's? Let's start with your reality.

HOW TO TEST YOUR DREAM AGAINST REALITY

You have an individual dream. But if you are going to turn that dream into reality, it must be something more than pure fantasy. You can dream of ruling the world, but frankly it's unlikely that you're even going to take over Scranton, Pennsylvania, and you'll just wear yourself out trying.

Corporations have rules for their daydreams, or what management boards call visions or mission statements. Not to take all the fun out of things, but these rules are useful here, and we might as well steal them as we've stolen so much else.

The first corporate rule is that you must be able to take some immediate action, however small, toward fulfilling the dream. If a corporation's daydream is a 99 percent perfect vacuum cleaner in three years, the corporation has to be able to take the first step: fixing that wiggly on-off knob they've been getting all the letters about. If you can't see the first step, you won't take the trip.

What's your first step? If you're going to become a charter captain, it could be taking a power squadron course. If you're going to be a clown, it could be buying the floppy shoes. If you're going to be a trapeze artist, your first step might be getting rid of that annoying fear of heights.

I know a fireman who wanted to build log homes for a living. His first step was a course in building with logs. The second step was to build his own small cabin in his spare time. His third step was dealing with the people who knocked on his cabin door asking who built it.

I have a neighbor who rents a Victorian coach house nearby. She wanted to become an artist. Her first step was to turn down the raise her company was offering her and take a day off a week instead. Soon she was working at her company for three days a week. Then it was two, and now she's only called in when there's work overflow. She found change a day at a time. I have a cousin who started his mail order company when he was disabled with a broken leg. His first step was breaking his leg.

You don't have to change everything overnight for all time. You can just take one small step for yourself. The step must be something you can do right away or very soon, not a step that requires you to win the lottery first. And it should lead to another step and another and another. This is why companies start pilot projects. If the pilot project works, they build on the success. If it doesn't work, they try something else.

Stop for a second. What's your first step? If you want to become an actuary, the first step is probably reading two books on the industry. If you want to move to Lima, Ohio, your first step might be to write to the Chamber of Commerce there. If you want to open a roadside stand on the Internet, the first step is probably to take up surfing. Don't get bogged down in the whole massive morass of change: start with one small step.

The second corporate rule is that you must be a credible source of your daydream. General Motors or Ford could probably make airplanes (and both of those companies actually have in the past), but would they be a credible source? Would you feel comfortable flying a Chevy Caprice or a Ford Crown Victoria? IBM could undoubtedly make home theaters with four-foot screens, but would Big Blue be a credible source? Seagram's has the technology to make fuel for your car, but how good would you as a consumer feel about filling the Chrysler with Chivas Unleaded Ultra? The person who grooms my dog could also probably do my hair but . . .

Companies have what they call core competencies. If you ask 3-M what its core competency is, you'll be told that it's putting thin surfaces on other thin surfaces. They put glue on cellophane and call it Scotch tape. They put layers of metal on plastic and sell it as recording tape. They put very weak glue on paper and sell it as Post-it notes. It's what they do: thin layers of stuff on other thin layers of stuff. And they stick to it (pun more or less intended).

Sony's core competency is the design and manufacture of electronic entertainment devices. When they got into the actual manufacture of the entertainment that would be played on the devices, they overstepped their bounds occasionally and lost more money than the GDP of Tasmania. You can name ten dozen other companies who have made the same mistake.

What really is your core competency? Are you creative? Are you essentially a strong back, a hewer of wood and a hauler of water? Are you, at bottom, someone whose core competency is convincing other people to do things? Are you most successfully a manager, someone who arranges chores for others to do and then motivates them to do them?

Can you match that core competency with your daydream? Heaven knows it's tough just maintaining credibility in the business you're in now. Launching a new one isn't going to be easier. You'll be underqualified. Or overqualified. Or you won't possess the right skill set. You'll be too old or too young, you'll be too regimented or not regimented enough, or you'll be too entrepreneurial or not nearly entrepreneurial enough. This is all true by definition. You're making a change and doing something different. Therefore, you are not necessarily suited to the task. You are not a credible source of supply. Your bank won't believe it, your suppliers won't believe it, and your customers won't believe it. You can't just talk the talk. You've got to be ready to walk the walk. You have to be credible. Otherwise, you're like Sony chocolate chip cookies or Bozo the chartered accountant.

> *Imagine yourself in a Middle Eastern bazaar. On one side of you a guy is selling falafel. On the other side there is someone selling cantaloupes. What have you got to sell? You can't sell twenty years with IBM or middle management at Ford. You have to sell the things that make you unique.*
>
> —DAVE MAGUIRE, FORMER CEO, JANNOTTA BRAY AND ASSOCIATES

Now wait a minute (I hear you cry). If credibility operates within such a narrow range, then nobody would ever change and everybody would stay in the same kind of job for life.

Well, no. Core competencies are not the same things as skills. Core competencies don't change; skills change all the time. Credibility means sticking to your core competencies, even if you have to change your skills to match.

I have met a fighter pilot who is studying became a doctor. Is that credible? Not on the face of it. However, when you start to parse the core competencies needed, it begins to make sense. Intelligence? Fighter pilots have it. Ability to deal with scientific knowledge? Yes. Ability to cope with emergencies? Yes. Understanding of complex systems? Yes. Dedication? Definitely. Endurance? Yup.

Warren Radtke, vice-president of a career consulting firm in Boston, puts it this way: "You have to think of yourself as a collection of verbs, not as a noun. Those verbs could be assembled in one way and the result would be a schoolteacher. Assemble the same verbs in a different way and you might get a market researcher."

Maybe the problem is that you don't know what your core competency is. We all harbor fond little illusions about our good points, so

The most successful people are those who don't have any illusions about who they are. They know themselves well and they can move in the direction of their best talents. They know the kind of culture they thrive in and how they can benefit from that culture. Unfortunately, most people don't understand themselves. Most people don't want to lose their illusions about themselves, although they may say they want to take charge of their career.

—BUD BRAY, FORMER PRINCIPAL,
JANNOTTA BRAY ASSOCIATES

it might be a good idea to ask around. You may think of yourself as an innovator. Others may think of you as a snail, sludging slowly ahead. It wouldn't hurt to ask. The question you're going to bother people with is, "Hey, Edward, Tanya, what do you think I do best?"

They'll tell you. I've seen the exercise done. I know of one executive who thought his core competency was a strategic ability to see the big picture. His wife, his friends, and his secretary gently broke the news that what he really had was an astounding ability to make things work by sweating the details and making sure that everyone else sweated them, too.

I know of a sales manager who thought her credibility was based on her management ability. Her own sales force disabused her of the illusion at a cathartic meeting. She was, they told her, a terrific and enthusiastic salesperson who simply infected others with her enthusiasm. Her management abilities were seen as iffy at best. "You couldn't manage a bun fight at a bakery," one co-worker told her cheerfully.

Companies often have a problem defining their core competency, too, if you find that reassuring. For example, in the 1930s, if you'd asked a railroad magnate what the core competency of his railroad was, you'd likely get an answer like "railroading." If you'd asked his customers what they actually bought from the company, the customer would likely say that they were paying the railroad to get their cabbages from California to Chicago. Trucks can't compete with railroads at building rails, but they can get things from California to Chicago. To survive in a dominant position, the railroads should have defined their real competency. If you get things from A to B on time, the customer won't care whether the wheels are steel or rubber.

Harry the printing salesman has *printing sales* engraved on his card. He likes the words. However, if you ask his customers what Harry really does, the customers will tell you, "Harry helps me get my advertising done." His core competency is helping get things done, particularly advertising. He'd probably do better in business if he had that printed on his business cards. What he does isn't what we usually define as sales and it may or may not require a printing press.

Ignore your own business card for a while and forget what it says underneath your name on the little plaque outside your office door or what's painted on the side of your truck. What do your customers really buy from you? Management? Enthusiasm? The ability to negotiate? A strong back? What does your employer really pay you for? Tactical smarts? Off-the-wall solutions? Dogged determination? The ability to take flak? Those questions are one way to help define your core competency.

This sometimes takes a while. I give you the strange case of Leona Mandeville. She'd worked six years in the offices of a multibranch travel agency in Chicago and was very happy there, despite the fact that travel counselors aren't paid much and large parts of the customer pool can be very demanding.

What's been happening in the travel business is that airlines have been cutting ticket prices, which cuts the amount of commissions available to travel agents. It's gone further than that: airlines have started capping commissions so that there's a firm top-end limit on them. That puts a limit on what underpaid agencies are allowed to make on a top-end client. There's more, but the result was that Leona's multibranch agency decided to cut down on its real estate costs by cutting locations and to cut down on staff by getting rid of everything but their relatively low-maintenance corporate work. In this case, it meant getting rid of Leona: six weeks' notice and a short, boozy party after quitting time on her last day.

Leona's not introspective, but she knows how to figure out how many beans make six. What had been the part of her job that she enjoyed most? "Getting people on a fabulous vacation they hadn't even dreamed about. They'd be cautious and ask about a cruise. I'd start talking about an escorted bicycle tour of the south of France. They'd want to go to one of those franchised hotels in the Caribbean. I could see they'd be bored by the second day, and I'd start talking up new rain forest tours in Belize. I had fun. They had fun. And they kept coming back for more and bringing friends."

What was her core competency? Not the usual travel agent business of getting on the computer and tracing out the shortest route or cheapest fare to Roanoke from Chicago and then wringing the most freebie air miles out of the deal. She wasn't a machine. Her core competency was getting a feel for what people really wanted and then mating it with a product that was fresh and alive.

What's she doing now? She's holding home travel parties: "I get ten people together and tell them about five really interesting vacations. I'll show them videos, guide books, references from other people. Even though they might not book a trip, we have a good party." That's another of her core competencies: throwing good parties.

Leona's normal route would have been to trudge the streets of Chicago looking for a replacement job that was exactly the same as what she'd been doing before. She found her second life—or at least a part of it—in mining her core competency.

PERSONAL ARCHEOLOGY 101: DISCOVER YOUR FUTURE COMPETENCY BY LOOKING AT YOUR PAST

There's another way to uncover (or confirm) your competency. It involves an intriguing exercise in personal archeology.

"The trouble with me is that I like too many things," says Brenda Davis. "I started out working in Human Resources because I had a degree in psychology. I got a degree in psychology more or less because my best friend got a degree in psychology and borrowing her decision was easier than trying to decide between modern languages,

> I could be anything if I only knew what it was
>
> —TITLE OF A BOOK BY BARBARA SHER

comparative literature, history, art history, musicology, and, believe it or not, math, which were all things I seriously considered during my last years of high school and my first year at college. I found everything fascinating. And I'm fairly intelligent, so I seemed to get good marks at whatever I took.

"HR was not too bad, and I quite enjoyed the job for about five years, in two different companies, although I was beginning to get a little restless. Then I was assigned to a project that had to do with our HR database, working with the MIS department and tracking people's careers through the company to see if we could identify particular educational qualifications that determined who moved up and who stayed still. It was a financial company and I was interested to note that the top people were not from the business, accounting, or commercial backgrounds, but tended to have degrees in the humanities or social sciences.

"Anyway, I got very involved with computers in that project and wound up making a lateral transfer into MIS. It turned out I had a knack for using computers. Also, unlike some of the people already working in this area, I was able to explain the systems to non-technical people. Non-MIS people didn't mind talking to me. I did that for another couple of years.

"Around that time I got married and my husband was sent to Germany. In a fit of desperation, I took a course in teaching English as a Second Language, figuring I could use it somewhere. I never did. Instead, by way of a series of lucky encounters, I fell into a job with an international management consulting firm that had an office in Frankfurt. I picked up German fairly readily, along with the vocabulary of management consulting. I had a daughter, but I went back to work after two months. Everybody kept telling me I was indispensable. The nanny got to see Sally's first steps.

"The next time we moved, it was for my job. I was offered a senior position at head office in New York. Tom agreed that it was my turn, and he found something he quite liked there, although I know it was not an ideal time for him to leave his job.

"And then, in New York, when Sally was about four, I hit a wall. Both literally and metaphorically. The literal part was that I fainted in a meeting in a hot, airless room and fell into the white board I was writing on. Knocked over a projector at the same time. Very dramatic. The reason I fainted was that I was pregnant again (I hadn't planned this one).

"They kept me in hospital overnight for observation. The doctor looked stern and told me that if I wanted another healthy baby I should re-examine my lifestyle. I lay awake all night thinking, 'Now what?'

"I took a leave of absence, most of which I spent at our place in the country. Sounds great, doesn't it? Well, in terms of my health, it was wonderful. I ate properly, got lots of exercise, and slept in late. In terms of figuring out 'What next?' it was a complete waste of time. I was just drifting, thinking that after I had my baby, I'd just go back to my job, only I'd try to pace myself better.

"The baby was born in the spring, a boy, and I started to make plans to go back to work. And then I started to procrastinate. I told myself it was the midnight feedings, I was just short on sleep. But even when Peter was sleeping through the night, I couldn't seem to get my act together. Deep down I knew that if I went back, I'd get caught up in the same old whirlwind and I'd miss Peter's childhood, just as I'd missed most of Sally's.

"Finally I began to think, 'Is there something I can do that won't use up all my time and make me crazy?' And that's where I nearly went nuts. Because there were dozens of things I could do, I mean, that I had the skills and experience to do.

"The books all said, do what you like best. I came up with a list of thirty-two things, based on the projects that had excited me most. I enjoyed working with people, working with computers, working as a consultant. I'd even enjoyed the teaching course and had been quite interested in teaching. I went round in circles. I asked other people and they all came up with different answers for who they thought I was and what I should do. What I learned from this is that I seem to be a chameleon and I change depending on my environment.

"Then I remembered the presentation I'd been giving the day I fell into the white board. It was a meeting with a client, and we were exploring the 'What business are you in?' question. I thought about what I'd told them before I fell over and thought, 'Well, if there is any merit at all in that idea, I ought to be able to do it myself.'

"So I stopped thinking about the jobs I'd had and the skills I'd used and I started digging into why I was good at so many different things.

"I realized that for years I'd been doing things because I could do them. I kept moving from one area to another, enjoying the feeling of picking things up quickly more than actually doing the job. I kept thinking, 'Wow, here I am in my suit, looking all serious, and all these important people are paying attention to what I say. And I learned some of this stuff only yesterday, reading up on it on the plane.'

"Some people might call it the impostor syndrome, but it wasn't. Instead, I prided myself on learning fast and on bringing a new perspective to some of the stuff I was learning. I didn't see any of the business theories as dogma or as immutable laws. I saw them as one way of looking at things because I knew there were others, some of which I already knew, some of which I was probably going to learn later. I didn't take any particular theory 100 percent seriously. What I took seriously was keeping an open mind and trying to find the right idea for the situation, whatever it was.

"Getting to this point involved sort of excavating what I liked to find out what I liked about what I liked, if you see what I mean. (Did I mention I'd considered archaeology at one point at university? The thought of excavation really appealed to me.) I eventually figured out that what

I was good at wasn't psych, or HR work, or computers, or teaching ESL, or consulting, or giving presentations with white boards to people in expensive business suits. What I was good at was learning fast and communicating my knowledge to others.

"I didn't stop there, though. I thought, 'Why do I learn fast?' And I realized that I had a knack for seeing essential concepts almost visually in my mind. I could see the shape of things underneath all the words. I guess you could say I can see the forest, not just the trees. It meant that I not only learned fast, but I could explain things to other people because I didn't get tangled up in the details. I could say, 'This is the most important idea to understand. Once you grasp it, all the other things will follow.' It made me a good teacher.

"Seems obvious, doesn't it? But that's 20-20 hindsight. At the time it was a major revelation.

"At the same time, I thought about my work environment. I thought about the bosses I'd had and came to the conclusion that, although some were better than others, and all had good experience, not one was brighter than I was, and a couple were quite intimidated by me. It occurred to me that I might be the best boss I'd ever had. I know that sounds braggy, but I was trying to be honest.

"I quit, eventually. I wish I could say that it was my idea, but actually Tom gave me an excuse by getting a better job offer that meant a move to Montreal. My first thought was, 'Great, now I can really polish up my French.'

"To make a long story slightly less interminable, I wound up starting a small company. Just-in-time research for executives and politicians. Everything you need to know on three pages or less or in a crash-course setting for people who aren't very good readers. I know that sounds funny, but some of my clients don't want the stuff on paper, they want me to tell them in person or tell a small group.

"I set my own hours. I got to see Peter's first steps. I do not work weekends. I've taken on some staff to do the paperwork. Not because I don't enjoy paperwork, but I'm so efficient at it that I could waste my time doing that instead of sticking to my particular job: research, writing, teaching. I still have to watch for that. I had to learn to delegate because it was always so tempting to say, 'Here, let me do that,' because I knew I could do it in half the time. It was hard to watch other people learning slowly, when I learn fast. But I told myself that I was a good learner and I could learn to delegate along with everything else."

WHAT ARE YOUR CORE COMPETENCIES?
AND WHY?

Look through the list below and check off what you can do. Then try a
little personal archeology. Why can you do these things?

- ☐ I can sell. Because . . .
- ☐ I can listen. Because . . .
- ☐ I love public speaking. Because . . .
- ☐ I can isolate the logic of a thing. Because . . .
- ☐ I can define the emotion of a thing. Because . . .
- ☐ I'm terrific with numbers. Because . . .
- ☐ I never have to use the manual. Because . . .
- ☐ I'll hire someone to use the manual. Because . . .
- ☐ I can analyze data. Because . . .
- ☐ I can work 18 hours. Because . . .
- ☐ I can pack 18 hours' work into eight hours. Because . . .
- ☐ I lead people. Because . . .
- ☐ I follow superbly. Because . . .
- ☐ I'm persistent. Because . . .
- ☐ I'm innovative. Because . . .
- ☐ I'm a team player. Because . . .
- ☐ I do really well on my own. Because . . .
- ☐ I'm physical. Because . . .
- ☐ I'm a thinker. Because . . .
- ☐ I'm creative. Because . . .
- ☐ I can make other people creative. Because . . .
- ☐ I get things done. Because . . .
- ☐ I get other people to achieve things. Because . . .

☐   I'm patient. Because . . .

☐   I like to find things out. Because . . .

☐   I adapt easily to new technology. Because . . .

☐   I understand the value of doing things traditionally. Because . . .

☐   I'm methodical. Because . . .

☐   I'm experimental. Because . . .

☐   I'm conservative. Because . . .

☐   I'm not easily frightened. Because . . .

☐   I'm loyal. Because . . .

☐   I lust to try new things. Because . . .

☐   People like listening to me. Because . . .

☐   People like me to listen to them. Because . . .

☐   People come to me often for advice. Because . . .

☐   People talk easily to me. Because . . .

☐   I prefer to work on one thing at a time. Because . . .

☐   I prefer to have five projects on my desk. Because . . .

☐   I manage by talking things out. Because . . .

☐   I manage by the seat of my pants. Because . . .

☐   I'm . . . Because . . .

This is just to get you started. If you need more guidance, there are all kinds of books and tests that will help. There's the Myers-Briggs test, which is based on Jungian ideas of personality type. It is not the final answer to your questions, however, it will at least point you in certain directions. You can find the Myers-Briggs in many different career planning guides, such as *Do What You Are*, by Paul Tieger and Barbara Barron-Tieger. There's Richard Bowles's splendid book *What Color Is Your Parachute?*, which is full of helpful tests and suggestions. There are workshops, seminars, and retreats and there are personal career counselors and therapists. There is no shortage of material on this subject, and if you are really having difficulty deciding what you are good at, I advise you to explore all the resources available.

MATCHING YOUR CORE COMPETENCY
TO YOUR DREAM

Now, what are the kind of competencies required by your dream? Suppose you want to be a clown. What essential qualities must you have? I'm not yet talking about skills that you can acquire, I'm talking about the kind of innate qualities that you need to be a clown. I'd say that just to survive the audition for clown school, you'd need the following:

- A sense of humor.

- A high pain threshold, so you can pratfall five times a show.

- Physical flexibility (and a lack of claustrophobia), so you can fit into a tiny car with 15 others.

- Physical coordination and a good sense of balance. You must be able to trip carrying a vase of flowers and not spill them.

- An ability to take direction, so you won't argue when you're the one that gets to be shot out of the cannon.

- An ability to work with others.

- A tolerance for small children.

- No allergies to greasepaint, circus animals, or seltzer.

Attributes like these are not things you can readily acquire if you don't have them already. If you don't have them, you'd be an incompetent Bozo.

Now think about your dream and the qualities it demands. Can you really turn yourself into an outgoing sales type and what three things do you need to do to demonstrate that to yourself? Can you work alone and remain motivated and how do you prove that before you make the change? You like furniture and you know about furniture, but does that mean you're going to be good at building it?

These are questions that go to the heart of compatibility between you and your dream. Ignore them at your peril.

Credibility and job fit are related to competencies. Other words for competencies might be *attitudes*, *qualities*, and *temperament*. Those things don't change. Skills and knowledge, however, can be acquired. You may need some.

That's okay. While it's hard to change a core competency, you can buy most skills.

SKILL-TESTING QUESTIONS

Skills can be acquired, but do you know which ones you need to acquire? A furniture maker may have the knowledge of wood and the craftsmanship to build a wooden boat, but lack the skills and know-how to install the electricals that even a classic boat needs. A cola company knows how to put fizzy liquids in bottles, but it will need new skills and knowledge to make champagne.

In every corporation where we're making large changes, we find that staff (and I include most managers) need to build new skills and enlarge their knowledge. Remember the companies that gave their people computers, but didn't train them how use the machines? Remember companies that kicked off a just-in-time system without showing their own people and their suppliers how to make it work? How about the organizations that announced they were going to empower their people without explaining the concept and or coaching employees in how to deal with it? They left staff wondering just what the heck empowerment meant.

Are you about to commit the same sin? Your current position may require research analysis skills and a knowledge of certain markets. But there are other skills that your current position doesn't require that will be required at your new circus. Imagine for a minute that you are a savvy human resources director at the circus. Your immediate job is to assess your current skills and knowledge to get you ready to be a clown. As a human resources director, you'd probably make up a list of the minimum clown skill prerequisites, such as:

Applying greasepaint and false nose

Carrying out slapstick routines

Riding unicycle

Balancing on stilts

Cleaning up after elephants

Running in floppy shoes

If you discover that you (the candidate) don't have the necessary training to be a clown, then you (the human resources director) will have to send the candidate down to Venice, Florida, to the Ringling Brothers' Clown College and have you the candidate registered for Full Immersion Foolishness 101. Ah, dear. Such a sad moment when you sit your mature adult self down and realize you haven't got the training to be a clown.

Now, what exactly is your daydream? Do you have the skills? Do you have the knowledge? Can you acquire them? To help you answer these questions, list in the skills required to live your daydream (for example, can ride the unicycle) and whether or not you have that skill. Then, list the knowledge required to live your daydream (for example, understanding the economics of a traveling circus) and whether or not you have that knowledge.

Be prepared to do some research to make this test meaningful. For example, if your version of running away to the circus means opening a beach bar in Forgotten Bay, St. Lucia, you might assume that you have a lot of the skills and knowledge needed. After all, you've washed dishes before, you make a pretty mean banana daiquiri, and you look rather dashing in a planters' hat. However, if you were to sidle up to the bar in Forgotten Bay and ask the proprietor what he did during the previous twenty-four hours, you'd come up with something like the following table.

IN THE LAST 24 HOURS I . . .	SKILL/KNOWLEDGE REQUIRED
Fixed the damn tap	Plumbing skills
Stopped the cash register leaking	Bartenders worldwide know 17 ways to cheat the owner. You need to know them, too
Fired Emily	Knowledge of local employment practices
Hired DJ for Saturday night jam	Knowledge of local music preferences, rates

IN THE LAST 24 HOURS I . . .	SKILL/KNOWLEDGE REQUIRED
Did taxes	Knowledge of local tax laws
Put an ad in the paper for Saturday night	Media and design skills
Talked with woman who swallowed bug	Negotiating skills
Ordered liquor, food	Knowledge of local consumption patterns, buying skills, kitchen skills, kitchen design skills
Gave the bartender his wake-up call	Employee motivation skills
Bought the constable a beer	Community relations

Without the relevant skills and knowledge, you can't run a profitable beach bar. Without certain skills and knowledge, you probably couldn't even be hired as a bartender in Forgotten Bay. This is truer than it seems: any number of very intelligent dentists and accountants have found themselves going broke with their investments in snazzy little bistros, the same way schoolteachers have gone broke opening flower shops and lawyers have gone broke running mail order businesses. They were intelligent people. They were energetic. They were ambitious. They just didn't have the skills. In the words of a breeder of exotic fish, they went fins up.

Do your homework. Survey people doing what you want to do. Ask them what they did in the last twenty-four hours. Ask them what they did in the past week. Ask them what are the five most important things they have learned and how they learned them. The answers are not always apparent from the outside. A graphic designer I know says her second most important skill set is negotiating contracts and copyrights. A dairy farmer will tell you about the need for computer savvy. The operator of a non-profit daycare has to know how to read financial statements and deal with a board of directors.

And don't think you can give yourself on-the-job training. You won't have time. For the proof of that, ask anyone who's made a major change. It's hard to learn the accounting you need for your flower shop when you're painting the walls at two in the morning. If you want that job in marketing, a willingness to learn marketing skills on company time will not get you very far.

You wouldn't hire someone who needed to acquire a substantial set of skills or a largish body of knowledge and wanted to do it on your time. If you wouldn't hire yourself to fill the position you're creating, you need training.

That leads to something you should mull over. You have financial skills. You have no lion taming skills. You want to run away to the circus. But would it be sufficient to be the accountant for the circus? Must you be the lion tamer? If your skills are in organizing people, would you be as happy getting the 15 people in the little tiny car as fulfilling your transient dream of being shot from a cannon?

What are your skills now? How would they fit in at the circus? List the skills you'll need and where you'll learn or borrow them.

Don't forget: you may not be the only one who will have to learn some new skills. You're probably not riding into the sunset alone. You're taking people with you, and those people will need some training, too. Name your daydream. Does your spouse have the skills to accommodate that? Your kids? Do your associates? Look at your dreams from their point of view.

13

families and fellow travelers

In which you will find that:

1. Your nearest and dearest may not want to run away to the circus quite as much as you do.

2. Companies also have difficulties convincing people that change is beneficial.

3. You need to think your dream through from the point of view of those who are going to live it with you.

4. You may have to negotiate and make some trade-offs around your dream.

You're ready to change. You're ready to innovate. You're ready to bust out, boldly go where no person has gone before. Alas, the rest of the world—spouses, children, friends, supporters, and associates—balk like kids headed for the

> There is no such thing as "Fun for the Whole Family."
>
> —JERRY SEINFELD

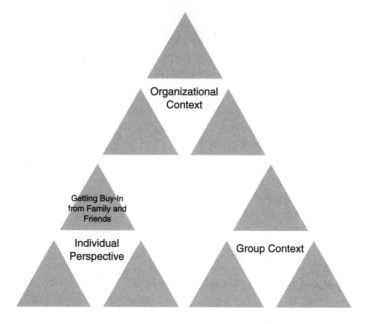

© *PeopleTech Consulting, Inc.*

dentist, even though you've patiently explained that this is a good idea (or thought you had). *Thought you had* is key.

Consider your dream of running away to the circus. Consider the people who can affect that goal, one at a time. How does the dream look to them?

As Seinfeld has pointed out, just because you're having fun, it doesn't mean that everyone is having a great time. And the person who isn't may let you know it at the least convenient moment. I call these people James Forsytes, after the elderly character in *The Forsyte Saga* by John Galsworthy, who was always muttering, "Nobody tells me anything."

Every family has at least one James Forsyte. Most of the time they're out of sight, out of mind, and out of touch. Then, just when you are making plans for something very important, James Forsyte complains that he was not consulted and digs in his heels. You may be able to carry on regardless, but depending on the position in the family, he may bring things to a screeching halt. Name the three James Forsytes in your family circle.

Organizations almost inevitably have their James Forsytes. Across the organization, you might have dozens or even hundreds of James Forsytes, endlessly complaining about the fact that nobody tells them what is happening. They don't listen and never call you, but woe unto you if you fail to keep them up to date. Some of them are quite capable of cutting you out of the company will.

Companies have spent billions keeping the flock informed. I know one organization with 5,000 employees, any one of whom will probably tell you that he or she is never told anything. Each of these people has a computer on his or her desk with an e-mail system brimming with the latest on what the company is doing. The company has three newsletters that everybody gets. The company has regular meetings at which the janitor is allowed to ask the VP of finance what's going on with his dental plan. All the office doors are almost always open. Yet still there's that Forsytian echo in the halls: "Nobody tells me anything."

Getting buy-in from people requires patience and good communication. No, let me rephrase that, it requires inexhaustible patience and endless communication. Without it, however, change is just somebody's wistful dream.

THE FORSYTE SYNDROME

You've no doubt seen the syndrome in corporations. R&D over in Bavaria wants to introduce the perfect coffee maker. It keeps coffee fresh all day. It doesn't make those little gargling sounds as it brews. There's an electric eye that monitors the coffee as it's dripping into the pot to make sure it's exactly as strong or weak as you want it. It has a small foot print that doesn't take up much counter room. And the carafe is elegant enough to be taken to the table.

The head of marketing in the United States, let's call him Jim, hasn't been consulted. This happens in a lot of companies. R&D has a permanent festering feud with marketing, whom they regard as Jurassic jerks whose role should be limited to revealing R&D's genius to the public and holding back the crowds so that the customers can buy in an orderly fashion. Marketing often sees R&D as a bunch of idle dreamers who don't really understand the consumer.

Jim in marketing gets his first look at the perfect coffee maker. He calls it a "nice experiment in technology," an "excellent example of how innovative this company can be," and a "good design exercise." Then he reaches into his top drawer and brings out the knife he keeps especially for this purpose and slips it neatly into R&D's back.

Jim's department produces letters from major chains saying that the buyers are dubious. He gets the corporation's tame home economist to say that Europe might be one thing, "but here in America, we make coffee differently." He has the lawyer draw up an opinion questioning the safety of an appliance that stays on all day and pointing to possible product liability lawsuits.

Result? We're still stuck with gargling coffee makers that turn the brew into oily acid after two hours. No change, no breakthrough, no progress.

Reason? Not jealousy, although there might be a little bit of that. The real problem is that R&D didn't get buy-in. There has been no real communication. Nobody got Jim on board, and Jim has some quite legitimate concerns. He wonders if the perfect coffee maker will make all the imperfect coffee makers that are currently in the product line suddenly obsolete, leaving them with much less shelf life. He wonders if the retailers will accept a coffee maker, however perfect, at this price point. He wonders how his team is supposed to sell something that is so advanced in a traditionally cautious market.

Here's another example. The CEO of a trust company comes up with a vision of a leaner, meaner, more consumer-responsive organization. He announces his vision at a meeting of senior management during a retreat at a resort with two golf courses, a lake, and a million pines.

As a first step, he challenges managers to produce plans within three months that will cut costs 5 percent within six months. The managers applaud, but if you've ever heard sweaty palms applauding, you'd recognize the real level of enthusiasm.

The managers head back to their various offices. Over the next month they meet in the sort of places where managers "just run into each other and start talking about the situation." Not so gradually, an informal consensus evolves. Cynics would notice that this consensus actually happens faster than any consensus is ever formed in favor of change. Cynics would be right.

On the appointed date, the managers submit their plans to get lean, mean, and responsive. The plans are enthusiastic. Their plans are well worked out. There are lots of charts, graphs, colors, and quotations. Much research is cited; many trees die. Cerlox binding shares go up.

What the plans say, almost without exception, is that the way to get lean, mean, etc., is to kill off those projects that the CEO likes best, the ones that really appeal to the board. This is a game bureaucrats often play with politicians: "Gee, Governor, we can cut the deficit if we stop all this gratuitous feeding of the orphaned and the elderly." Senior bureaucrats play the game well. Middle- and upper-level managers don't do it badly either.

Result? The organization gets meaner but no leaner. Managers have protected the fat that gives them status and the reason for their salary level. They have protected their reputations. And a lot of times they've acted just because they weren't part of the original decision. It isn't their dog and they feel honor bound to kick it.

GETTING BUY-IN FROM YOUR NEAREST AND DEAREST

Teddy Livvy is a person I run into at the cottage. He'll tie his fourteen-foot aluminum boat with its ancient motor to my dock and come in to look in my fridge: he's that kind of friend. Back in the city he manages (or tries to) a medium-sized company that makes herbal soaps and shampoos. He takes my beer, he leaves shampoo. It's a good deal. At my fighting weight, I need shampoo more than beer.

He started the company about ten years ago after he found that most soaps and some shampoos were making him sneeze and irritating his skin. He didn't have much money, but he did have an incredible array of relatives, all of whom bought a little stock and most of whom are glad they did. The exception is Aunt Diana, who had a large windfall in the form of the insurance policy payout on Uncle Frank. She bought more of Teddy's stock than most.

When Teddy comes up with a new idea, Aunt Diana is usually against it. Teddy wants to package a line of small soaps and little bottles of shampoos to go into the inns that are developing in recreational areas. It's modest volume, but the exposure to a fairly upscale consumer would be great. Aunt Diana is against it: "Nobody we know goes to those places."

Teddy thinks there's a good case for trying a test market in direct-mailed gift baskets of soaps and lotions, like gift baskets of flowers, possibly even marketing through florists as a nontraditional means of distribution. "You're going to send me soap by messenger on my birthday?" asks Aunt Diana. "What does that tell me? Next you'll send me knives."

Teddy thinks strawberry scented. She thinks roses, so the hand lotion won't "make me smell like jam."

All of this makes for lively board meetings. Teddy could have lived with that if the fuss ended with the board meeting. But Aunt Diana has a phone and knows how to use it. She'd lobby and she had a lot of time in which to do it. A bludgeoned extended family would start phoning Teddy and asking if strawberry was really such a good idea. Teddy would be beaten down.

He finally figured out, as so many of us do, that his greatest enemy could be his best friend. There have been 4,000 movies built around this concept. When he had a new idea, he'd immediately go to Aunt Diana. He'd bring the facts and figures. The conversation would go something like this, although I've made it much briefer: "Aunt Diana, in California and Minnesota they're finding that banana-scented conditioners are taking .05 percent of the market. If we did this in our market, we'd sell 22,000 units at a profit of eight cents per unit. And there might be a similar market for banana shampoo. So that would be about 50,000 units. It wouldn't interrupt our production. In fact, with the new machine we bought, we wouldn't have to buy any extra equipment, but the filling line would have to move a little faster. But, I don't know . . . bananas? Who likes bananas? A lot of people are against bananas. And should we make the filling line people work harder?" Within twenty-four hours, Aunt Diana would be on the phone to the other relatives saying things like "Teddy needs a little support for his bananas."

I've simplified the story. The whole truth is even stranger. Teddy makes a great half hour dinner-time recitation out of it. But the whole truth would boil down to the same thing. He gets his way by inviting people on board, involving them, and telling them all the facts. They were involved in the decision, and practically nobody I know would ever quit a decision they were involved in making. Pride of ownership is a beautiful thing.

A FEW OF THE REASONS THEY WON'T GO ALONG WITH YOU

In a book called *Why Employees Don't Do What They're Supposed to Do and What to Do About It*, Ferdinand F. Fournies gives a whole smorgasbord of reasons why individuals dig in their heels when somebody suggests doing something different or new. Here are just a few:

- They don't know why they should do it.

- They don't know how to do it.

- They don't know what they are supposed to do.

- They think your way won't work.

- They think their way is better.

- They think something else is more important.

- There is no positive consequence to them for doing it.

- They anticipate a negative response for doing it.

- There is no negative consequence to them for not doing it.

- They think they are doing it but they aren't.

- There are obstacles beyond their control.

- Their personal limits prevent them from doing it.

- They have personal problems that prevent them from doing it.

- No one could do it.

This is not a complete list, you understand, but it gives you an idea of what corporate change promoters are up against. And the list is just as true of a single-outlet donut shop as it is of a multinational. It is also true of your family.

So let's look at your particular case. Start with your spouse—or your bank manager. Why should he or she contribute to your running away to the circus? How should he or she contribute? What is he or she supposed to do? Isn't what you're doing now good enough? Isn't paying off the mortgage more important? What's been the matter with the way you've been living up till now? What's in it for him or her?

I remember a father who announced a change, a divorce, to his pre-teenage son. The son thought about it for a moment and then asked, "Will I still get my allowance?" You announce that you're going to transfer into the operations part of your organization. Your spouse asks if you'll still get every second Friday off in summer. You tell them you're being transferred to Denver. The family worries about the cottage.

Your change affects others, a whole host of others. And unless they can see the benefits to themselves, unless they see your reasoning clearly, they're going to stick out a foot and you're going to trip over it. You're enthusiastic and energetic about the possibilities; they're dubious, perhaps even checking with the lawyers about whether you could be committed before you ruin a life that seems perfectly good to them.

This is important. Most corporate changes fade away, not from lack of vision, but from lack of explanation and buy-in. A colleague of mine once visited a company to do some consulting work. As he stood chatting to an executive in the reception area, he asked casually about the company's mission statement. "We don't have one of those," said the executive. Beside them, the receptionist politely cleared her throat and pointed to the wall behind her head, where the mission statement was written in large letters. My colleague correctly concluded that the CEO had a little explaining to do—to her own people.

Sharing the vision is the first step, but only the first. The next step is talking about the benefits that change will mean to individuals. Management assumes that the troops will intuitively understand that the changes management wants to make will result in better lives and happier days for everyone. The troops immediately assume that the changes mean downsizing for some and longer days for others. They may be wrong, but no one has persuaded them otherwise.

You have a dream. Admirable. We should all have them, and the best ones possible. The dreamless make the world a duller place. But that dream is going to have to be sold. Or in the language of consultants and politicians, you're going to have to achieve buy-in.

HEY, WHAT ABOUT ME?

The first step in achieving buy-in is to make a list of all the people your dream is going to affect. Then you list the downside for each of them. This is important because it may alert you to the fact that there *is* a downside for them. If you want to leave your job as director of R&D to be a juggler or a farmer, they may lose face, for example. It may be hard for your kids to explain to their fellow creatures that Daddy's a juggler in a circus or Mom has started to raise llamas. I know that during one of my internships, it was sometimes hard for my father to explain to the neighbors that Marti was explaining sex to couples who were having difficulty with it. Sex needs no explanation on most farms, not to the animals and very seldom to the people.

Obviously, achieving buy-in may require some energetic thinking. You have to find or create a definite upside, and it would be better, in the words of Doctor Kissinger, if the explanation had the additional advantage of being true. "Daddy will be much happier," or "Think of the fun we'll have feeding the llamas every morning before we comb their wool for the sweaters we'll knit," don't quite cut it. You need solid, credible reasons:

- We'll work shorter hours.

- We'll have control over our destiny and won't be worrying about being fired.

- We'll be building up equity.

The more specific you can be about the benefit, the better. So as well as saying, "We'll work shorter hours," add "Starting on March 1, we'll work from 10:00 to 4:00." As well as saying, "We'll have control over our own destiny," add, "Over the next five years it's been estimated that my company will outsource 75 percent of the things I do for them now. I have a three-to-one chance of keeping the job I'm in now. An independent research company says that 82 percent of the people who buy the kind of franchise I plan to buy succeed and make a profit in two years."

One nice thing about using hard facts to make your case is that the James Forsyte in the crowd will need to have equally strong arguments to counter them. Otherwise, he's just blowing bubbles. The other nice thing about hard facts is that you'll learn more about the circus while you gather them. Start with the following table.

THE PERSON AFFECTED	THE DOWNSIDE	THE UPSIDE
Spouse	_____	_____
Child A	_____	_____
Child B	_____	_____
Child C	_____	_____
Parents	_____	_____

THE PERSON AFFECTED	THE DOWNSIDE	THE UPSIDE
Relative A		
Relative B		
Boss		
Assistant		
Partner		
Co-worker A		
Co-worker B		
Co-worker C		
Mentor A		
Mentor B		
Mentor C		
Banker		
Lawyer		
Source of Funds A		
Source of Funds B		
Source of Funds C		
Creditor A		
Creditor B		
Creditor C		
Friend A		
Friend B		

THE PERSON AFFECTED	**THE DOWNSIDE**	**THE UPSIDE**
Friend C	_____	_____
Neighbor A	_____	_____
Neighbor B	_____	_____

Look at your change from their point of view. Suppose your spouse announced one rainy Monday that he or she had decided to go out the door, turn left, and keep walking until he or she found the personnel manager for Barnum and Bailey. Your first reaction would be, "What have you been smoking?" Your second reaction, following rapidly on the heels of the first, would be, "Hey, what about me?"

"Hey, what about me?" What's going to happen to the lost income? Who's going to mow the lawn/make dinner/walk the dog/discipline the kids/handle the paperwork/remember if it's recycling day for bottles or for papers? The answer is to have first thought the travel out and then have a credible solution—or to be open to someone else's credible solution.

"Hey, what about me?" How do I explain this to my Mom/the kids/the Laughtons down the street/my boss/the person who approves our line of credit? You have to be ready with the explanation. You can't gloss it over. People are really worried, and it's no use saying they shouldn't be.

"Hey, what about me?" What did I do so wrong that you want to change everything? Why wasn't I consulted? Don't you care what I think? A large and understandable part of the hey-what-about-me's is emotional. We are all of us emotional animals, and emotions are real. Your course is to consult beforehand and build a chain of agreement.

Another reaction you may get is denial: "Honey, I know things have been difficult lately what with the recession/family illness/job uncertainty/unexpected debts/roof leaks/downsizing/transfer/daughter's wedding, but sooner or later things will go back to normal. Everything's fine the way it is. We don't need to change a thing." If you get this reaction, you will have to make your case for change carefully and patiently. You can't simply blurt out that there's a problem and there's going to continue to be a problem. You have to take it easy, explain the situation in detail, and be prepared to repeat your explanation many times.

Behind some of these reactions may be a little bit of envy. The person announcing the change is bound for a new adventure, a new beginning.

The person listening to the announcement may feel all the more hemmed in by his or her life in comparison. I remember how I felt when a colleague told me she was taking up a job offer in Geneva. I'd been stuck in meetings all day, and she was waxing lyrical about ski weekends in the Alps. I don't think my reaction was as enthusiastic as it might have been.

How does the prospect of someone else's change affect you? Suppose your child came in and said, "Yo, I'm out of here and into becoming a trapeze artist." After the urine test, what would your reaction be? Try it out loud, right now.

Suppose your executive assistant came in and said, "I'm going back to university to study medicine." After thinking about where you're supposed to pull a replacement out of a hat, what would your reaction be?

Or suppose a business associate dropped by your office and said, "We have to talk. I've decided I want to spend the rest of my life as a scriptwriter." Or your lawyer phoned and told you she wanted to be a reflexologist? Or a former mentor said that he had decided to take early retirement and take up boat building?

You'd be at least initially uncomfortable. You'd quite possibly get an attack of the hey-what-about-me's. You might be consumed with envy because your life suddenly seems very tame by comparison. And you'd start saying things like, "Admirable notion, Smithers, but is this the best possible time?" or "I understand where you're coming from. Let me get you a straitjacket." You might say, "Nobody tells me anything."

One of the problems with the surveys we did before undertaking this book was that we had very little response from those who had tried to change and failed. Presumably, this was for the same reason that very few people talk about losing at poker or about having an empty bucket at the end of a day of fishing. Failure to succeed, especially in such a pivotal decision as this, has a very quiet voice. But from my corporate experience, I can tell you that resistance to change is what usually sinks any good idea. From the dozens of interviews we had with those who successfully found their respective circuses, I can tell you that resistance was a major stumbling block. Reactions from aghast parents, nervous children, or associates who felt threatened could rattle even those with the steeliest wills.

The successful found ways to overcome the resistance. Not surprisingly, the ways they found were similar to the ways successful corporations have found to understand and overcome resistance to organizational change.

How to Break the News You're Bound for the Big Top

First rule: Don't break the news. Running in and yelling happily, "I've quit my job, but everything's okay: I've bought the floppy shoes and the red nose!" is going to run you into a wall of trouble before you've practiced your first professional pratfall. What you must do first is create a common understanding of the need for change.

First, you pick a time when nothing much else is going on and there will be an opportunity to talk. Just before Thanksgiving dinner, during your child's graduation, or on the eve of a family member's major surgery are all bad times to bring these matters up.

Then you explain the problem before you embark on your plan for the solution. For example: "I'm unhappy. There are a bunch of reasons I'm unhappy. I'm unhappy because I'm feeling professionally insecure because companies all around us are downsizing and our own company isn't handing out lifelong jobs any more. I feel I have to make a change so that we have more power over our own future. I trust us more than the company."

Or it could be: "I'm unhappy. The reason I'm unhappy is because my work is demanding but dull as dishwater and as repetitious as minimalist music. I feel like a record skipping into the same groove again and again. I want to make a change because I need to learn and grow instead of stagnating."

Or: "I'm unhappy because I don't like where we're living. I don't like the crime rates. I don't like the climate. I don't like the costs and I don't like the school system or the direction the local economy is headed. I think we should consider moving."

All of these are valid reasons for change. All of them have a corporate parallel that organizations have acted on. Organizations make changes because they're insecure about the economic climate, because they felt the need to revitalize themselves, and because they had business objectives in changing locations. But those companies that have made those kinds of changes have found that explaining the reason for the change is essential. They've put it on the record and made overcoming their variety of unhappiness an objective that everybody can understand and even sympathize with.

Second rule: Involve all the affected parties in the planning stage. People move more happily into a house when they've had some say in choosing or designing it. People enjoy a meal more if they've had a hand in preparing it. People get more out of a vacation if they've had some say in planning it.

Some decisions are yours to make. If you feel your true vocation in life is to be a lion tamer, then you should try to make it happen. It's your life—well, mostly. At the same time, however, it's strategically wise and just plain kind to talk to the people in your life about how you're going to get to that point, so that their lives aren't tossed in the air.

Involving them in the decision means more than asking for their opinions. One good and meaningful way is to ask them to collect data. Ask Person A to find out how many circuses there are and where they travel. Ask Person B to get the facts on how much a lion tamer gets paid and how many days off there are. Ask Person C to track down how much the chair and whip will cost. This has a couple of benefits. First, after looking into the situation, they won't be shooting from the hip or dealing in stereotypes: they'll either be aided or constrained by the facts. Second, you do actually need to know the price of equipment and a lot of other things. Third, the process of fact gathering could make them enthusiasts for reasons of their own.

Involving people also means asking for their ideas. I don't mean things like, "I don't think you should be a lion tamer." That's not an idea, that's an opinion. An idea would be: "I think the best place to study lion taming would be . . ." or "Let's go to one of those safari zoos and talk to the people there about what it's like to work with lions."

As I suggested in the previous chapter, part of getting people involved is getting them to assess what new skills they'll need and how and when they'll get them. Their decisions should be based on research: reading the books, surfing the Internet, and meeting face to face with people who currently have the responsibilities.

Involving people should additionally mean (and this is something some executives find difficult) actually incorporating their good ideas. If you're not going to use suggestions, don't ask for them. You'll buffalo the troops, and they'll know very quickly they're being buffaloed and start behaving accordingly. Plus you'll have demonstrated that you're a thick-eared bonehead.

Third rule: Be prepared to negotiate. Your teenagers don't want to leave their school, your spouse doesn't want to leave his or her job, your dog has a favorite fire hydrant, and the people in the next office don't want to have to look for someone who can write their reports. The rule is to disrupt only what needs to be disrupted. The more of what they like and need that they can hang on to, the more they'll let you change what you want.

You have to make trade-offs. I'll let you run away to any circus you want as long as it has a Jacuzzi. You'll let me run away to any circus I want as long as you can still see your folks on a regular basis. Ask people what they can't give up. See if you can fit it into your new life. Suggest alternatives. Make some trade-offs. It's called negotiation. You probably did it when you bought your last house or condo. Do it now.

Fourth rule: The best trick is no tricks. There are any number of manipulative executives at any number of corporations and organizations who cannot make a straightforward announcement without putting some kind of spin on it or are less than completely honest about how and why change will occur in the organization. This behavior inevitably encourages unions or groups of employees to start putting a spin on what they do and keeping their own secrets. The result? The entire organization winds up in a spin and nobody has the faintest clue what is going on.

No tricks means that you have to be open and honest. You don't overstate the upside. You don't ignore the downside. You don't hide evidence pro or con. The benefit of open and honest communication is that it usually forces people to be open and honest with you. In an open, honest situation, you can solve problems more easily.

This doesn't mean you should be slow to accentuate the positive. State the downside, but if you can honestly match it with a credible upside, get the words out of your mouth: "Yes, I'm going to be a circus clown. And when I become a clown, this family of five will have 20 percent fewer duodenal ulcers."

The alternatives to open and honest are closed and dishonest. And isn't that the circus you're trying your hardest to run away from?

Fifth rule: Look continually for areas of agreement. If you're a salesperson, you know that you have to narrow down the areas being discussed so that areas of contention can be handled more efficiently. You can do the same thing with your family. "We agree on moving, we agree on keeping the dog, and we agree that it isn't necessary to have a new Mercedes every three years. All that we're arguing about is whether I tame lions or tigers. Let's see if we can compromise on those." Keep to sweet reason. Ten times out of ten, at least in the business situations I've been in, attacking doesn't work.

Think about the last three people who've gone ballistic in business meetings you've been in. Where are they now? Think about the last three people who tried to achieve a realistic consensus. Where are they now?

Sixth rule: Be flexible. You are not charting an unchangeable course. There will be crossroads at which you can adjust your direction. Tell people this and define those crossroads if you can. Tell them that at those points you're willing to consider alterations in the change you're making. Be relentlessly reasonable. It makes unreasonable people nervous.

Your line is not, "I intend to open a pet shop and stick to it forever because that is where my heart is now and has ever been." Try this: "My target is $5000 a month after three months. If we aren't getting that, I'll explore three areas where we can make some alternative income. If we are taking in less than $3000 per month, I will have kept up my contacts at my present company and be keeping a weekly eye on what the job market is." Selling test drives is easier than selling cars and it's also more upfront.

This is not just for the benefit of your family. It will also help you plan better. You may be all set for a career as a professional gardener and landscaper, but you throw your back out after the first week. Because of the negotiation process, you have already worked out plan B.

14

throw away the manual

In which you will find out that:

1. Starting a new life will mean thinking for yourself, a notion that frightens some people.

2. It's a good idea to spell out what can go wrong and plan for it ahead of time.

3. You don't have to wait until you are forced to change: you can start by firing yourself from your current life.

4. You should decide what baggage you will take to the circus—and what you will leave behind.

Starting any second life, whether you choose to be a sword swallower, a jazz musician, a librarian, or the company's production manager, is going to require you to take responsibility and authority in

> When you're competing on knowledge, the name of the game is improvisation, not standardization.
>
> —JOHN SEELY BROWN AND
> ESTEE SOLOMON GRAY

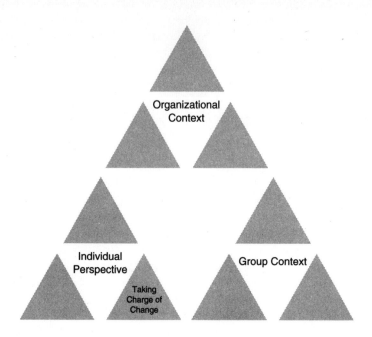

© *PeopleTech Consulting, Inc.*

some new areas of that life. You may have to assume authority for marketing your services rather than relying on another department to do that for you. If you are going to run any kind of business, however small, you will have to take on more responsibility and authority for financial decisions, location decisions, purchasing decisions, staffing decisions, and scheduling decisions. Are you ready for this? If not, how are you going to get ready?

When corporations ask employees to take on responsibility for decision making in their area of work, they often use the buzzword *empowerment*. I hate that word. It smacks of the Big Guys Up There being all generous and condescending to the Little People Down Here. I use the word *response-ability*, meaning the cut-the-mustard ability to do what needs to be done in the circumstances and the responsibility for making sure it gets done. What you need right now is the response-ability for seeing through the changes you want to make.

There's a catch to this, though. Response-ability isn't always an easy thing to master. I'll give you an example from a financial company. Financial companies do not always have visionary or dynamic CEOs. They do not always have charismatic ones either. This one had a CEO who was all three and not afraid to show it.

In a not-very-major branch office, there were a group of employees who were sincerely interested in their customers. Their customers were being ill-served by the company's policies and procedures manual, that fat book that told them in excruciating detail what to do in case A and what to do in case Z-12/076.

The CEO visited the office. He asked the people there whether there was anything they thought should be changed. The bravest, or it might have been the most honest of the group, said that there was. The policy and procedures manual was seriously out of date. It was based on high inflation, younger families, and two-tone cars.

The CEO asked for a copy and a copy was brought. The CEO took the policy and procedures manual, ripped it in two, and put the pieces into the recycling bin. The employees looked at the bin and then they looked at the CEO. The bravest of them asked what they should do now. The CEO replied, "You'll just have to think."

Radical suggestion. It would have been unthinkable in many organizations because the need for that skill has been taken away. You don't think, you follow directions, obey the standard operating procedures, comply with the dress code, hum the elevator music, and don't talk with your hands in your pockets.

I think that this particular rot set in years ago with Taylorism, scientific management, and the application of assembly-line techniques to processes that were anything but routine and repetitious. Really, it's enough to make you weep with frustration at the waste of human brain power. The idle capacity of corporate intelligence wouldn't be tolerated if that capacity were something like a computer or an airplane or even a grommet punch sitting there and gathering dust. And we've been keeping this capacity idle for years.

Now, after years of preventing employees from making use of all of their intelligence, we tell them that there's no such thing as job security and that they've got to add value every day of their lives or they'll be in the next wave of downsizing. Employees are desperately scrambling to find the new manual that tells them how to add value in six easy steps. Talk about a recipe for complete confusion and demoralization.

What does your job demand of you? What does it reward? And how much opportunity do you get to take meaningful decisions (really meaningful, not just the difference between ordering green file folders or yellow file folders)? Because, if you don't have that opportunity, you may need some practice before you open your own circus.

FACING UP TO THE WHAT THENS?

Let's take three examples of people who are considering making a change, but have not yet made the decision to leave their current jobs.

I'm an administrative assistant in my company's legal department. I don't get to organize my days. I do what the legal staff need me to do, when they need me to do it. I've actually learned quite a lot about the law just from dealing with the material and working on their reports and correspondence, but I'm not qualified to use my knowledge. I would love to go to law school and learn to be a lawyer myself, but the idea scares me. What if I failed? What then?

—JANET, AGE 37

I'm a teacher. I've worked in elementary schools for twenty-three years. I used to spend hours developing creative lesson plans and coming up with new ways to teach reading and spelling. But the methods I used to rely on are considered old-fashioned, and I've got to stick to the set curriculum, which I think is a joke. It doesn't challenge kids. And it doesn't challenge me. I'm just going through the motions now. I want to get out, but this is all I know. I think all the creativity has been drained out of me. I've considered teaching adult literacy classes where I might have a bit more leeway in choosing how I teach, but I can't seem to get myself moving. I might find that all my ideas have dried up. What would I do then?

—TERRY, AGE 43

I've been in accounts payable since the beginning of time. I need about a quarter percent of my brain to do my job, it's so routine. The trick to getting through the afternoons around here is learning to sleep with your eyes open. Doesn't seem to affect my productivity. I want to try something different, I really do. But I have no idea what to do. All anybody's going to do is just hire me for my accounting experience, and then it starts all over again. I've considered working part-time and taking the time off to learn the antiques trade, which is kind of an interest of mine, but I keep procrastinating. Next year. No, the year after that. One day I'll find that next year is the year I'm due to retire anyway. What happens then?

—EPHRAIM, AGE 42

Three bad cases of the what thens? When I hear these kinds of comments at a client company (and I hear remarkably similar comments about everything from removing management layers to relocating the cafeteria), I usually sit down with the senior management team and get them to spell out all the possible disasters that might result from that change. We write everything down in detail, putting it in black and white. It's depressing sometimes, but also cathartic. People say things like:

- "We'll run down our credit availability."

- "We'll really be stretching our production capacity."

- "The union will never accept it."

- "It will confuse the customers."

We then go around the table and make contingency plans: "If this happens we will . . ." For every single disaster, we have a disaster action plan—a real one. These are not hypothetical problems, and we don't make up hypothetical responses. We put a lot of care and thought into disaster action plans.

- "We'll get the suppliers to help us finance by going into partnership with them."

- "We'll build in a productivity bonus."

- "Let's see how the union will react when we tell them about the potential new jobs."

- "We'll launch a public awareness campaign to explain the new procedures and train the front-line staff how to deal with the changeover."

We put in lots of detail. People start to look a bit more positive. They're not just looking at the problems, they're starting to look at the solutions. And it often turns out that the solutions they're coming up with can be used in other areas of the company.

Then we look at the change again. And we look at the one disaster that nobody ever mentions the first time around: the disaster of not changing at all. What are the downsides of staying exactly in this position? Same work processes, same market share, same product line. Now everyone is wide awake.

Comparing the disaster scenarios with the prospect of remaining unchanged is interesting. Because there is no contingency plan for the effects of staying still, other than carrying out the change, *the only contingency for the appalling prospect of staying the same is change.* And you've made sure that all the angles of the change program have been covered.

At this point, the senior management team has painted itself into something of a logical corner. The basic decision has been transformed from whether or not to take action to what type of change should be made. In the face of that kind of decision, the people who usually scream "whoa!" start actively attempting to find the best change possible.

Try this yourself. Look all the possible disasters squarely in the face and then design a way around them. Suppose Janet fails law school? Well, she might, although I think she's already better qualified than a lot of law students. But suppose she failed some of her courses? What then? Well, she could retake those courses. She could transfer to a course for paralegals that might be easier. She could study part-time and minimize her risk. She could do some word processing and other tasks for law professors in return for coaching. There are quite a few options.

And if she stays put? She'll never even become a paralegal. She'll spend the rest of her life wondering if she would have made it and feeling that somehow life shortchanged her, when all she's done is shortchanged herself.

Should Ephraim, the accountant, open an antique store? Suppose nobody comes? Well, then he's lost some money, although we doubt he's going to fail altogether. Worst comes to worst, he can do accounting for other antique stores. If Ephraim stays put, he will not be happy. Eight hours a day wondering if you could have done it is a long time to be unhappy. How does the cost of the antique store compare with ten more angry years? What contingency plan is in place to deal with the fallout that would come from not changing?

If you stay put, what's your contingency plan for dealing with your frustration or unhappiness?

First, Fire Yourself

"Being fired is a liberating experience, so I decided to fire myself. I didn't like my attitude. My work habits were getting bad: I was coming in late and leaving a touch early. I was getting really good at doodling plans of the perfect garden during meetings. I was depressing my fellow employees. They used to rise to my level and now they were sinking to it. I wasn't a team player. My last good idea at work had been to extend lunch by an hour. I was getting stale. So I gave myself two hours to clean out my desk and went downstairs to hand in my security pass. I was tempted to tell the security people never to admit me again to the building, but I didn't quite have the nerve.

"I went home and told my wife I'd been fired. She said the usual things, sympathized, cursed the person who'd fired me, and then said, 'You know it's probably for the best. You didn't fit.' True enough. I used to fit, but I didn't anymore.

"So in a matter of hours I was shopping for a destiny, new beginning, whatever you want to call it. I think if I hadn't fired myself, if I'd hung around that place for a few more years, I'd really have been stuck. I would have become one of those bi-monthly salary junkies, a status quo addict. You meet a lot of them. So here I am with a garden center instead. Want an azalea?"

I have talked to dozens of counselors who work with people who have been fired. They help the downsized, the dispossessed, the outplaced, and the de-hired. They see a lot of pain and turmoil. They know that some people will never completely get over the shock. On the other hand, they very often see people turn their severance packages into their dreams and go to work happy.

Getting fired is, for a lot of people, an experience in liberation equivalent to leaving the army or getting your final divorce papers. At first your time is fully occupied coping with the transition. But gradually you come to realize that new options are opening up. Only one option has closed: returning to the job, the army, or the marriage. Everything else is possible. You don't have to compare these opportunities with your present job because you don't have a job. That adds to your freedom of choice.

Is it ever advisable to fire yourself? That's a complicated question, and I fall back on my time-proven answer: is the pain of remaining the same great than the pain of changing? This hard question demands an answer.

In large companies that have gone through major downsizings, I've noticed that a sizable percentage of those who were shown the door found exciting and entrepreneurial pursuits to replace their old positions. I've seen a survey that found about 75 percent of these people now felt they were working harder. Most felt they were making less money. But most said firmly that they were happier.

So perhaps firing yourself isn't such a crazy idea. It's the ultimate move in response-ability. It puts you, slam! right up against the situation. You have to face it. You have to innovate. You have to put afterburners on the change process because otherwise you're going to start getting those whining calls from the folks who carry your mortgage.

Firing yourself also helps you face one of the essential truths of our millennial age: we're all on our own. Like outplacement or divorce, it's both scary and liberating. It's not a solution for everybody because it is drastic and dislocating, but I mention it because it is, in a sense, the ultimate act of response-ability.

NOT WANTED ON THE VOYAGE

Change, however, is not just about taking charge, it's also about letting go. Any change means giving up something. You're excited about leaving a boring job but apprehensive about losing the steady paycheck that goes with it. You can't wait to move to Taos, but you're going to miss your neighbors in Cleveland. You're looking forward to working from home with no boss breathing down your neck, but you're not quite so happy about leaving behind your well-equipped office and your administrative assistant.

We all carry baggage. That baggage might be well loved or it might be the kind of stuff you hope they'll lose at O'Hare so you can be rid of it without blame. Whatever it is, you have to scrutinize it carefully and imagine life without it.

A lot of people are having difficulty with the shift from the entitlement mentality to the "earn-it" mentality. These days you have to constantly think of yourself as providing a service, not just filling a job. You have to present yourself as a solution to the employer's problems or needs, and you have to keep proving yourself. It's a daunting prospect, but those who can adapt to the new way of working will be successful.

—DOUG MATTHEWS, EXECUTIVE VP, RIGHT MANAGEMENT CONSULTANTS, CINCINNATI

What are you prepared to give up and what are you going to take with you? Consider the story of Robert Louis Stevenson.

He wrote the poem opposite when he lived in Edinburgh, Scotland, where the pubs are warm but your bedroom isn't heated and the latitude is the same as southern Alaska. In 1883 he wrote *Treasure Island* and with the proceeds, he was able to take a chartered schooner in 1888 to the islands of

> *I should like to rise and go*
> *Where the golden apples grow;*
> *Where below another sky*
> *Parrot islands anchored lie.*
>
> —ROBERT LOUIS STEVENSON,
> "TRAVEL"

the Pacific to pick out one that would be his own personal paradise. He chose Western Samoa, complete with a house on the hill, deferential servants, cooling breezes, wide porches, and the fragrance of tropical flowers.

The change from Edinburgh to Samoa was propelled by pain. In with all the rest of the baggage, Stevenson brought tuberculosis. He also brought his wife and children and his job. He had chosen Western Samoa because it was one of the few Pacific islands with regular (monthly) postal service, so he could write and continue to earn money. I did say he was Scots. He even brought a few quaint customs from his homeland: he insisted his Samoan servants wear kilts. He made the change, his doctor didn't give him much choice, but he never left Scotland behind completely.

Let's take another example: Paul Gauguin, the painter. Before I dug into his story, I'd been carrying around a vision of him as a nineteenth-century Parisian stockbroker who craved a new life and a new way of painting that the world wasn't quite ready for. He cut himself off from his mundane and middle-class existence and fetched up on a beach with oil paints, fresh coconut milk, and a fourteen-year-old girl without a training bra.

The facts are these. Gauguin dithered. He went back to France for a couple of years before returning to the islands. He couldn't decide which island to return to. He fumbled between Tahiti and the Marquesas.

He abandoned his job (and family) not because of an artistic vision but because the brokerage business was in the dumper. He bailed out because of business pain.

He didn't even seem to enjoy paradise all that much, at least according to the letters he wrote back to France. They sound like the usual moanings of the inconvenienced tourist who can't get the brand of mineral water he or she prefers.

And he brought baggage: venereal disease and a drug problem. To quote the brain surgeon, "You can run but you can't hide," which I always thought was a pity because some days I'd like to do both. However, your baggage will seek you out as relentlessly as a Swissair luggage agent.

The question becomes which baggage do you want to take and which will you leave behind? Imelda Marcos left behind a huge collection of shoes when she left the Philippines. Stevenson wanted to keep his postal facilities. Kids take teddy bears on vacation and leave their insulin behind.

Take the following test. It's sort of the game you play in which you imagine your house is on fire. Do you save the cat, the last picture of Gran, the prom corsage, or the stock certificates? If you're changing completely or even partially, you're not allowed to take all of it. Maybe you could try this at a party: "What would be the first thing you rescue when the hurricane arrives?" It's an interesting piece of entertainment and, like asking someone you just met what they'd like to hear on the jukebox, it's just as defining.

We'll make the game a little easier. We'll let you rescue two or three things—four, if that'll make you happy.

What I'd rescue

☐   My family

☐   My pet(s)

☐   My job

☐   My sector of the economy

☐   My present body

☐   The place I live in

☐   The area I live in

☐   The way I spend my spare time

☐   My collection of _____

☐   My clothes

What I'd rescue

☐ My personal papers

☐ My social life

☐ My salary

☐ My benefits

☐ My perks

☐ My boss

☐ My friends

☐ My colleagues

☐ My car

☐ My status symbols

☐ My fitness program

☐ My cell phone

☐ My bad habits

☐ The policy and procedures manual

You also can play the game—ideally after a few Martinis—reversing the process: what would you immediately chuck in the fire? Either way, the game is (if you play it honestly) an instructive way of assessing just how much you really want to change. What you rescue is the way you define yourself, the things that you probably think help make you who you are. What you throw in the fire and maybe douse with a little gasoline is what's causing you pain, what's surplus to requirements.

Warning: there are at least five things wrong with this test.

1. It's too simplistic. If it were that easy, we'd all be at the beach, canoeing down the Nahanni, or doing whatever we define as fun. And the world's office towers would be deserted except by those who love office towers.

2. It doesn't address what should be new about your life. It's all *delete* or *save* but no *insert*. You're burning bridges instead of building them. You're running away or running with instead of running to.

3. Because it doesn't address what should be new in your life, it doesn't get down to decisions about your positive urges like learning something new, finding a new place to live, or becoming a vegetarian.

4. It doesn't give you a plan with targets and dates and all that good stuff to make sure you're on track.

5. Life isn't really like this. Even if your house is on fire, you don't get to choose what you keep. Even when you run away to the circus, some things will follow you whether you want them to or not. This game is just to make you think about your current life and how well it fits you.

GUILT-EDGED CHANGE

Change involves guilt at some point. Leaving a mate, selling a house, downsizing your aspirations, giving up the job Mom always wanted you to have, or changing your barber all have serious guilt quotients. The size of the guilt will be reflected in your stress levels. Those stress levels have been quantified by research.

You are no doubt familiar with the Holmes-Rahe stress scale. Different life events are assigned numbers: If you add up the events that you are going through at any one time, you come up with a probability of health problems in the next year.

EVENT	VALUE	YOUR SCORE
Death of a spouse	100	____
Divorce	73	____
Marital separation	65	____
Death of a close family member	63	____

EVENT	VALUE	YOUR SCORE
Personal injury or illness	53	___
Marriage	50	___
Being fired at work	47	___
Marital reconciliation	45	___
Retirement	45	___
Pregnancy	40	___
Business readjustment	39	___
Change in financial status	38	___
Death of a close friend	37	___
Change to a different line of work	36	___
Mortgage foreclosure	30	___
Change in responsibilities at work	29	___
Outstanding personal achievement	28	___
Spouse begins or stops work	26	___
Change in living conditions	25	___
Revision of personal habits	24	___
Trouble with boss	23	___
Change in working hours or conditions	20	___
Change in residence	20	___
Change in schools	20	___
Change in social activities	18	___
Vacation	13	___
Christmas	12	___

If you score more than 300 points for the changes going on in your life right now, there's an 80 percent chance you will have health problems in the next year; 200–300 points is a 50 percent chance; 150–200 is a 37 percent chance.

The numbers are a bit arbitrary and could be weighted according to the importance you place in your work life versus your home life or your financial situation versus your social situation. Still, they give you an idea of how stress can mount up.

You will notice that both good and bad changes are included, from bereavement to outstanding personal achievement. This may have something to do with the guilt factor. Success can be as difficult to cope with as failure because you may feel that you haven't completely deserved it, that you are getting all the credit for something that was a joint effort, or that you achieved it at the expense of someone else's failure.

If you are going to take response-ability for your life, you have to face the guilt and the stress fairly and squarely. You will feel the change, and so will the people around you.

Play the "What I'd rescue" game anyway. It helps you focus. If you've been daydreaming about running an electronic cottage industry in Provence, it'll reveal what you must give up to start actually doing it. If you've had a compelling vision of yourself as a fishing guide in Muskoka, it may kick you into thinking about the possibilities more clearly. You may discover that you don't really want to change at all. All you want are the daydreams and you want to keep all the baggage.

Baggage you can check. Reality . . . no. And reality, sometimes, is beyond our control. Weather, the economy, political events, and natural disasters will affect how and whether we get to live our dream. I have to tell you a story about a German looking for Paradise. The story is stolen from an out-of-print book called *Blueprint for Paradise*, which is a slim but potent volume of how to build a house on a tropical island. The German in the story was looking for the best possible place to settle. Perfect climate. Perfect topography. Good for growing food. A dash of civilization. After much searching he found it and settled there in a hut made of the native vegetation. Inside there was a table covered with local fruits and vegetables and the occasional roast pig. The sunrises were beautiful. The sunsets were calming.

The year in which our hero settled there was 1939. The island was Guadalcanal.

Sometimes you don't just carry your own baggage, but you have to carry the world's as well. That doesn't make it not worth the effort, but it does make it worth realizing that whatever course you take you're occasionally going to find a roach in the strawberries.

part three

at the circus, there be tigers

15

it doesn't happen overnight— not with the corporations, and not with you

---

In which you will find out that:

1. People and organizations going through change usually experience it in five stages.

2. Just because you haven't completed all the stages doesn't mean you aren't making progress toward your goal.

3. People hate to change, but love to experiment.

Corporations don't change overnight, even when they face a crisis. We've found that corporate change happens in five stages (no, I'm not talking about denial, anger, bargaining, depression, and acceptance). People, too, need time to deal with change. How long did it take you to transform yourself from a student into a professional or to adjust to marriage, divorce, or children?

If you can identify which of the stages you're in, it will help you get a view of what's going to happen next. It's one way to get a more

People are impatient. They want results right away. Business people are trained to work towards objectives and accomplishments, but making significant change is more like a marathon than a sprint and the objective is often uncertain. When we're in the middle of the journey it may feel like failure. We aren't sure where we're going or if we're doing the right thing. It's important not to give in to that feeling of failure, to let go of the need for certainty. Lots of people are miserable for a few years before they get the gift of change. It's also important to realize that we cannot force the pace and make the change go faster.

—REBECCA MADDOX, PRESIDENT AND
FOUNDER, CAPITAL ROSE INC.

organized view of what sometimes appears to be a disorganized process.

Of course, the minute you suggest to anyone that this is going to happen to you in predictable stages, people's backs go up. People pride themselves on being distinct individuals, with an individual way of doing everything. They dress individually, they eat different foods, and they watch different television shows.

Ah yes, but we're all human. We grow up in a series of fairly predictable stages from ankle biters to angst-absorbed bundles of hormones to adults (we hope). Take it as a given and get over it. You will change in these predictable steps.

STAGE ONE: IGNORING THE NEED FOR CHANGE

Companies do it; people do it. They do it because they're unaware of the need for change: "We will always have a 50 percent share of the cat litter market because we've reached a size where nobody can take that away from us" or "Mabel would never divorce me." They live in the present, if they're not living in the past.

Companies and people also ignore change because they reject the need for change: "If it ain't broke, don't fix it" and "Why leave such a nice home with such a great view of Three Mile Island?"

Or they may ignore the need for change while giving the idea lip service: "We're a dynamic, forward-thinking organization; it says so right here in the manual" or "I've always prided myself on keeping myself current; right now I'm learning Esperanto."

Some people work very hard to ignore the need to change because their lives are so painful that considering the alternatives might make it feel even worse. I've known men and women who scraped themselves out of bed each day at 6:00, ate some kind of granola bar while reading the business section of the newspaper, and drove themselves to their office or

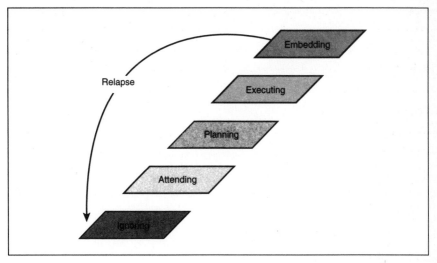

© *PeopleTech Consulting, Inc.*

their factory screaming at the traffic. They'd miss a doctor's appointment for a meeting on organizational revitalization. They'd miss a day's fishing for "An Executive Retreat on Our Future on the Internet." They thought lunch was a luxury they weren't allowed and family dinners were optional. They couldn't sleep well. They woke up rehearsing meetings in their minds or wondering about the state of health of some machine on the shop floor. And if you asked them, they'd say something like, "Things are going really well, really great."

It isn't easy to admit that you no longer fit into your own life. How long you stay in the ignoring stage depends on how sensitive you are to changes in your environment and on your own belief in your ability to change that environment or find a different one.

STAGE TWO: ATTENDING

I'll repeat the mantra: "Nothing changes until the pain of staying the same is greater than the pain of changing." The fact that I've trotted it out so often that it's beginning to develop slightly flat feet doesn't change the fact that it's true.

Most people don't pay attention to losing weight until the inconvenience (both social and physical) of not losing weight is greater than their love of Reese's Pieces. They may have filled the top shelf of their library with diet books, but there's dust on them until that moment that they can't fasten any of their belts or they catch sight of themselves unexpectedly in a mirror and mistake themselves for a sumo wrestler.

Most companies don't start to think about change until they notice that the bottom line has taken on the color of blood. They may readjust the corporate management chart, adopt a new slogan, or add a product line, but they don't really notice the need for real change until they hear the shareholders making guttural noises in the back of their throats.

Most politicians don't think about change until the pollsters tell them that voters are taking an inordinate interest in the opposition. Most dogs will continue trampling your tulips until you convince them that the pain involved in continuing this pastime is greater than the pain involved in having a nice nap on the patio.

The pain can involve money, social pressure, status, or even physical pain. Ask someone who gave up Camels when the pain of breathing got to be too much.

Pain prompts the realization of the real need for change. It propels you into the attending stage, where you seriously intend to change something sometime in the future but you haven't quite picked out what or when. You don't deny the reasons to change and, in fact, can recite them:

> "The work isn't fulfilling."
>
> "Competition is taking away 3 percent of our market share a year."
>
> "I'm gaining eight ounces a month."
>
> "The average age of our customers is now 58 years old and is going up by nine months annually."
>
> "I'm always tired."
>
> "I'm bored witless."

At this point, you may spend a lot of time dreaming about change, from the unlikely (winning the lottery, inheriting a castle in Spain, being elected president) to the simplistic (everything would be perfectly fine if you could just get enough sleep/reduce the mortgage payments/get your boss to see reason).

It takes time and a hard look at yourself to go beyond this wouldn't-it-be-nice-if stage and actually start weighing the benefits involved in change against the reasons you have for not exchanging your first life for a second chance. You have to go from "Wouldn't it be nice if I ran away to the circus?" to "If I ran away to the circus, I'd have fewer corporate benefits but more psychic benefits; I'd have less status but more fun; I'd have to clean up after the trick ponies but I wouldn't have to kiss butt."

Still, we procrastinate. Some corporations get stuck at this stage. Their engines might be roaring and the memos might be flowing, but they're not getting anywhere because they still have one foot on the brake. People meet. They discuss possibilities for change. They report to each other. They do everything but make progress.

Two ideas might get things jump started. One comes from People Tech's experience. One other I stole from a delightful book by Dale Dauten called *The Max Strategy*. It's okay for me to steal it because Dale had the wit and wisdom to steal it from a man called Max Elmore. Read the book.

The People Tech technique is to ask those involved at the company to quantify the benefits of changing. One example includes a large insurance company that was stuck in the attending mode toward a quality control program. They were saying things like, "It'd be great because then we could do a nice ad campaign about it" and "It wouldn't be great because then we would be sort of admitting that we didn't have a quality program before."

The consultant asked each of the participants to figure out what would be the financial benefit if the program were given the go ahead. He reduced the discussion to something that was measurable.

Members of the group reported the lowest benefit of establishing the program was $50,000. The top end was $1 million. That kicked them out of the attending stage and into action. A possible bottom line got them off their asses.

The benefits of running away to your circus might not be reduced to dollars and cents as easily, but it isn't dollars and cents you're necessarily after. Your motivations are deeper and broader. Write down your core values. Write down what drives you daily. Then write yourself a report on how the change you think you want to make would improve those things. Putting it in black and white should help you move your process along. And it'll give you an interesting document to show your stakeholders and the board of YouInc.

Dale Dauten's valuable stolen idea is based on this premise: *People hate to change, but people love to experiment*. This is a fairly spectacular insight. People hate to change ("I don't want to get married . . .") but they love to experiment (". . . but would you care to fool around in the back seat for a while?").

People hate to change. You'll get rock-steady votes against running away to the circus. However, people love to experiment. You'll get enthusiasm for spending a week at the circus.

Dauten—and his mentor, Elmore—add a further insight to this principle. They claim that experiments never fail. A week at the circus or a 15-minute tussle in the back of the car both tell you something. It may be good news. It may be bad news. But at least it's news and it lets you know something, if only about yourself.

STAGE THREE: PLANNING

At the next stage, the future gets nearer: You actually begin to plan specific actions to reach specific goals. You acknowledge the headache. You're deciding on the remedy.

There are two potential dangers in this stage. You can rush it or you can prolong it. People are tempted to rush through the planning stage when the pain of the present has become so insistent that any alternative at all seems better than staying the same. This is usually the route to bankruptcy in business and unhappiness in personal life. People buy franchises without researching the market, the product, the competition, or the location. People sell up and move to a new country only to find that they hate it for reasons they could have foreseen if they'd taken the time to do their homework.

Perhaps the tendency to skimp on planning comes from a misunderstanding about what plans are. They're not what you do before you change, they are part of the change itself.

> Plans are important in organizations, but not for the reasons people think . . . . Plans are symbols, advertisements, games, and excuses for interactions . . . . They are symbols in the sense that when an organization does not know how it is doing or knows that it is failing, it can signal a different message to observers . . . . Plans are advertisements in the sense that they are often used to attract investors to the firm . . . . Plans are games because they often are used to test how serious people are about the programs they advocate . . . . Finally, plans become excuses for interaction in the sense that they induce conversations among diverse populations about projects that may have been low priority items.
>
> —KARL WEICK

Read the quotation in the box above. What Weick says is true, not only for organizations, but for individuals. You need personal plans to symbolize where you want to go, to advertise YouInc. to the rest of the world, to flirt with ideas about the future, and to act as talking points with your friends and family. As you plan, you start to change, and your ideas about change start to change, and the people around you start to look at you a little differently. It's an important part of the process.

However, don't have such a good time planning that you stay in this stage forever. You're likely to get run over by the future while you stand in the road gazing at a map. Remember John Lennon's remark that life is what happens while you're making other plans?

Corporations often put major efforts into their plans, attacking every possible glitch, addressing every possible benefit, and listing every possible tactic. At one company I worked with, the planning took over a year, involved hundreds of people, and cost over $1 million. And by the time the plan came out, nobody had enough energy to execute it. The product turned out to be the plan rather than the change. It's not much use when the show car never hits the road.

I knew a very careful man who was in the broadloom business. It was the family business, and he was the eldest son. Although he didn't choose the business for himself, he gave it everything he knew how to give. He took presentation courses so he'd be able to sell better to corporate accounts. He was one of the first people I knew who understood how computers could handle inventory control and he put his ideas into action. He spent weekends showing broadloom to couples in housing developments. He was succeeding in terms of his family's expectations ("We're going to build a dynasty!"), but he knew he wanted something different in his life. His dreams were about importing certain gourmet products from Europe that weren't easily available in his part of the country. He studied the field. He wrote down everything that would happen in a critical path. He talked to people. He read magazines. And for about four years that's what he did with his dream: he planned it, improved it, and then improved the improvements. Planning the dream became his main focus outside of his job, and those plans became more and more elaborate. He could tell you costs, suppliers, customer demographics, trade patterns, and computer resources—everything but the date. He never got to the date.

This book says that you should spend more time planning than most people do. However, this book also says, right here, that you should remember that the plan is not the ultimate goal. So give yourself a time limit.

STAGE FOUR: EXECUTING

At the executing stage, you make sure the stove is turned off, the newspaper delivery has been canceled, and the post office knows where to forward mail. You lock the door and head for the circus. The future's in your face.

You might as well know right now that you will be tempted to turn around, unlock the door, check the stove again, sit down for a few minutes, and decide that maybe you won't make it to the circus today. Tomorrow, maybe. Maybe Thursday would be better: then you could be really sure you'd canceled newspaper delivery, too.

The largest corporations have done this. Ask the Chevrolet division how long it took them to bring out their new Corvette—or read about the painful process in a book called *All Corvettes Are Red*. Intelligent governments have done the retrograde stumble, announcing the brave new vision and then having sober second thoughts, aided by broad consensus and abetted by a failure of will or guts.

Anyone who has ever tried to quit smoking or change any other habit recognizes the syndrome. You've joined the fitness club. But after four workouts, you have a day when working out seems too much trouble and effort. You have a couple or several of these days in a row. You rationalize that you have to save your energy for thinking or painting the backyard fence and besides you don't have time because . . .

Of course, you're probably under stress right now. You may think you couldn't possibly handle a lot of change at this point in your life.

This is a dangerous period. Ask a smoker. Ask a yo-yo dieter. Give me a call.

STAGE FIVE: EMBEDDING

The embedding stage is where you cajole yourself, kick yourself, cheerlead yourself, reward yourself, or do whatever it takes to keep the execution stage going, progressing, and even accelerating. You struggle to avoid relapse. It is a struggle. Anybody who says she was able to change overnight is lying through her teeth. Ever gotten anything really good without a struggle?

Relapse happens in organizations all the time. People suddenly find that section 82A of the plan can't be put into effect right now and so they'll continue acting under the provisions of the former procedures manual for the immediate future. The immediate future turns into years.

Alcoholics Anonymous and the other twelve-step groups spotted the problem long ago. They realized that to embed change, people need constant reminding of the benefit of the change. Weekly reminding works; daily is even better. Corporations do this, too. Tracking demonstrable progress made over such-and-such a time period and reporting it to everyone involved keeps people motivated.

You can do the same thing for YouInc. and you should. It's not just to remind the others, it's to remind you. And you should keep on reminding yourself until the change is embedded, until the new becomes as comfortable as the old.

> *Someone said that when willpower and imagination lead in two different directions, imagination will always win. Imagination is more powerful than sheer willpower. Therefore, to have a high image of what one is to become and concentrate one's attention upon it is to move toward it almost automatically; but to spend all one's time fighting against the evil impulses is to keep one's mind so much upon them that they have a better chance to get hold of one. What gets your attention gets you, finally.*
>
> —G. ARTHUR CASADAY

16

you don't have to do it all at once: how to test drive your second life

---

In which you will find out that:

1. You can experiment with your second life during vacations or weekends or even part time during the week.

2. Experimenting may infect you with the desire to change more permanently. It may even infect your nearest and dearest with the desire to change.

Eleven months of every year, Don Brown gets up, shaves nicely, combs his hair nicely, puts on a superior white shirt and a superb suit, gets into the Jaguar, and drives to the glass tower where he dispenses advice on mergers and acquisitions in a calm, charming manner.

Ask his secretary about him and she'll say he's "Steady. And kind." His clients think he's insightful and innovative, "The kind of man who's going to get himself through with logic and fairness and not by bullying. He's going to get his way, however, and he's very worthwhile because of that ability."

His peers will say he's "Professional. Interested in what you say. Very persuasive in what he has to say." Ask one of his competitors in the game, a person who has fought with Don's client for control of two large corporations, and he'll say "Don is unbeatable. If you lose against him you've lost. But if you win you still lose because the street thinks you're a crass, unethical dork, just on the street's principle that anyone who beats Don must be one. He's no fun to play with. He's probably nice on purpose. The same way I'm a dork on purpose."

> The human mind, once stretched to a new idea, never goes back to its original dimensions.
>
> —OLIVER WENDELL HOLMES

Hah. I am one of the few who know what Don Brown does the other month of the year.

He gets up, shaves nicely, combs his hair nicely, picks up a suitcase, gets into the Jaguar, heads to the airport, and jets to another city. He gets off the plane, gets into a rented car, drives to a writer's colony, and spends a month in a hut in the woods writing rather gory action thrillers that are published under a name I can't reveal to you.

I asked him why. "I like to write." No further explanation.

Don Brown is only one of a few people I've discovered who run away to the circus once a year. Another is the chief executive of a privately owned company. Each year he takes a month to six weeks off and runs away to a different circus. One year the circus was being a sous-chef in a restaurant in northern California. Another year it was being a tour guide in New York. A third year he was leading a secret life as the assistant to one of those house painters who can make your living room wall look like marble or compressed straw.

"The first year taught me that fast cooking doesn't have to taste like reheated Play-Doh. That was valuable to me and it was valuable to the way I run this company. Who's going to argue with me in a meeting when I can say I'm the only person in the room who's been a professional chef in a restaurant where they're paying more than $1.89 for an entree?" Good point.

"The weeks doing the tour guide thing in New York were terrific! You'll learn more about things about people from across the country than you'd learn in most boardrooms. There's a presumption in a lot of boardrooms that all Americans drive BMWs or want to drive BMWs. Board members confuse Americans' aspirations with their own. I like bringing it up in meetings. You know, 'Last year when I was a tour guide in New York, I noticed real people didn't really dress the way they do in our ads.' It disconcerts people. The experience certainly disconcerted me.

"And when I was a painter—well, more of a paint mixer and a can carrier—last year I learned a lot. About how people feel about their houses. About how a house painter can feel as wild and agitated and professional about his job as I do about mine. The man had more passion for his job than some of my VPs. And I also got to learn more about sandwiches. The man's wife made really great sandwiches. I borrowed some of her ideas with her permission. She was a little shocked when she found out who I was when I went over one night for dinner. She got over it. She said 'You know, I never really thought that all you presidents of things were really assholes. Despite what it indicates, you know, on the news.' That was better than getting my face on the cover of *Fortune*.

"One month a year, I get to be somebody else. One month a year, if they can make it, my friends go to Bermuda, play golf. I go pretend I'm someone else. I have figured out I have the better deal. They get to be themselves: I get to be somebody else. Anybody who knows me knows that that's an improvement."

He spends eleven months a year working for the company store and one month a year being someone else. I've thought a lot about those two conversations since. It's not a bad idea. The idea of having a part-time secret identity intrigues me, even if it doesn't come with a secret decoder ring. And it struck me that both men were learning more, looking at things in new ways, and finding new metaphors they could take back to the company. They stretched their minds and, as Oliver Wendell Holmes suggested, their minds retained the larger size.

Why wouldn't it work the other way around? If, say, a Gulf of Mexico shrimp fisherman could be in charge of Kimberley-Clark's Kleenex product line for a week, wouldn't he learn a lot? Wouldn't Kimberley-Clark? What insights would a Generation X entrepreneur bring to a board of directors that a Fortune 500 CEO wouldn't have? Suppose that bright young graphic designer you met at the art gallery came to the next three Compaq board meetings? Imagine the possiblitites. What kind of difference might this make to the companies involved?

GREEN ACRES: SATURDAY NIGHT BUCOLIA

You can also do it on weekends. Seriously. I'm not talking about the chief executive of something who hops in the Range Rover on Friday night and runs away to play farmer of 30 acres in a scenic part of the countryside. There is "back to the land" on his or her lips, but there are copies of *Town and Country* magazine on the Mission coffee tables right beside *Barron's*.

Mind you, there's nothing wrong with that. Ever since the Roman Empire, city dwellers have had country homes. It's human to want to raise up your eyes unto the hills and see somebody growing canola. And it contributes a lot to some rural communities. Farming's expensive. It sometimes takes a stockbroker to be able to afford the freight.

However, I've also known people who become serious, not just earnest and talkative, about farming. They find their circus waiting for them every weekend, usually under attack by mealy worms, blossom-end rot, or seagulls. They sweat the details. They argue at the seed stores. They sit in their offices during the week and look at the weather rolling out and wondering what those clouds are going to do to their tomato mosaic or their Colorado potato beetles. They get on the energy-sapping end of an idiot stick and do the shoveling themselves. If you think that this diminishes their energies or unnecessarily diverts their attention from whatever the corporate mission is, you couldn't be more wrong. The two people I'm talking about walk into the office on Monday morning tanned, fit, and directed.

The same is true of the woman I know who runs a small town restaurant on weekends. Dealing with patrons and servers and the local cook who grills her salmon gives her new ways to deal with her support staff in the downtown renovated red brick mansion that is headquarters for the corporation she works with. It certainly works better for her than spending the weekend reading Lawrence Saunders. Her weekends have just grown to three days.

The same is also true of a man who lives down my street during the week who grinds lenses for telescopes on his weekends in a warehouse district loft. Grinding lenses imparts patience and a reverence for the universe, whereas golfing imparts a vocabulary consisting mainly of muttered four-letter words. Some things are just a continuation of what you normally do. Others things constitute a circus, if only briefly. The difference is the level of involvement and the passion involved.

Passion is the key word here. For many people, success actually takes them away from passion instead of closer to it. You started out passionately committed to working with handicapped children. You did so well that you got promoted and now spend your life in meetings, doing paperwork, and having very little direct contact with the children who inspired you. You may have started out as a talented graphic designer. You did so well that you kept getting bigger and bigger assignments and had to take on more staff. Now you spend your days dealing with clients and overseeing the work of younger designers, doing less and less of the hands-on design work you love. According to career counselor Katy Piotrowski, "It's a variation on the Peter Principle. People who do well and are ambitious typically get promoted outside of the passion area."

What drew you to the career you are in now? How far have you strayed from that original attraction? How could you get it back?

Moonlighting at the Circus

Some people escape to the circus at night. They climb out the window, go down the road, and slip under a flap of the tent. By day, a mild-mannered accountant; by night, a professional bass player in jazz bands. That expands to two-week gigs in winter when the accountant plays on cruise ships. Who would you rather be on the cruise ship: one of the two thousand passengers or the bass player in the ship's jazz ensemble? (The bass player does some accounting for me.)

By day, a high school geography teacher; by night, two and three nights a week, a police volunteer patrolling subways. Some people watch *NYPD Blue*. Others live it. By day, IRS bureaucrat; by night, country singer. Easy change: who'd know more about hurtin' music?

The point is, you can test-drive your circus for a month, for weekends, or at night. It's more fun than doing it only in your dreams.

The Change Virus

Sometimes, when we are asked to help a large, traditional company implement organizational change, we'll say to the CEO, "This is a big place with a lot of baggage. Don't expect us to turn around the whole corporation all at once. Let's start with one division that has an ambitious manager. And make it a division where change will produce quantifiable results." We get hold of the small entity and effect the kinds of changes that are the objectives for the company as a whole.

We use that one division as a virus. And we make sure it's as infectious as a cold in a kindergarten. Other divisions raise their eyebrows at the beginning, but then they start paying attention for a range of reasons.

First, the change isn't being visited on them by a bunch of consultants. It's being executed right here at home. Second, showing that a part of the company can change overcomes a lot of inertia problems and trashes the usual excuse "that it might work other places, but it'll never work here." Third, other division managers become restive and competitive when they start seeing quantifiable results. Those managers start phoning us, taking us to nice lunches, and asking us to help. This is a lot better sometimes than the CEO standing up at a meeting and telling managers that they have to fall into line with the outside consultancy. The latter course can often lead to a lot of resistance.

In one corporation, part of the change we were implementing involved a move to new technology. Company wide, division managers had been opposing the idea for months. We heard: "It would whittle away our independence," "The technology's going to be obsolete in two years anyway; technology always is," "Too expensive," and (my favorite) "This division doesn't play with toys." The echoes are still ringing in the meeting room.

We found the right division with the right manager: gutsy, tough, and ambitious. We helped pave the way for the installation of the new technology. The results came in: orders were being shipped faster, the right stuff was being shipped more often to the right places, and shipping costs were down because it was easier to consolidate shipments. Warehousing costs went down because the division could order more intelligently. Financing inventory costs went way down. Our division manager's stock started going up. Other division managers began phoning us. A few nice lunches later, we were helping them.

Looked at in hindsight, the creating-a-virus technique seems pretty obvious, but it wasn't at first. Our own people questioned it: "Hasn't been done before," "Costs more per employee than installing a company-wide program," etc. I listened carefully to the objections because I am famously attentive to the opinions of others and because some of the objections were coming out of my own mouth. In the end, we had to infect ourselves and prove it to ourselves before I got into line.

INFECTING OTHERS WITH THE CHANGE VIRUS

You've probably done this before in your life: gotten other people enthusiastic about something you discovered. It could have been camping, Chilean wine, a sport, or "Fawlty Towers." You started on a minor note:

overnight in a tent not far from home instead of a two-week trek into the mountains, a glass of wine instead of a case, etc. Works every time.

You don't offer people a meal of squid if they've never tasted it before. You offer a bite. You can get people to become part of your change to a second life if you remember that people hate to change but they love to experiment.

How will you get them to experiment with your circus for an hour, a half day, a weekend, or a month? It shouldn't be just a chat. Chat's cheap, unless you're using a 900 number. Make whatever you're doing a real engagement in the actual environment. If you want to give over the rest of your life to building cedar strip canoes, start with the first one, or start with a model. If your vision of the future has you becoming the sales manager in New Mexico, start with a one-week vacation there.

Testing: that's what companies do with new products and new services. If they aren't ready or financially able to plop the product on every supermarket shelf in the country, they test market it. They pick a small center with the demographics they feel are right, put the product on the shelves of the supermarkets there, run an advertising campaign of a size that would be proportionate to what they'd have to run if they mounted it nationally, and monitor the results.

If you wanted to infect your family with the virus of an actual circus, what would you do? Have them staff a charity booth at a trade show? Get them to enter their famous dill pickles at a small town fair with a carnival attached and hang around for the results of the judging? If you wanted to go into the antique business, start with a smallish collectible like antique corkscrews and see how many of the brood became interested. If you wanted to become a writer in your field of expertise, start by having the people close to you read your first article for a trade journal.

And how will you get yourself to experiment? Will you offer free labor? Will you volunteer to work after hours with the brand manager, if that's where you're headed? If you want to start a bed and breakfast, will you offer a current owner your skills in return for a week's experience behind the front desk? Will you start a smaller version of the same thing in your spare time? If you want to start a mail-order trout-fly company, will you kick the idea off by offering just your favorite fly in a local market and filling the orders on weekends? Will you take a course? If you want to open a Thai restaurant, will you pay to see how they ferment the fish sauce at a school and then stay after to learn more?

Start your own virus. Change a half hour of your day, three hours of your week, two weeks of your year. Viruses are catching.

17

the moment of . . . um . . . you know, decision

In which you will find out that:

1. It's time to take the first step. Yes. You there. Now!

2. If you won't set a deadline for action for yourself, I will.

3. If you wait for a crisis to set change in motion, you may have to wait too long.

At some point, you have to make the decision. At some point, you have to hurl yourself off the diving board and get wet. At some point, you have to sign your name to the contract. At some point, you have to square your shoulders, take a deep breath, and say, "Let's do it."

You can't have all those NASA countdown interruptions in which they say, "Minus 18 and holding." Age forty-seven and holding?

I have a friend. He has a son. The son is twenty-nine. The son is convinced that he will become a film director. To further his dreams, the son goes to two movies a day. He also wears a beret, which I didn't realize was a prerequisite, but which seems to be.

I was having lunch with them the other day. "Byron," the man asked his son, "What are you going to do?"

"Dad," the son said, "As you know I'm going to be a director, like Hitchcock, but less manipulative of the audience."

> Whether things will be better if they are different I do not know, but that they will have to be different if they are to become better, that I do know.
>
> —GEORG CHRISTOPH LICHTENBERG

"No, son," said the Father, "I meant, What are you going to do this afternoon?"

The question is not when you will complete whatever transformation you have in mind, but what you're going to do tomorrow. Will you still be stuck thinking about the whole thing or will you be taking the first steps?

To get you moving, I have a suggestion. Send me a five-dollar bill ($8 in Canada) and a SASE. I will send you the date when you should start your change. The envelope should be addressed: Marti Smye, President, PeopleTech, 175 Bloor Street West, Suite 1801, Toronto, Ontario M4W 3R8.

I will pick a date completely at random. Fraud? Maybe. But on the other hand, you will have a voice of authority telling you exactly when you should take the leap. You will be able to say to other people, "I must do this on such and such a date. I spent good money to get the advice of a highly paid consultant who pinpointed it exactly."

Take the first step. I have seen a change process that's intended to result in a new life for a company fail simply because there was no first visible step. There were a lot of speeches, many meetings, myriad memos, catchy slogans, employee badges, and then . . . nothing. No visible first step was taken. There was a month of sizzle but no steak and everything went back to being just the way it was. "Ah yes," the staff say as they contemplate the new buzzword, "*this* year's five-year plan." They file it with all the other five-year, long-range, leading-edge, change-the-company plans they've seen in the past year.

So, what is your first step? That's a question that either challenges you or makes you nervous.

I think that today would be an absolutely fabulous time to take the first step. It's earlier than tomorrow, which puts you ahead of the game. The weather's okay for taking a first step—no matter what the actual weather is. You have half an hour free. You must have, you're reading this book.

Take a few minutes. Make the call. Buy the magazine. Write the letter. Get the textbook. Make the appointment. Sign up for the course. Visit the shop. It doesn't matter which one you do first, as long as you start doing something.

Then, tomorrow, take another step. And the same the day after. Within a few weeks—apparently suddenly—you'll be on the trip.

"I'd been thinking about starting a canoe rental company for years. I'd done a bunch of canoeing myself. I had a vague location in mind. I read other peoples' advertising. But it had all been sort of passive experience. I wasn't really out doing anything.

"One day I had a lunch cancellation. I was driving by a real estate place when the guys called me on my cell phone to reschedule. I stopped in front of the real estate place with nothing to do. And then suddenly I felt a need to go into the real estate place and talk to somebody about waterfront property. Half an hour's chat, and I had a general idea of my options.

"Next day, lunchtime. I get out one of the magazines and I start phoning 1-800 numbers to places they build canoes. You don't get any experts on the line, but people are willing to send you a ton of information.

"Next day, lunchtime. I was starting to look forward to this and starting to plan for it. I phoned canoe outfitters: Florida, Quebec; all over. Yes, they'll send the info. Yes, they'll send the rates. They tell me what their low seasons are and when the cost is high. They give me detailed information on what sort of service they're offering.

"And the day following that I phoned some prefab cabin people. And then the next day I called the state tourist board to see what they've got. You start to make some friends; make arrangements to go up and talk to them, let them know what you're thinking of. People will be really helpful. They're enthused about the kind of business they're in and they like to share their enthusiasm and their ideas.

"It took me two years to get into the canoe business the way I wanted to get into it. But most of it I did at lunch."

ARE YOU WAITING FOR A CRISIS?

It's no big secret that many people have change thrust upon them when they are fired, have a heart attack, or get a letter from their spouse's lawyer. Crises certainly precipitate change, but sometimes the change that occurs in the midst of trauma is more a reaction to the trauma than a move toward the positive. Many people who are undergoing a personal crisis cling desperately to the safe and familiar when the foundations of their world are rocked. They do change, but it may take longer and it may involve more false starts.

This is a problem for companies, too. Rosabeth Moss Kanter, an astute observer of such things, points out that "The ability of organizations to change significantly appears when the inclination to change is least."

I know a man, we'll call him Luke, who was unhappy in his job because of a boss that he disliked. He felt his boss was more concerned with personal gain than with the welfare of the company and its employees. Eventually, inevitably, Luke and his entire department were laid off because the boss felt he could make more money personally as an agency that sold goods produced by other companies than as a producer of the goods.

> *Deeply troubled companies don't usually seek help. And when they do, they have a hard time benefiting from it. The situation parallels one in psychotherapy. Psychotherapy is usually ineffective for severely mentally ill people; it works better for well people. The healthier you are psychologically, or the less you may seem to need to change, the more you can change.*
>
> —RICHARD FARSON

Luke could have seen this coming, but it still hit him like a ton of bricks. He became depressed and that made him ill for several months. When he recovered, he looked for a job and eventually found a position working for a large museum in which he worked very happily and creatively until his retirement fifteen years later.

Luke waited for a crisis and then spent months recovering from it. If Luke had simply started job hunting after he'd noticed the writing on the wall, his reaction would have been very different.

Lukes abound in many organizations. They carry on until the bitter end, as if they were somehow required to go down with the ship. And as anyone knows who has ever been shipwrecked, it's hard to free the lifeboats and get them into the water when the ship is already on the rocks.

Would it help if I told you that according to an American Marketing Association survey of Fortune 500 companies, 84 percent had at least one "major business transformation" in the works? Those transformations may well be somebody's crisis sometime soon.

Or would it help if I told you the grim joke about an elderly couple who walk into a lawyer's office and ask him to draw up divorce papers. They tell the lawyer that they've been meaning to get a divorce for years. "Why did you wait so long?" the lawyer asked.

"We were waiting for the children to die."

What are you waiting for?

18

making change a constant in your life

In which you will learn that:

1. You need to develop the habit of changing.

2. Alternatively, you need to break the habit of not changing.

Whatever we have now, we want something else. When you were six, you wanted to be eight so you could play real baseball. When you were thir-teen, you wanted to be sixteen so you could get your driver's license and mess around in the back seats of cars. When you were eighteen, you wanted to be twenty-five so you could have your own place and play the stereo just as loud as you wanted, order pizza at three in the morning, and eat it with a side of tequila. When you hit fifty, you started to dream about retiring to somewhere warm.

> *Some people are completely unprepared for retirement. I asked one man what his retirement plans were, and he said, "I just hoped they wouldn't notice I was sixty-five."*
>
> —KENNETH M. "PETE" HENDERSON, JR., RETIRED VP AND DIRECTOR, JANNOTTA BRAY ASSOCIATES, CHICAGO

We crave change—or we think we do. Walk to a magazine stand and read the titles:

Rewriting Your Resume for the Millennium

Constructive Divorce

Just Quit

Lose 20 Pounds and Get Washboard Abs in Two Months!

14 Stunning Makeovers

The Changes Your Company Must Make to Survive

The New Computing: What You're Missing

Retirement as Renewal

New Car Fever

20 Coming Careers

The glossy magazines—after considerable investment in consumer research—do not believe there's any money in advising you to stay in your job, maintain your present weight, stand by your spouse, keep the car you've got, remain with your current decor, or be true to your spiritual values. They know that you want to spend a couple of hours wallowing in the idea of becoming a thin, blonde, self-employed entrepreneur looking for love in entirely new places. They know you crave change the way a hound craves road kill.

The companies we consult for also crave change. It's true. I've read their memos.

Both you and the companies find it hard to make the changes you crave. They're still using policies and procedures manuals that were written in 1965. You're still five pounds heavier than you wish you were, married to the same spouse, and driving that car you thought you wanted four years ago to the job you swore you'd leave. After years of diet books and "lite" foodstuffs, is the national median bathroom scale less challenged? Have you even started flossing yet?

The average company is in the same boat and up the same creek. If somebody hasn't taken a whip to it, it still thinks it has put a whole new face on itself by introducing dress down Fridays, a new employee motivation campaign, and decaf at the coffee machine. I saw my first Honda automobile in 1967: how long did it take GM to respond? I am on my fifth computer: how many executives don't know how to keyboard yet? They have laptops, but many of them are the most expensive paper-weights they've ever bought.

Change is hard. Continuous change is even harder, but just as necessary.

People who have experienced change are apt to be the best at dealing with it again. A person who has visited thirteen countries is more likely to deal with the four-teenth successfully than the person who is making a trip abroad for the first time. A person embarking on a third career will know how to adapt to the next one: how to prepare,

> Most executives in their forties and fifties haven't done a very good job of thinking about the next thirty years of their lives. They don't realize that those thirty years usually represent a period longer than the period they've already worked.
>
> —JOE JANNOTTA, FORMER PRINCIPAL, JANNOTTA BRAY ASSOCIATES

how to accommodate, and what expectations to have. Anyone who has tried changing one thing once (stopping smoking, learning French, con-trolling stress, leaving a bad marriage, or moving to Oslo) develops a skill for making other changes.

If you haven't made any major changes in your life so far, you will need practice. I recommend that you get started soon, before major change is inflicted on you involuntarily.

Thirty years. Think of all the things that you achieved in the first thirty years of your life. You learned how to walk, talk, tie your shoes, do math, talk to the opposite sex, drive a car, get a job, pay bills, deal with foreign airlines, and raise children who were going to be smarter than you were. What are you going to learn in the next thirty years?

I am changing more often now. I do not have lunch every day with the people I had lunch with. Minor point. I do not clock in and out at the hours I used to have my timecard stamped. Minor point. I don't work in the same way I used to, eat bran every day for breakfast, or read the same papers. Minor points. I do not have the same box on the org chart I used to. A more major point, according to my accountant. I don't

> When I turned sixty, I wrote a twenty-five-year plan. I didn't want to spend the rest of my life playing golf. Maybe I'll write a ten-year plan when I'm eighty-five.
>
> —TOM MULLANEY, BUSINESSMAN

have the same future I used to. A major point, which fascinates me. I have a new dog, a new house, and some new goals. I have broken a set of habits. I am going to break more. I am afraid, sometimes. I am going to get more afraid. I'm doing hard things I've never done before. I'm going to try to do even harder things. I am having more fun than most people.

To get you started, I've put together some of the exercises from this book and some additional exercises in the workbook that follows. Take some time to think about them. I wish you good luck, a strong heart, and the best possible second life.

workbook

I. Do you have enough dreams yet?

Using the brainstorming techniques described in this book on pages 54–56, come up with ten possible circuses you'd run away to. Start by setting an objective by filling in the blanks in the following:

I'd like to be in a geographic area where _____
_____.

I'd like to live in a _____
with _____.

I want to work _____ hours a week in this sort of
setting _____.

The people I'd work with would be _____
_____.

The work would guarantee me satisfactions like
_____.

In the chain of command I'd be _____
_____.

I'd be wearing _____
_____.

Ten circuses that satisfy those objectives are:

1. _____

2. _____

3. _____

4. _____

5. _____

6. _____

7. _____

8. _____

9. _____

10. _____

Now, go away for a week.

When you come back, look at the list and answer this question: Which circus have you been thinking about most?

II. Research: How to shatter your own illusions

People have illusions about the kind of work other people do. You likely have illusions about the kind of circus you're going into, but you don't know what they are. It's time to track them down. Some suggestions:

1. The leading magazine on the subject is _____ _____. Get a copy. Subscribe.

2. The three best books on the subject are:

a. _____

b. _____

c. _____

Order them.

3. Check the video store. Is there a video on the subject? Is there a movie? If you want to run away to the circus, seeing Burt Lancaster in *Trapeze* will spark some ideas and park others.

4. Does the local college have a course in the subject? When are you going to take it?

_____

5. What is the leading company doing this in your area? How are you going to get to visit them? What's the next best? How are you going to visit them? What's the third best? How are you going to get to visit them?

a. _____

b. _____

c. _____

6. Is there an organization that works in this area? When will you meet with a representative from that organization?

_____

_____

7. What can you learn about the issues from suppliers, shareholders, and customers? How will you track them down?

Suppliers: _____

Shareholders: _____

Customers: _____

8. How would you spend a day or a week actually doing what you want? Who would make that possible? Why would they make that possible?

How: _____

Who: _____

Why: _____

9. Where are the two Web sites that tell you most about the issue?

a. _____

b. _____

(If you don't have a computer, enlist a fourteen-year-old to help.)

10. Can you identify someone who has retired from a similar situation? When will you talk to that person?

_____

_____

Go back over the list above and make two phone calls before you dare move to the next item. Now.

III. Carry-on bags

What are you going to take to the circus with you?
Your decoder ring? Your dog? Your fame, wealth,
home, city, knowledge?

   Tick off the items in your escape kit from the list below.
Add a few if you want to. Then, to focus your mind, pick out
five things you'd take if you could take only five.

☐ Family members

☐ Friends

☐ Pets

☐ The place I live in

☐ The area I live in

☐ The way I spend my spare time

☐ My collection

☐ My clothes

☐ My car

☐ My personal papers

☐ My social life

☐ My status symbols

☐ My fitness program

☐ My cell phone

☐ My bad habits

☐ My church

☐ My club

☐ The industry I work in

☐ The company I work in

☐ The group I work with

☐ The kind of work I do

☐ The hours I work

☐ The days I work

☐ The system I work under

☐ I'd definitely take

1. _____

2. _____

3. _____

4. _____

5. _____

If you're all alone in the world, you've completed the exercise. If you're not, have those who are important to you—those who'll be going on whatever voyage you're taking—do the exercise, too. Give them some time and a quiet room.

Then compare lists. What are the commonalities? What are the differences? Don't argue about it. Explore.

IV. Left luggage

It's the same list as the last exercise. But this time note what you'd definitely leave behind. List them all. But then whittle the list down to your least-favorite five.

I'd definitely leave:

1. _____

2. _____

3. _____

4. _____

5. _____

Again, have your fellow travelers go through the same exercise and again look for commonalities.

V. What makes you work best?

Throughout this book I've been pushing you to define what kind of work environment suits you best. If the pushing has been successful, you have a pretty good handle on it. But it's better to get it out of the corridors of your mind and set it down on paper. That makes it official. And just doing the exercise will make the definition more precise. Keep it short and then check the truth of it by remembering your best past experiences.

1. Whatever organization I work with must share my beliefs that:

a. _____

b. _____

c. _____

2. The immediate group I work with must be like the group I worked best with in the past. Three characteristics of that group were:

a. _____

b. _____

c. _____

3. The three biggest rewards or satisfactions I've ever gotten from my work life were:

a. _____

b. _____

c. _____

VI. The logical circus

Would you (as a human resource director) hire you (the nervous job applicant)? Please fill in the following application form.

YouInc.

The organization demands the following core competency:

_____

_____

The candidate offers the following core competency:

_____

_____

The organization demands the following core competency:

_____

_____

The candidate offers the following core competency:

_____

_____

Skill set offered by candidate	Skill set demanded by organization
_____	_____
_____	_____
_____	_____
_____	_____

Job environment offered by company	Job environment desired
_____	_____
_____	_____
_____	_____
_____	_____

VII. Appointing your board

YouInc. needs a board of directors. It's best if they're qualified and motivated.

Qualifications	Name	Motivation
1. _____	_____	_____
2. _____	_____	_____
3. _____	_____	_____
4. _____	_____	_____
5. _____	_____	_____

Skill sets needed:

1. _____

2. _____

3. _____

4. _____

5. _____

Board meetings will happen every _____ for the first _____ months and then every _____ thereafter.

VIII. Eight ways I could test drive my dream . . .

If you wanted to open a bistro, you could be a busboy for a week. If you wanted to be an organic gardener, you'd start with a 10 × 10 plot. If you wanted to be a doctor, you could start by volunteering at the hospital for two nights a week.

How could you test drive your dream?

1. _____

2. _____

3. _____

4. _____

5. _____

6. _____

7. _____

8. _____

Now, which one are you going to do first? When will you do that? And which are you going to do second? When?

IX. Welcome to your new daytimer

Let's take a little excursion to five years from now. Fill in the following daytimer with what you'd like to be doing. One person I gave this exercise to looked at the page and then tore it in half. He gave me back the bottom part and explained, "I don't intend to work after lunch ever again."

7:00 _____

7:30 _____

8:00 _____

8:30 _____

9:00 _____

9:30 _____

10:00 _____

10:30 _____

11:00 _____

11:30 _____

12:00 _____

12:30 _____

1:00 _____

1:30 _____

2:00 _____

2:30 _____

3:00 _____

3:30 _____

4:00 _____

4:30 _____

5:00 _____

5:30 _____

6:00 _____

Evening _____

To do tomorrow _____

Left undone_____

In case this daytimer is lost, please return to

_____

at_____

X. Write, when you know where you are going

This isn't my last book on the subject. It's worth more than one book to explore how people genuinely change themselves. And that means I'd like to hear from you. Some topics I'd most like to hear about:

1. What were the most valuable parts of this book to you?

2. What were the five biggest problems you found in running away to your circus?

3. What unexpected delights did you find along the way?

4. What person helped you the most? Why?

5. What person proved to be the biggest obstacle? Why?

6. What stage—ignoring, attending, planning, or executing—did you find the most difficult?

7. What other book helped most?

8. What other sources of information helped most?

Drop me a note. Drop me several.

references

Introduction

1995 Gallup poll: Reported in Ronald Henkoff, "So You Want to Change Your Job," *Fortune*, January 15, 1996, pp. 42–64.

1996 National Career Development Association poll: Reported in Ann Hornaday, "How Do You Know When It's Time to Go?" *Fast Company*, premiere issue, p. 134.

Survey of 300 women: Betsy Morris, "Executive Women Confront Midlife Crisis," *Fortune*, September 18, 1995, pp. 60–86

Dream Society: "Report from the Futurist," *Fast Company*, October/ November 1997, p. 40.

Chapter 1

How difficult it is to accept: Jack Hitt, quoted in Tom Peters, *The Pursuit of Wow! Everyperson's Guide to Topsy-Turvy Times*, New York: Vintage (Random House), 1994, p. 179.

Even 50 percent of the Japanese: Cited in Faith Popcorn and Lys Marigold, *Clicking: 16 Trends to Future Fit Your Life, Your Work and Your Business*, New York: HarperCollins, 1996, p. 225.

World Economic Forum: William Thorsell, "Thoughts from the Mind Patch," *Globe and Mail*, 8 February 1997, p. D3.

Think back in your career: Clifford E. Montgomery, "Organizational Fit Is Key to Job Success," *HRMagazine*, vol. 41, no. 1, January 1996, p. 95.

Studies are starting to show that a poor fit: quoted in Glenn Rifkin, "Stress in the Workplace," *Harvard Business Review*, September/October 1994, p. 10.

Eleven thousand days: Richard Koonce, "Becoming Your Own Career Coach," *Training and Development*, January 1995, p. 18.

Chapter 2

Fastest-growing occupations: *Monthly Labor Review*, vol. 105, June 1982, pp. 18–28; vol. 108, November 1985, pp. 42–57; vol. 118, November 1995, pp. 60–84.

More than 40 percent of the 1980 Fortune 500: Oren Harari, "The New Job Security: You!" *Management Review*, September 1995, p. 29.

What the future predictors: Robert A. Nisbet, "The Year 2000 and All That," *Commentary*, June 1968, pp. 60–66.

Table showing organizational changes: "Paradigms for Modern Managers," *Business Week*, special issue on "Reinventing America," 1992, pp. 62–63.

The new economy will return to a hunter-gatherer society: Charles Winslow and William Bramer, *FutureWork: Putting Knowledge to Work in the Knowledge Economy*, New York: Free Press, 1994.

People are beginning to ask about secure employment: See Sally Lerner, "The Future of Work in North America: Good Jobs, Bad Jobs, Beyond Jobs," *Futures*, vol. 26, March 1994, pp. 185–96, or Jeremy Rifkin, *The End of Work: The Decline of the Global Labour Force and the Dawn of the Post-Market Era*, New York: Putnam, 1995.

Work is moving to unconventional sites: Joseph Coates, *Future Work: Seven Critical Forces Reshaping Work and the Work Force in North America*, San Francisco: Jossey-Bass, 1990.

Chapter 3

Don't expect toothpicks to pry you: Tom Peters, *The Pursuit of Wow! Everyperson's Guide to Topsy-Turvy Times*, New York: Vintage (Random House), 1994, p. 189.

Sometimes in the course of our lives: E. Annie Proulx, "House Leaning on Wind," *Architectural Digest*, October 1997, p. 48.

In the global economy: Jeremy Rifkin, *The End of Work: The Decline of the Global Labor Force and the Dawn of the Post-Market Era*, New York: Putnam, 1995.

Bertolt Brecht: from the poem "Questions from a Worker Who Reads," in *Selected Poems*, New York: Harcourt Brace, 1947, 1975.

Chapter 4

All I can see as I look back: Joanna Field, *A Life of One's Own*, Los Angeles: J.P. Tarcher, 1981, p. 19.

Daydreaming by midlife executives: Doctoral thesis by Judith Meyerowitz, cited in Robert K. Otterbourg, *It's Never Too Late: 150 Men and Women Who Changed Their Careers*, Hauppage, NY: Barron's, 1993, p. 8.

I began to have an idea of my life: *A Life of One's Own*, p. 89.

Our thought is incoherent: David Bohm, "The Special Theory of Relativity, 1965," quoted in Peter Senge, *The Fifth Discipline: The Art and Practice of the Learning Organization*, New York: Doubleday, 1990, p. 239.

Chapter 5

Organizations don't learn: Patricia Pitcher, *Artists, Craftsmen and Technocrats: The Dream, Realities and Illusions of Leadership*, Toronto: Stoddart, 1995, p. 150.

Chapter 6

Corporations differ as much as species of animals: Henry Mintzberg, quoted in Robert Fulford, "Regarding Henry," *Report on Business* magazine, October 1995, p. 74.

If you're not willing to enthusiastically adopt: James C. Collins and Jerry I. Porras, *Built to Last: Successful Habits of Visionary Companies*, New York: HarperCollins, 1994, p. 121.

Jeffrey Edwards: quoted in Glenn Rifkin, "Stress in the Workplace: Rethinking Job Fit," *Harvard Business Review*, vol. 72, September/October 1994, p. 10.

It fuels the fire of revolution: Richard Farson, *Management of the Absurd: Paradoxes in Leadership*, New York: Simon & Schuster, 1996, p. 92.

When a psychological need is met, it recedes: quoted in Julie Connelly, "How to Choose Your Next Career," *Fortune*, 6 February 1995, p. 145.

A study carried out by the Association of Theological Schools: Reported in Joseph N. Boyce, "Leaps of Faith," *Wall Street Journal* (eastern edition), 9 August 1995, p. B1.

The feeding and crafting of the soul: Gail Sheehy, *New Passages: Mapping Your Life Across Time*, New York: Random House, 1995, p. 172.

At the end of the day: Quoted in Betsy Morris, "Executive Women Confront Midlife Crisis," *Fortune*, September 18, 1995, p. 78.

Chapter 7

An estimated twenty million Americans: Barbara Bailey Reinhold, *Toxic Work: How to Overcome Stress, Overload, and Burnout and Revitalize Your Career*, New York: Dutton, 1996, p. 1.

Chapter 8

If you see a carpenter: Studs Terkel, *Working*, New York: Ballantine Books, 1972, p. 672.

Provices and serducts: Michael Schrage, "Provices and serducts," *Fast Company*, August/September 1996, p. 48.

The new physics of work: Charles Fishman, "We've seen the future of work and it works, but very differently," *Fast Company*, August/September 1996, p. 55.

It's like the old saying: Quoted in Melanie Warner, "Working at Home—the Right Way to Be a Star in Your Bunny Slippers," *Fortune*, 3 March 1997, p. 166.

The rise of work is not confined: Juliet Schor, *The Overworked American: The Unexpected Decline of Leisure*, New York: Basic Books, 1992, p. 5.

She'll go for anything: Reg Theriault, *How to Tell When You're Tired*, New York: Norton, 1995, p. 64.

After years of listening to me talk: Ken Englert, "Close Contact," *Boating*, July 1997, p. 66.

A college education doesn't make the bags any lighter: *How to Tell When You're Tired*, p. 68.

As someone who has spent: George D. Cohen, "No Job for a Grown-Up," *Utne Reader*, January/February 1997, p. 47.

Chapter 9

Collaboration is called for: Michael Schrage, *No More Teams! Mastering the Dynamics of Creative Collaboration*, New York: Doubleday, 1989, p. 4.

Chapter 10

Shared visions: Peter Senge, *The Fifth Discipline: The Art and Practice of the Learning Organization*, New York: Doubleday, 1990, p. 208.

Do it yourself: Rebecca Maddox, *Inc. Your Dreams*, New York: Viking, 1995.

What you primarily need is not advice: William Bridges, *Transitions: Making Sense of Life's Changes*, Reading, MA: Addison-Wesley, 1980, p. 80

Chapter 11

Nothing is as invisible as the obvious: Richard Farson, *Management of the Absurd: Paradoxes in Leadership*, New York: Simon & Schuster, 1996, p. 25.

False collectivization: William Whyte, *The Organization Man*, New York: Simon & Schuster, 1956, p. 49.

One can either work or meet: Peter Drucker, *Management: Tasks, Responsibilities, Practices*, New York: Harper & Row, 1973, p. 403.

A 1997 survey of Fortune 1000 companies: Reported in Mary Gooderham, "Electronic messages burying workers," Toronto *Globe and Mail*, 14 May, 1997, p. A6.

In the workplace, home office, sales floor: Ellen Ullman, "Out of Time: Reflections on the Programming Life," in *Resisting the Virtual Life: The*

Culture and Politics of Information, edited by James Brook and Iain Boal, San Francisco: City Lights, 1995, p. 143.

Chapter 12

Book by Barbara Sher: *I Could Be Anything If I Only Knew What It Was*, New York: Delacorte Press, 1994.

Myers-Briggs test: See, for example, Paul D. Tieger and Barbara Barron-Tieger, *Do What You Are: Discover the Perfect Career for You Through the Secrets of Personality Type*, Boston: Little Brown, 1995.

Book by Richard Bolles: *What Color Is Your Parachute?* Berkeley, CA: Ten Speed Press, annual.

Chapter 13

Why individuals dig in their heels: Ferdinand F. Fournies, *Why Employees Don't Do What They're Supposed to Do and What to Do About It*, Blue Ridge Summit, PA: Liberty House Books, 1988.

Chapter 14

When you're competing on knowledge: John Seely Brown and Estee Solomon Gray, "After Reengineering," *Fast Company,* premiere issue, p. 79.

The island was Guadalcanal: Ross Norgrove, *Blueprint for Paradise: How to Live on a Tropic Island*, Chico, CA: Moon Publications, 1989.

Chapter 15

Stages of change: Wendy Potter, "The Stages of Change: A Theory and Model of the Process of Organizational Change" (unpublished paper, People Tech, 1993). This paper builds on the work of Kurt Lewin, who proposed three stages—unfreezing, movement, and refreezing—in *Field Theory in Social Science* (New York: Harper & Row, 1946). Claes Janssen suggests four stages: contentment, denial, confusion, and renewal; his work is cited in Marvin R. Weisbord, *Productive Workplaces: Organizing and Managing for Dignity, Meaning and Community* (San Francisco: Jossey-Bass, 1987), p. 266. Five stages in individual change have been identified by James O. Prochaska, Carlo DiClemente and John C. Norcross, in "In Search of How

People Change: Applications to Addictive Behaviors," *American Psychologist*, vol. 47, no. 9, September 1992, pp. 1102–14.

Experiments never fail: Dale Dauten, *The Max Strategy: How a Businessman Got Stuck at an Airport and Learned to Make His Career Take Off*, New York: Morrow, 1996, p. 49.

Plans are important: Karl Weick, *The Social Psychology of Organizing*, Reading, MA: Addison-Wesley, second edition, 1986, pp. 10–11. Weick is paraphrasing an argument by Michael Cohen and James March, first published in *Leadership and Ambiguity: The American College President*, New York: McGraw-Hill, 1974.

Corvettes: James Schefter, *All Corvettes Are Red*, New York: Pocket Books, 1998.

Someone said when willpower: G. Arthur Casaday, quoted in Peg Bracken, *I Didn't Come Here to Argue*, Greenwich, CT: Fawcett Crest, 1969, p. 65.

Chapter 16

It's a variation on the Peter Principle: Katy Piotrowski of Bernard Haldane Associates in Denver, quoted in Shari Caudron, "Pursue Your Passion," *Industry Week*, 2 September 1996, p. 27.

Chapter 17

Whether things will be better: Quoted in Dietrich Dorner, *The Logic of Failure: Why Things Go Wrong and What We Can Do to Make them Right*, New York: Henry Holt, 1996, p. 50.

The ability of organizations to change significantly: Rosabeth Moss Kanter, Barry A. Stein and Todd D. Jick, *The Challenges of Organizational Change: How Companies Experience and Leaders Guide It*, New York: Free Press, 1992.

Deeply troubled companies don't usually seek help: Richard Farson, *Management of the Absurd: Paradoxes in Leadership*, New York: Simon & Schuster, 1996, p. 85.

American Marketing Association survey of Fortune 500 companies: cited in Lesley Alderman, "How You Can Take Control of Your Own Career," *Money*, July 1995, p. 37.

Index